# The Marine Fish and Invert Reef Aquarium

Published by Dupla (USA) Press
575 Broad Street
Bridgeport, CT 06604

Printed in the United States by :
Remar Printing Co, Bridgeport, Connecticut

Edited by : Sarah R. Thiel

Copyright holder : Albert J. Thiel

88-MMMMM-03


First Printing        February 1988
Second Printing       March 1988
Third Printing        May 1988

9 8 7 6 5 4

The second and third printing contains materially the same text as the first,
about a dozen pictures have been added however.


Library of Congress
Cataloging in Printing Information      88-70195


ISBN     0-945777-00-0

# The Marine Fish and Invert Reef Aquarium

## Advanced Techniques and Instrumentation

Albert J. Thiel
Norwalk, Connecticut

To Sarah my loving and supportive wife

To W. Sprokkreeff

To our ten Furpersons who give unconditional love

# Acknowledgements

We express thanks to the many hobbyists
who, through their many questions, have
contributed to the content of this book

Special thanks to

Sarah
George

my MacSE and NEC Multispeed EL

# Table of Contents

**Preface**

# 4. Instrumentation

# 5. Water Quality Criteria

# Appendix 2  Manufacturers

# Appendix 3  Bibliography

# Preface

Although several books on the subject of keeping Marine Fish, Invertebrates, and Macro-Algae already exist, and even though many articles have appeared in hobby and other such magazines, especially since the introduction of elaborate and sophisticated new "Systems", there still seems to be a void in the areas of what type of equipment to use, and the purpose of a number of the more expensive instruments that have recently appeared on the market.

Much of this equipment is imported; the instructions that accompany the merchandise are not always easy to understand, and the translation of the instructions could often be improved. This is very frustrating for many a hobbyist, since frequently the price paid is much higher than one is used to spend on aquarium equipment. Then again, the type of equipment that we refer to here is much more advanced too.

On the positive side however, the availability of this equipment, e.g. the instrumentation introduced some time ago by companies such as Dennerle, Dupla, and Tunze, and the multitude of "Reef-duplicating Systems" now available, as well as the much more efficient trickle filters, permit the implementation of more novel ways of aquarium keeping.

These Reef-like system tanks allow every aquarist to maintain his or her aquarium under near ideal conditions, resulting in Fish and Invertebrates that not only look healthier, but more importantly, survive for much longer periods of time.

And is that not what we should all be concerned with? Indeed, the longer we can keep Fish and Invertebrates alive in our aquariums, the less the "real" Reefs will be depleted. Presently, every time a Fish or Invertebrate dies, we head for the nearest pet store and acquire new ones. We may not think of it as such, but this keeps up demand unnecessarily, and forces abnormal and superfluous depletion of reef stock; and as true Hobbyists, we should concern ourselves with the long term effect that our hobby has on the Reefs as well.

Marine Fish keeping still has "mystique" attached to it, either because it appears to be more difficult than freshwater fish keeping, or perhaps because of the perceived higher expense involved. Fortunately this is changing slowly, thanks perhaps to the ever growing number of articles written about the marine hobby, and thanks certainly to the magazines that publish such articles, e.g. Fresh and Marine Aquarium, Tropical Fish Hobbyist, and a late comer, Marine Fish Monthly, dedicated exclusively to the marine side of the hobby, and which seems to be enjoying growing support amongst many hobbyists.

To popularize the hobby to the levels seen in the fresh water hobby, many more gains need to be made however. This will start to happen when the mystique surrounding the marine hobby is lifted, and when hobbyists are finally able to keep their tanks looking healthy for extended periods of time.

Advocates and manufacturers of sophisticated aquarium systems have had great difficulty convincing aquarists and store owners alike, that besides the basic maintenance practices, the ones recommended in many books, other factors have to be kept in mind when dealing with an eco-system so delicate as the marine aquarium. Indeed, although marine tanks have been around for many years now, the keeping of such livestock still holds numerous unknowns, mostly because there are, or have been, few trend setting systems and few aquariums that aquarists can look to as good examples of how things should really be done.

Little is still known about the feeding habits of most Invertebrates and of many fish. Correct water parameters are elusive and can in many cases only be approximated. Protein chemistry, as applied to the aquatic environment still holds unfamiliar, and even many puzzling mysteries.

This is very much unlike what has happened in the fresh water hobby, where maintenance practices have held few secrets for years now, where examples of "near ideal" aquariums abound, and where a multitude of books can be referred to for solutions to possible complications. Most experts in the fresh water hobby also agree, most of the time, on what needs to be done to improve conditions. In the marine hobby this happens unfortunately only infrequently.

Conflicting information, plain contradictions and un-truths, have confused many of us, and have led to what we consider the appearance of "hybrid" systems. By this, for lack of a better word, we mean systems in which the aquarist, because he or she cannot find a better and definitive way of doing things, has resorted to using a "little" of the many different methods advocated, borrowing some from one author's recommendations, and some from others. It is as if he or she is buying "insurance", by combining different techniques, in the hope that such combinations will in the end result in better working aquariums.

Such is of course a fallacy, and will only lead to problems somewhere down the line. Techniques used in one system may be detracting from the efficiency of the other one or ones.

Moreover such systems are usually developed to be modular and synergistic, a situation where all components work together towards a finer aquarium. Combining portions of many systems together can therefore ob- viously no longer result in the kind of outcome that one is led to expect by the individual manufacturers.

Consequently the hobbyist becomes frustrated and has the impression that the products he or she has bought do not perform as expected. Not only does this thwart the hobbyist's efforts, but in the long run it makes many potentially serious hobbyists lose patience with keeping tropical Fish. They then dismantle their aquarium, and store it in the garage or attic, with the many other aquarium products that are no longer being used.
This not only ties up untold dollars, but unfortunately works against the hobby being the enjoyable and fulfilling pastime it should be.

Sadly so, store owners and their sales personnel eager to make the sale, can not always be relied on for accurate information, and so- lutions to the many problems facing the aquarist. Neither does he or she always get accurate responses to the many questions requiring answers.

Store owners and their personnel can however not be made the scapegoats of our frustrations. To illustrate this, just think about what you do when you buy a car. You buy the car from a sales person, which acts very much like our pet store personnel. When you have problems with this car, you go to a mechanic, not the salesman.

You should use a similar approach when it comes to tank problems. Look for what you consider to be a knowledgeable sales person in your favorite pet store. Or talk to a friend who has been in the hobby for a long time. Alternatively go to an Aquarium Society meeting and try to find the answers there. Such Societies exist all over the country, and are an untapped source of wisdom that has in most cases been empirically arrived at.

If you take the time and the determination, you will find the answers to many of your questions, without having to re-invent the wheel, at great expense in both Fish and Invertebrate lives and dollars.

This book, then, is an attempt to demystify the reasons for the newer equipment, and explains how such instruments and control practices fit into the overall "optimal" aquarium picture. Of course, and although this book implies that these techniques relate to the marine aquarium, they can just as well be used on any fresh water tank, except for a few perhaps that do not make sense, e.g. protein skimmers. Most of the chemistry is the same, especially when it comes to filtration and water quality, save that in one case we are dealing with water of low dissolved salts content, and in marine tanks a high one.

As time goes on, newer or more advanced approaches are always uncovered. Therefore, even though this book is up-to-date inasmuch as techniques and equipment are concerned at the time of its printing, it is highly likely - or should I say desirable- that over the months and years to come, additional equipment, control instrumentation, tests and so on, will appear. These will make the aquarist's life easier and conditions in the aquarium better controllable. This is the reason why an up-date on such techniques will be issued in the spring of 1989.

This will ensure that hobbyists can benefit from additional information as it becomes available and practical to use. Such information will therefore only be disseminated once the techniques have proven them selves to be worthwhile, and easy enough to implement.

Applying the techniques advocated in this book, will not only save many fish and invertebrates lives, but it will also give you much greater joy from this wonderful hobby of ours.

Acquiring all the instrumentation that is discussed in this book at once, is obviously one way to go. Experience however has shown that most people buy the pieces of the complete Reef set up, one at a time, and build up their Reefs over perhaps months .
This seems indeed the most sensible way, and makes the financial involvement much easier to bear.

Complete Reef set ups are not cheap by any means. Anyone wishing to get into the hobby, at this level, should therefore "budget".

We welcome any suggestions, and comments on the subjects covered in this book. Send your letters to Dupla Press.

Writing this publication was quite an undertaking, especially because the marine hobby has progressed so rapidly in the last year. Most of the methods advocated will be new to hobbyists in the United States and are therefore likely to generate a lively debate. We welcome such a debate, as it improves communication between hobbyists and spreads information faster than any other means. The book was not intended to be a "text book", and some of the chemistry is therefore very simplified.

Those scientists, and other chemists out there, will forgive us for having tried to keep the explanations as simple as possible, we hope. We wish you all good luck.

Albert J. Thiel
Norwalk, Connecticut
December 1987

**Note regarding the Second Printing :**

Except for some typographical error corrections, and a few changes of graphs and pictures, this printing is materially the same as the first one.

We have also changed to point setting of the typeface, and reduced it to 10 from the original 11.

We thank our readers from bringing some of the typos to our attention.

Thanks to the overwhelming success the second printing occured within 6 weeks of the first one. The third printing of the book will include several revisions, mainly in the light and micro and macro-algae sections.

As more evidence on the relative benefits of the use of Actinic lighting becomes available, it will be included in that revision.

We wish to thank Pam at Remar Printing for her dedication in the complete re-setting of this book.

**Dupla USA Press has started a NEWSLETTER called :      "Marine Reef"**

Marine Reef is available from Dupla USA Press, starting May 1988, and is issued every three weeks.

It is a technical newsletter dealing with the keeping of Reef Aquariums only. It is not for everyone. If you are serious about the Reef tank you keep you may wish to subscribe. The cost is : Post-paid $ 48.00 for 17 issues, Dupla USA Press, 575 Broad Street, Bridgeport, CT 06604.

# 1. Introduction

The keeping of Marine Fish and Invertebrates, as a hobby, has grown in great strides in the last couple of years.

Books by such recognized authors as : Stephen Spotte, Martin Moe, Horst Kipper, Kaspar Horst, Frank de Graaf, Peter Wilkens, Guido Huckstedt, and articles by such authors as George Smit, Don Dewey, Albert Thiel and many others, have greatly contributed to the spreading of more sophisticated techniques of keeping aquariums, and a dramatically increased knowledge on the part of Hobbyists. In this respect John Burleson also deserves much credit.

Aquarists everywhere have greatly benefited from these suggestions and techniques, with the overall result that the hobby advanced considerably, and has become more "professional".

This has not only made aquariums look better, but has resulted in greater satisfaction from the hobby, as aquarists implemented newer techniques and were able to see rapid results on one hand, and keep their stock alive for much longer periods of time, on the other.

It has also contributed to a desire to "perfect" the aquarium, as manufac- turers, noting the trend, were able to bring better equipment to the market, at reasonable prices, as the hobbyist was, and is, ready to invest in such products.

This same trend was helped as well by more restrictive legislation on the importation of fish, corals and invertebrates in certain countries, making it necessary to produce equipment that allows the livestock in our aquariums to be kept alive for much longer periods of time. This is perhaps more so in Europe than in the United States, but lately even here such trends are noticeable, and restrictions are being imposed, especially on the importation of corals and the like.

This is obviously a very positive trend, one that we should all support by applying these newer methods, thus giving everyone involved the necessary incentive to produce even better instrumentation, at more affordable prices. Such instruments not only make the fish and invertebrates live longer, but make our hobby much more enjoyable as well.

In this book we will look at these instruments, techniques and methods, and substantiate why they benefit the aquarist and the aquarium; the reason for them; and how to apply them safely and with the knowledge required to interpret the results obtained accurately.

This is important, as just having a set of numbers or values, and not knowing what they mean, or how to correct the situation, is like sitting on a pile of gold, and not knowing it is worth money. It is hoped that the Hobbyist will derive worthier knowledge from reading this book, and apply it to his or her aquarium.

Some of the topics covered include :

Redox potential, Ozone, Protein skimming, Temperature control, Oxygen reactors, Carbon dioxide reactors, Trickle filtration, Filter media for trickle and wet dry systems, a multitude of tests, Trace Element and Fertilization requirements and control, and many other such areas of interest.

Hobbyists wanting to implement these and other recommendations will find answers and guidelines in these pages. If, at first, some of these concepts seem esoteric, do not get discouraged, as reading these pages will give you the necessary knowledge to understand and use them safely. They will not only allow you to get a better grip on your aquarium, but they will, in addition, allow you to obtain the results that derive from good maintenance and control practices.

This book can be read from front to back, or you can go to any chapter that interests you particularly, immediately, without loss of understanding. It would appear however that starting from the beginning will give you more progressive information,which we believe is probably a more desirable approach. The choice is yours.

For those with a specific interest in Macro-algae, there is an thorough section at the end of this book that deals with the keeping of such algae, what to expect, and the nutrients and nutrient levels required to keep them alive and growing. Lighting requirements and fertilization are covered in depth as well.

The lighting section, as you might expect includes sections on metal halide, actinic and other lighting types.

The section on redox potential is especially detailed because we felt that this concept is not very well understood by Hobbyists yet. Since it has gained so much attention, in the last few months , we have added the results of an experiment in redox potential analysis. We believe that this will prove to be of help, in understanding this rather difficult chemical concept a little better.

Last but not least, a very detailed section on tests, and how to correct situations that are not within the parameters given, is included as well. This was the result of the large number of questions that hobbyists from all over the United States have been asking us over and over again. This includes for instance dealing with excess phosphates and nitrates.

Obviously no book can be complete. We apologize for any omissions that might have been of interest to you. Perhaps, if they are pointed out to us, we can include them in the up-date that will be published in the spring of 1989.

One section that is hardly covered is ultraviolet radiation parasite control equipment. This is on purpose, as we do not advocate the use of such intrumentation. This does not mean that such equipment does not work. It does, but we prefer natural ways of dealing with diseases. We also feel that the environment becomes too sterile as as result. This is a personal choice, and you may disagree. We certainly do not recommend combining ultraviolet and ozone.

Since only a very short has elapsed between the first and second printings we have not been able to document more findings on the use of Actinic lighting, and have therefore not changed our comments in the lighting section.

# Ten Golden Rules to an Optimum Aquarium

 1. Tropical warmth in the water and in the substrate

 6. Strong water movement

 2. Aquarium-specific lighting

 7. Dense planting

 3. Chemically stable water

 8. Harmonious fish population

 4. Natural plant fertilisation

 9. Tropical fish care

 5. Biological filtration

 10. Control of all variables

The Ten Golden Rules Courtesey of Dupla Aquaristik Gmbh

# 2. The Basics

It is not the intent of this book to cover all the basic requirements of marine tanks in depth.

If you are unfamiliar with these, you should refer to a book dealing with such basics before setting up your aquarium. It is assumed that if you read this book, you either already have a working marine aquarium, or that you are familiar with how one is set up.

You may want to refer to the list in Appendix 2 for suggestions, if you wish.

For that reason we are only covering some subjects superficially, and assume that you know how to set up a Reef aquarium and what basic equipment you will need to do so.

Setting up a Reef is exciting, looking at it will give you many hours of pleasure. Maintaining it is a little more challenging however.

We hope that reading this book will answer most of your questions.

## 2.1 The Aquarium :

Typically the type of aquarium that you will be using is made of either glass or acrylic material. The latter is usually referred to by one of its trade names : plexiglass. Both have advantages and both have disadvantages. Those who have tried both ,will, we are sure, agree.

Aquariums made out of combinations of wood and glass, or concrete and glass, and other such tanks are not covered as they are usually only found in very large set ups, often in Public Aquariums, and do not really concern the average aquarist. Of course the older type aquariums, made of iron, should no longer be used. Although you might still see them around, they should no longer be considered solutions for Reef tanks.

Iron dissolves over long periods of time, rust settles in the tank, enters the motors, and generally results in slow deterioration of tank conditions. Stick with the basic tank made out of glass or acrylic material.

Since acrylic aquariums have become so popular lately, we conducted a few experiments with them to determine their relative merits, and how well they perform, in true conditions, compared to the traditional glass ones.

### 2.1.1. Glass Aquariums

Glass aquariums are heavy and very reliable. They are not as easy to drill as acrylic tanks. They are however easy to clean and withstand some abuse. Moving them around, as well all know, is a chore. Glass tanks seem to last longer in rough environments, although one would think not, because glass is "fragile". Glass aquariums are totally inert and do not bow, providing the right thickness of glass has been selected when building the aquarium. Tempered glass cannot be drilled; keep that in mind when buying an aquarium that you plan to install as a reef system, with an overflow, leading to a trickle filter.

Glass aquariums are easy to seal, and the silicone bonding remains pliable, and can be removed if necessary. This would be the case if you decided to make changes to the tank, or move it, in pieces, rather than as a whole. Toluene and Xylene for instance will dissolve silicone. These products are usually available from paint stores. You should use them after you have cut out the glass panels, to clean up the glass and remove any residual silicone, the left-overs that are normally so hard to scrape off.

Taking the tank apart requires little more than cutting the silicone out with a razor blade knife, and then removing the rest with one of the above compounds.

The thickness of the glass used is determined mostly by the top to bottom measurement, and not so much the length or width.

Whether a brace, or several braces, across the top are used, also influences the glass thickness. Most tanks nowadays are made out of 1/4 to 1/2 inch glass, and some have bottoms made out of 5/8 or sometimes even 3/4 inch thickness.

Glass does not easily scratch, and is easy to clean, especially on the inside, where algal growth sometimes requires drastic scraping.

## 2.1.2 Acrylic Aquariums

Acrylic tanks on the other hand are light, can easily be drilled, and do not require too much effort to move around. They can be abused, but unfortunately scratch easily.

If the outside is scratched, such damage can be repaired by using one of the many special compounds sold to do so.

When the scratches are on the inside however, it is a different matter all together. Acrylic is not easy to clean, particularly on the inside; this is especially so if micro-algae have started to grow on the panes.

Your only way to solve that problem is to lower the water level, and use the special products that are available to clean acrylic material. This is a tedious job, and one needs to be very careful not to make scratches as, once the tank is filled again, algae will grow in these scratches, and will be even harder to remove.

Buffing is possible, but one needs to be very careful not to turn a visible scratch into many more invisible ones which, over a period of time, will result in a translucid area forming where you used your buffer.

Some acrylic bonding agents "blush" over time, meaning they change color, usually to a yellowish milky patch. Acrylic tanks, once glued together, cannot be taken apart. Many of them are braced on the top in such a way that light is restricted.

This is not a problem in the beginning, because acrylic lets the light through without too much loss of lumens, but after salt deposits itself on the bottom of the brace, the light reduction can be pretty substantial. Acrylic tanks tend to be more expensive than glass ones.

Which type to buy or use is a very personal decision. Weigh all the plus and minus factors, and then go for it.

If the aquarium will be placed in an area where it might get roughed up, it is probably better to go with the glass type. But that is a personal preference.

Of course price is also a consideration, and based on available information, acrylic tanks still seem to be more expensive than glass one.

This could of course change over time.

## 2.1.3  Sizing

Size-wise you should buy as large an aquarium as you can afford. It is much easier to keep a large aquarium in balance, than a small one.

Take for instance the effect of just one dead fish in a ten gallon tank, or the same in a one hundred gallon aquarium. The result of the decay in the smaller tank will obviously be much more dramatic than in the larger one. The larger water mass can better deal with the pollution than the smaller one. This comparison does not apply to dead fish only but to any kind of pollutant that is introduced in the water, either by accident or as a natural occurrence, e.g. food decay, airborne pollution, or for instance filters that are not performing properly.

A large aquarium gives more sense of depth, especially the ones that are 18 or more inches deep, front to back, and looks much more like a real reef. You probably have been able to observe that in the pet stores that you have visited, in public aquariums or at a friend's house.

They are easier to decorate, and made to look like a "reef" easily, using reef rock, and similar products sold in pet stores, and sometimes called cave rock, coral rock, etc.

When deciding on the size, keep in mind that high flow rates are advocated for marine tanks, and that several instruments may need to be added, besides the filter.These include amongst others : a skimmer, cooler, ozonizer, and perhaps a number of pH and Redox potential control instruments.

High flow rates require large tubing or pipe which takes up space. Corner filter boxes that lead to trickle filters reduce the overall size of the aquarium as well. It is therefore much better to buy, or build, a larger aquarium than you had originally planned. The minimum size we recommend is 55 gallons. Larger, 125 gallons and up, are a much better choice in our opinion.

You can of course elect to set up smaller ones, but the overall effect will be less dramatic. We have however seen quite stunning looking 55 gallon tanks, with trickle filters and instrumentation. Such were using a syphon overflow box, such as the ones made by Summit Aquatics, which not only act as a syphon, but also skim the surface and have an automatic re-starting feature. The reason we are mentioning this particular unit, is that it is quite affordable, and works exactly as the manufacturer promises. We have tested the unit thoroughly and can highly recommend it.

Dead coral rock, and the so-called live rock that you place on top of it, easily fills a smaller aquarium, and rather faster in fact than you probably think. Plan ahead, and buy the aquarium after you have decided what you would like to keep in it. This will avoid unpleasant situations, and perhaps redundant equipment and an unused tank.

Deep, top to bottom, aquariums might look nice and impressive, but keep in mind that they are hard to service. Hard to service aquariums get neglected in our experience.

It is much better to stick with a size that you can easily service, meaning that you can reach all parts of the aquarium including its bottom without needing a ladder, a chair, taking some of your clothes off, or having to "hang" over the edge to reach the lower parts of it. This is important in a reef tank, because you need to be able to look behind the rock and other forms of substrate regularly, to make sure that no dead or decomposing material is present.

Of course size is often determined by the placement of the aquarium in the house or apartment. This might make it worth considering a custom, rather than one of the standard sizes.

It is a misconception to believe that custom built tanks are not affordable. Plans can be bought for perhaps a few dollars, and any custom glass shop should be able to build such an aquarium for you. You may even wish to build it yourself, which is not all that difficult, especially after you have talked to a few people who have done so before, e.g. at an Aquarium Society and enlisted their help. The extra yardage achieved by having a custom tank, might just make the whole difference. "How to" books are often advertised in the hobby magazines.

The measurements needed to build a 180 gallon aquarium are :

6 feet, by 2 feet , by 2 feet, using half inch glass, braced across the top, in the middle section. A total of approximately 45 square feet of glass. will be required. Scrap, or left over pieces of such glass, can usually be bought for 7 or 8 dollars a square foot. The long front and back panels are each 6 feet by 2 feet, the side panels are 2 feet by 2 feet, the bottom is 25 inches wide and 6 feet long. The side pieces fit on the inside of the front and back. All pieces are on top of the bottom piece. The brace is 4 inches by 25 inches. You will need approximately 2 large tubes of aquarium silicone.

You may also build such a tank by placing the bottom inside the side pieces. The bottom plate would then be 23 inches wide, and 5 feet 11 inches long. In Germany aquariums are built using thick beads of silicone between the glass panes.

Should you decide to use this technique, you will need to add 1/4 inch in your calculations to account for twice a one eight of an inch bead.

The advantage of this technique is that the bead prevents stress from building up in the glass, as any stress is absorbed by the thickness of silicone between the panes, which always stays more pliable that the glass itself. It also increases the overall strength of the tank. This technique is nowadays so common in Germany, that it is hard to find an aquarium that is built differently.

In this country aquariums are rarely built that way. It would appear that manufacturers either do not like such a technique, or are not convinced that it improves the structural integrity of the tank.

Germans have built and used such tanks for many years, and talking to them has convinced us that they are definitely a better tank.

The measurements for a 225 gallon aquarium are as follows :

6 feet by 2.5 feet, back to front, and 2 feet high. The glass measurements in this case are : front and back panel 6 feet by 2 feet, the sides are 30 inches by 2 feet, the bottom is now 6 feet long by 31 inches wide, and the brace is 4 inches by 31 inches. In this case we would still use half inch glass, but we would brace the top in 2 places rather than one. You may also use 5/8 inch glass for this tank, if you wish to make it a little stronger, and enable it to withstand a little more abuse.

If you opt to use the 1/8 inch silicone beads, add one quarter inch to your measurements.

It is better to use black rather than the common, clear, variety silicone. Indeed algae will not grow on, or try to push there way behind it. Black silicone does not let light through. Algae on and behind silicone looks very unsightly and they are hard to remove.

Very important for the durability of the aquarium is the cleanliness of the glass at the time the silicone is applied. Correctly built glass aquariums, using silicone, can easily last for eighty or more years, without showing any signs of undue age (Kipper, 1985).

Do not buy aquariums that look shoddily built, or that are made out of thinner glass than you would use. You are looking for problems if you do; they will not hold up in the long run, and cost you much more money than you thought you were saving.

Acrylic tanks are not easy to build yourself; you should therefore rely on the workmanship of people who make a living handling such materials. They have the expertise required to do it right and with the appropriate bonding agents.

Acrylic material is somewhat hygroscopic, it absorbs water to some extent, and as a result it builds up internal stresses. The bonded seams must therefore be of superior quality.

Tanks or trickle filters that crack after a few weeks or months, were either built using the wrong bonding agent, or a variety that did not give enough strength to the bond. This can easily happen if you are not an expert at working with acrylic.

We do not advocate that you try building one, unless you are convinced that you have the necessary qualifications and expertise, or know someone who has, and can help you . A filter box that splits, or a tank that breaks, are experiences no one needs!

## 2.2 The Stand

Any wooden or metal stand will do the job, providing it can support the weight of the aquarium, and leaves enough space underneath for the type of filter that you plan to use.

Installing a trickle filter requires more space in the cabinet than if you were using cannister filters, or other more traditional methods of filtration.

It is important to ensure that the tank is absolutely level on the stand. This will prevent stress inside the glass or acrylic material, and prevent premature leaking, and cracking. Inserting a thin sheet of styrofoam between the tank and the stand will alleviate possible stress. Quarter inch should do.

Stands come in many finishes : wood, or metal covered with wood, plain wrought iron, and even fancy ones in oak, or a nice laminate material. You are the sole judge of which type you will buy. Price is obviously a consideration, but since you will be looking at the stand for many years to come, you might wish to invest in one that looks aesthetically pleasing.

Since the filters will need to be cleaned, and since easy access to them is a consideration, you may wish to have place your trickle filter next to the aquarium, in its own small cabinet that can be drilled to accommodate all the piping and tubing. This is often done in Europe and makes the maintenance of the aquarium that much easier. Perhaps you can even place the filtration in your cellar, and, using a strong enough pump, return the water using piping that comes through the floor.

One can also operate a trickle filter that is higher than the tank. In such a case the water is pumped to the the top of the filter, and it returns by gravity, through pipe that is at least one inch wide, to prevent water backing up. If high flows are needed, this return may need to even larger.

There is no magic to setting up a system in this fashion. Simply place the trickle filter on a firm shelf, perhaps inside a cabinet, at a level that is a few feet higher than the aquarium itself. Water is pumped to the top and flows back to the aquarium, from the front or side of the filter, into the tank. Running the filter this way, might perhaps not be as aesthetic, as when it is hidden inside a cabinet, but is just as efficient. We ran a 55 gallon tank that way for over a year, and built a slide over type cabinet to hide it from view.

## 2.3 Aquarium Substrates

It is important to select the right kind of substrate. The choice you make will depend on your personal preference, but you need to take the type of filtration you will be installing into account.

E.g. you cannot, of course, use sand in combination with an undergravel filter. Nowadays one can buy a variety of substrates that have high carbonate and bi-carbonate contents. These are the best ones to use, since they will assist in maintaining the buffering system of the water, resulting in a more stable pH. More details on buffering, alkali reserve and pH are to be found in later chapters. Spotte in his book "Seawater Aquariums" does however indicate that such substrates will not perform as such for extended periods of time.

It is therefore better to use an additive (Thiel,1986). Several manufacturers sell carbonate hardness builders, and tests, that allow for the easy control and determination of exactly how much of an additive is required, to build up the carbonate hardness to the right level. More on this in a later chapter.

It is very important to ensure that the substrate used is unadulterated, meaning that it does not contain impurities; other elements mixed with the basic material you are buying.

This is often the case if you buy these items from stores other than pet stores. It has been found, for instance, that the oyster shell mixes sold in animal feed stores contain so many impurities, that they will create damaging breakdown products that will harm the Reef Aquarium. These mixes might be cheaper than what you find at the pet store, but just are not worth the risk.

Crushed coral, dolomite, calcite or aragonite –an unstable form of calcite– are probably your best choices. All these can be bought either at pet stores or from specialized firms that advertise in the hobby magazines you probably regularly read.

If you plan to use egg or oyster shell, make sure that it is of the purest quality that you can find. Various combinations of of the above available materials are of course in order, but the resulting mixture might look unappealing and unnatural.

Composite substrates are not easy to clean either. The substrate in Reef tanks need not be thick. One quarter to half an inch is usually plenty. Do not forget that since the substrate does not have to function as a biological filter, you can get by with much less material.

Thinner substrates will prevent the formation of anaerobic areas, which as you well know are very detrimental. They reduce oxygen in the water, and may produce Hydrogen Sulfide, which will kill the fish and invertebrates.

Spotte (1979) also indicates that the grain size is important, especially if the substrate is used as a medium for bacterial growth. The recommendations is 2 to 5 mm, which is the size of most of the commercially sold mixes in pet stores anyway. More on this can be found in Spotte's "Seawater Aquariums, A Captive Environment" book.

If you still use an undergravel filter you may wish to read up on such filters in Stephen Spotte's classic book.

## 2.4 Other basic Implements

If you plan to run your aquarium the traditional way, you will need under-gravel filter, (see a later chapter), a heater, perhaps a cannister filter, or a box/outside filter, some nets, rocks for decoration, perhaps live rock.

Of course you will need a good quality salt, some trace element additive, a superior research grade carbon, and some fine filtering material such as floss, and a good air pump.

Since it is not the subject of this book to look at all of these in detail; we will assume that you have these at your disposal, and know how to use them.

If not, once more, please refer to a book that deals with how to set up an aquarium from the start.

Those of you who already have aquariums, or have had one or more of them in the past, probably have a cellar full of such implements anyway. No pun intended, just trying to be realistic.

## 2.5 Artificial Sea Salts

Salt in the form of NaCl, is one of the most important elements present in the water in which the Fish and Invertebrates that we keep have to live. Yet little attention is paid to the type of salt used. Many types of salt are now commercially available. Some are more "basic" than others. This can usually be determined from the way they dissolve in water, and from the amount of residue found in the tank after they have dissolved.

### Should you therefore buy the most expensive salt?

Not necessarily, it depends on what you plan to keep in your Reef tank.

More sensitive forms of life require better types of salt, meaning purer, containing more complete and or better mixes of trace elements.

What then determines the price and the quality of artificial sea salt? The salt that we use in our marine aquariums consists of 2 important groups of elements elements. NaCl or Sodium chloride, the salt itself, Carbonates and bicarbonates, and a mixture of usually 70 chemical elements, in different quantities, each in very minute quantities. Besides these elements the salt mix contains carbonates and bicarbonates which are also of great importance to us, as we shall see in the section on buffers and pH stability in the aquarium.

For a detailed chart listing the composition of natural seawater, we refer you to one of Stephen Spotte's books.

To prepare the salt mixes aquarists buy, manufacturers make composites of all the main elements and impregnate that mix with trace elements. The quality of, and the way the latter are produced, determines to a large extent their price, and the resulting price of the salt mix.

The other factor to be reckoned with that enters into the price equation is the purity of the sodium chloride and of the other compounds, the carbonates and the bi-carbonates. The purer they are, the more expensive the salt will be.

The better forms of trace element mixes are "chelated" as the chemical process is known, usually with EDTA. This ensures that they will stay in solution for much longer periods of time, which is in essence what we are looking for. By staying in solution, and not falling out, or precipitating, they are available to whatever forms of life we keep, be it Fish, Invertebrates and Macro-Algae of all types.

Use a high quality salt, especially if you plan to keep very sensitive biomass forms, e.g. soft corals, many types of Invertebrates, and Fish that are known to require a high water quality. Fortunately, most salts that are nationally sold are of excellent quality and can safely be used in reef-like environments. Many experimental tanks have been set up with them, and have enabled hobbyists and scientists to keep stock alive for extended periods of time, and even make certain fish spawn, as for instance reported by the Instant Ocean Company, in their publication called SeaScope, which is available from many good pet stores.

Stay away however from salts that seem shoddily packed, carry no labels, or come in "generic" form. You might be getting plain salt and no trace elements whatsoever. Several excellent salts such as Cora, Instant Ocean, Tropic Marin, and Hawaiian Marine, to mention only a few, are widely available and will give you consistent quality.

It is important to mix the salt and the water in a separate container first. Do not add the salt directly to the aquarium. Do not either prepare the salt mix just before you are planning to use it. Salts must be dissolved in advance and require time to do so completely.

Check the recommendations the manufacturer puts on the packaging. Short cuts are definitely out. After mixing the salt and water, you should aerate the mixture and let it stand for at least several hours before using the mix. This might seem trivial. It is not. Following this method will give even mixes, of the right salinity, that are free of any residual chlorine or chloramine that might have been put in the water by your local water treatment plant.

Carefully monitor the salinity of the aquarium for, as evaporation occurs, only water is lost, not water and salt, and as a result the salinity will have a tendency to rise. This is important to remember because natural seawater, the water the stock we keep comes from, is particularly stable in its composition. The life forms in our Reef tanks are therefore not able to cope with many changes, especially changes that occur too rapidly. Stability in all matters is the key to success for a reef tank. You may have read this before, but not paid much attention to it. In Reef tanks stability is the key to long term success (Thiel,1985).

## 2.5.1 So what about salinity?

Seawater contains on the average 35 mg per liter of sodium chloride. We should attempt to keep that same level in our aquariums at all times. This can also be expressed as 35 ppt (parts per thousand) or per mille, because 1 liter =1000 grams, and 35 grams equals 35 per mille.

Because the salt contained in the water makes that water heavier, the salinity can also be expressed by a number that indicates how much heavier than pure water it is. Pure water has a specific gravity of 1 in our case, since it is used as a reference. This is the measurement that we know as "specific gravity", usually known as "s.g."

The specific gravity we need to maintain is approximately 1.023. It is important to remember that the specific gravity is temperature dependent and can therefore change although the salinity is correct. Reefs can be kept at slightly lower salinities, as some hobbyists do, without any damage. We do not recommend however that the s.g. be lower than 1.019 and not higher than 1.027. This does not mean that you can vary it at lib however. Decide on one number and keep the s.g. there at all times. We have personally had excellent results at 1.021 with fish and corals alike.

Martin Moe has published a chart of the effect of temperature on salinity, to which you may wish to refer.

As mentioned, the salt mixes all contain trace elements, sometimes also referred to as oligo-elements. Some of the ones found in seawater are: Nickel, Zinc, Vanadium, Cadmium, Titanium, Molybdenum, Chromium, Germanium and many many others.

The exact nature of their importance is hard to gauge, but it is known that they are important for biological activity, for macro-algae growth, and are required by most Invertebrates. That is the reason that the salt you buy contains such a mixture of trace elements in the first place.

It has been determined from the scientific study of algae, that they can store 10 and even 100 fold the quantities of many such elements contained in seawater. For instance Fucus spiralis contains 1000 times more Nickel than the seawater it lives in, 300 times more Vanadium, 10 000 times more Titanium (deGraaf).

This has obvious implications for those of us keeping macro-algae. Indeed in the event of a die-off, great quantities of such elements are released very rapidly in the water of the aquarium, which can lead to a massive die-off of Invertebrates and sometimes even Fish, especially the sensitive ones. More on this in the chapter on trace elements, and also in the one on Algae.

A die-off has occurred when the macro-algae have turned whitish. In our experience this often occurs during the night, and although the reasons for this are not entirely clear, reduced oxygen levels and the lack of light are some of the causes.

This may lead you to refrain from keeping macro-algae, because of the danger that you perceive. This is in fact exactly the opposite of what you should do. Macro-algae perform many important functions in the Reef tank, as we shall see later. What you need to concentrate on therefore is the techniques necessary to keep such macro-algae alive and growing in the Reef tank.

You may wonder why we keep referring you to charts published in other books. The reason is that we elected not to reprint, with permission, material that is already widely available.

Drawings and charts are found in this book, they are new and germaine to the material discussed, not just re-statements of facts that can be found easily enough elsewhere.

We hope that we have not inconvenienced you in doing so.

## 2.6 Tap or Distilled Water?

When it comes to our reef aquariums, we start with the best of intentions, make water quality tests, buy the best equipment we can, read several books and magazines, in short, try to optimize all our actions to do things the right way. Strangely enough, no one seems to pay much attention to the type of water used to make the mix that will ultimately fill our tanks, and to its properties. Neither is this done for top-off water used.

This is a trend that we would like to see change, as in many areas tap water can be of very poor quality, and either needs to be "cleaned up" before it is used, or it must be treated in some way, before we can actually fill our tanks with it.

Every aquarist wishing to keep sensitive corals and invertebrates, as well as fish, should request a complete water analysis from his/her local water supply company. This will in most areas be sent to you free of charge. You might have a few phone calls to make to get to the right person, usually the manager of the local water treatment plant, and you might have a little explaining to do, as to why you wish to receive such an analysis. I have found however, that in most areas where I have been involved in this process, such plant managers are very cooperative and really take an interest in finding out what exactly it is that we are interested in, in terms of analysis.

Experience has shown that in many areas the water supply contains many undesirable compounds such as phosphates, nitrates, ammonium, even nitrites, and in quantities that are too high for our purposes.

Knowing what we are working with, enables us to better gauge what the results of the tests we will do on our aquarium water later, really mean. For instance, if we determine that after 3 months our aquarium has a NO3 content of 15 mg/l and we know that the water we use to do water changes contains on the average 6 mg/l, the aquarium has in effect added 9 mg/l. Also keep in mind that evaporation that occurs removes only water, and not the compounds already dissolved in it. This leads to an increasing concentration of such compounds, unless of course water changes, with water that does not contain them, are made on a regular basis (see water change section).

The same reasoning applies to other compounds such as phosphates, which as we will see later, are also undesirable as they stimulate the growth of many undesirable types of algae, especially of the micro types.

Evaluating how well our reef aquarium is performing will become much more accurate, and we will be able to judge how efficiently the combination of all filtration is affecting the water quality.

Does this mean that we cannot use our tap water if it contains high levels of such compounds; certainly not. However it might demonstrate the need to aerate it for some time to remove chlorine or chloramine; the need to filter it over carbon first, to remove certain other pollutants; the need to add carbonate hardness generators, to bring it in line with recommendations; the need to remove copper that might be present; the need to mix it with some distilled water to reduce levels of nitrate and or phosphate; or the need to aerate and ozonize it, should it contain organic material. The latter is unlikely, however it might be the case in certain areas where water quality is notoriously bad.

If, on the other hand, you are using well water, it pays to perform some of the testing yourself, to know exactly what the water that you are using contains. Then effect the required modifications following recommendations given in this and other books. If you decide to use well or rain water, it may be necessary to aerate it first to remove dissolved gasses which may otherwise lower your pH levels.

To sum it up, analyze the water before using it, and keep notes. These notes will then be available at a later date when you wish to compare actual tank results with the data obtained from testing the initial water. Adding distilled or chemical free water might seem farfetched. It is however not, and generally the quantities required are not substantial anyway. Many aquarists in Germany do, at least to some degree. Topping off with distilled or chemical free water is certainly to be recommended, and will not cost an arm and a leg.

It might however save you a lot of future trouble, and for instance avoid outbreaks of micro-algae blooms, invertebrates that look unhealthy because of excess nitrate in the water, and fish that die . This is particularly so in areas where the quality of the tap water is notoriously bad. This would be a pity, especially since chlorine is so easy to remove by just aerating the water for 24 hours or so. Although you can buy dechlorinators, we do not advocate their use, because they have a tendency to increase the sulfate hardness of the water. More information on acceptable levels of the compounds mentioned, and how to perform some of the tests can be found in later chapters.

Later in the book, a section on water changes deals with the recommended amounts, using distilled water, and the new water purification reverse osmosis filters.

To sum it up:

° Test the water used for both water changes and top-offs
° Get a complete water analysis
° If need be, mix the mains water with distilled or chemical free water
° Alternatively purify the water before using it. This can be done by flowing it over carbon, forcing it through a carbon cartridge, or using reverse osmosis filters.

# 3. Filtration Techniques

There are essentially three types of bacteria that decompose organic matter (protein) : Bacterium coli, Bacterium proteus, and Bacterium subtilis. Proteins are broken down first in peptides, and subsequently in amino-acids. This activity can have very nefarious results for the aquarium, and could be the cause for the infamous "wipe-out syndrome". Indeed certain of the bacteria excrete toxins which are very noxious.

If, due to increased activity, because of a dead fish that is decaying, which results in an explosion in the growth of such bacteria, the levels of toxins suddenly rises rapidly, a massive loss of biomass could occur in the tank. It is therefore important to regularly check the aquarium, to ensure that no such decay is taking place.

This is also one of the reason why thick layers of sand should be avoided, as these bacteria usually inhabit the substrate. A sign of their presence is typically black spots, that when stirred up, give off a very strong smell, hydrogen sulfide (rotten egg smell). If sand is used, one should always make sure therefore that the layer is thin, moved around regularly, e.g. by hermit crabs or horse-shoe crabs, and that any dead fish or other dead material is taken out of the tank quickly. Check especially behind rocks and corals.

Amino acids belong to several groups. Some are the result of the breakdown of protein, others are the result of fish excrements.

Oliphatic amino acids are of no real concern to us, as they do not usually pose any danger. Amino acids containing Sulphur however are, as they can give rise to the presence of strongly reducing compounds, as opposed to strongly oxidizing compounds, which raise the redox potential. Sulphur containing amino-acids will lower the redox potential (see later chapter) of the water. Low redox potential is therefore an indication that problems exist, and that tank maintenance is urgently required, before damage occurs.

Low redox is also associated with lower levels of dissolved oxygen, which in itself is not desirable as it puts a lot of stress on the fish and can give rise to anaerobic activity. This can lead to the formation of the black spots mentioned earlier, when after forming organic acids these intermediate breakdown products combine with iron. The amino acids referred to that have strong reducing capabilities are methionine and the cystine-cysteine redox group. Ozone can greatly reduce their presence and decrease any such dangers (see Ozone)

Aromatic amino acids, although not posing a danger are oxidized by bacteria and result in the presence of phenols and cresols, the latter can be removed with good quality activated carbon. Phenols and cresols are the reason for the yellowing of the water as a matter of fact. Water that is heavily loaded with phenols and or cresols is detrimental to Invertebrates, corals and also to the more sensitive types of Fish.

Phenols need to be dealt with at all costs, as if nothing is done, their levels will rise over time to a typical 0.1 to 0.2 mg per liter. Invertebrates will suffer very quickly at these levels. Anemones will not open, or start decaying, corals will seem droopy, tube worms lose their crowns, and all invertebrate life looks as if something is wrong (Thiel,1986). None of the tests that you perform indicates shows anything wrong with the water. Of course phenols and cresols are not factors we test for.

Excess levels of amines, the result of bacterial breakdown of amino acids, are toxic, at least some of them. If these amines are not broken down serious problems can occur in the aquarium. Their levels build up when the normal break down processes are interfered with. This could result from the use of e.g. antibiotics, or other medications that destroy bacteria.

Do not therefore add any medicine directly to the aquarium, rather treat any Fish that needs to be treated in a separate tank, known to most of you as a "hospital" tank. Having such a small tank set up at all times is always a plus. Keep it running with just a box filter, and perhaps just one or two small Fish, thus keeping the water free of ammonia and nitrites. When treatment is necessary, add medicine and change water as recommended by the drug manufacturer. It is both wise and a great advantage to have a hospital tank set up somewhere continuously. Keep this recommendation in mind.

The amines get further broken down into organic acids and ammonium. The organic acids pose no threat to the reef aquarium, except if an excess of them lowers the pH. Kipper (1987) however writes that acidity due to organic acids is easily tolerated by Fish and Invertebrate life.

Nitrosomonas further break down the ammonium into nitrite, which in turn is turned into nitrate by the Nitrobacter. The whole process described so far is a highly aerobic process, meaning that it requires the presence of oxygen at all times. If the process occurs in the absence of, or at low levels of oxygen, even in parts of the filter or of the aquarium, the decomposition follows a different course, and noxious fatty acids as well as carbonic acid, are formed. The latter mixes with water to form $H_2CO_3$.

Anaerobic mineralization can produce several other noxious elements as by-products : indoles and scatoles. This process is easy to avoid however, by ensuring that no anaerobic activity exist in the tank and in the filters. This comes back down to superior maintenance practices. Keep it in mind! Indeed, anaerobic activity can occur in parts of the mechanical filters, without it being noticed.

Chemical filters, especially carbon in bags that just lie in the water and are covered with slime and dirt, can also give rise to some anaerobic activity. When this occurs, and when such indoles and scatoles are formed, problem might come for which the aquarist cannot find a reason.

We mentioned that ammonium is produced as a result of aerobic activity, however additional quantities come directly from the fish and from other lifeforms we keep. There is therefore always an abundance of work for our biological filters. We should ensure that their performance is not interfered with in any way.

For this reason, cleaning biological filters is extremely detrimental to tank conditions, and this is contrary to what you might believe or have heard. If you are not convinced yet, read this section on the breakdown of organic material a few more times, until you are satisfied that you understand the importance of maintaining extremely high levels of biological filtration. It will save many a fish and invertebrate and make the tank look much better overall.

Depending on the pH of the water, ammonium ion becomes ammonia, a gas, that dissolves in the water, and is extremely toxic. The higher the pH, the higher the percentage of ammonia. This is important to know, as only slight variations in pH result in much higher levels of ammonia, the toxic gas. Ammonium hydroxide $NH_4OH$ does not seem to be harmful to fish, although various theories on this co-exist, some alluding to possible noxiousness.

Nitrates are another matter altogether, and will be covered in a separate chapter, both in terms of quantities and possible ways of reducing their levels, which is a must in a healthy Reef.

While we have covered the breakdown of organic matter somewhat in detail, books could be written just on this subject, as so many other factors enter into consideration, especially in a closed system such as a reef tank. For instance, one of the end breakdown products is present in the water in the form of phosphates, PO4.

Phosphates accumulate in the water up to the level of maximum saturation, this in itself is already a problem as we will see in the chapter on microalgae. Once the phosphate saturation levels are attained, phosphates fall out, precipitate, in the form of magnesium phosphate or calcium phosphate, this in turn reduces the buffer of the water and affects the pH stability. Keeping phosphates low is therefore an important task for us to perform for more than one reason. You will find more on this in later chapters.

DeGraaf also indicates that a certain type of bacterium that is extremely dangerous to fish, can kill off a whole tank in a very short period of time, grows in filters that are not properly maintained, in tanks that are high in organic load.

These "Shigella" bacteria (which cause food poisoning in humans), do not normally grow in our aquarium because conditions there are not propitious, but they proliferate easily in filters if the latter are not well cared for. This has a major implication for us, indeed we can prevent the existence of these bacteria by regularly cleaning any mechanical filter in the tank, making sure that there are no dead spots in the aquarium where material can accumulate and decompose, and change our carbon regularly.

To check for efficiency of the carbon, use either the Dupla carbon efficiency test, or take two pieces of plastic, one white and one just very slightly yellow. Put both in the aquarium holding them next to each other, look from approximately 1 to 2 feet away through the front pane, and you should be able to still see that one piece of plastic is white, and that the other one is yellow. If you cannot see the difference you definitely need to change the carbon. Make sure that the yellow piece of plastic is only faint yellow, not strong yellow as this will falsify the test somewhat, and you might be changing carbon more than you should. This is of course not detrimental, but it involves a greater expense to you.

We have already mentioned the term "mature" filter, or cycled filter as it might be known to you, several times. Cycling a tank is described in great detail in every aquarium book we know. You should therefore not have any problem in understanding the concept, and know what you have to do.

However, cycling is just a process, a word used to define the fact that bacteria are now growing that break down ammonia and nitrite. This is not the whole picture, as we are sure you can appreciate. It should be clear that the more Fish there are in an aquarium, or a combination of Fish and Invertebrates, the more nitrogen compounds are produced, and the more efficient the filter needs to be to be able to cope with this ammonia-nitrite presence.

When you cycle your tank, the biological filter adjusts itself to the amount of "pollution" that is present in the water. This means that if there is little such pollution, your filter cannot cope with heavy loads of it immediately. By pollution, in this case, we mean the ammonia-N, which becomes present as protein has been broken down to some of its end products.

Example : let us assume that you have cycled your tank with 5 Damsels and a Hermit Crab. After about 30 days you determine, through the tests you conduct, that both ammonia and nitrite levels have peaked, and then gone down to practically zero, or to levels that are not detectable with the test reagents that you use. You deduce from this, and rightfully so, that your filter has cycled and that the tank is now ready to accept more life.

Careful ! You have a filter that is mature, and can handle the load produced by 5 Damsels and one Hermit Crab. That is all it can safely handle. When you now add Fish or other Invertebrates, more pollution is created and the filter has to adjust itself to this new and higher load. This takes time ! And this is the reason that you have to go very slowly when adding new Fish and new Invertebrates, even though your filter has matured.

Our recommendation is that you do not add more than two medium Fish, or one large Fish, or one invertebrate at a time, and that you wait at least 4 days between each subsequent increase in biomass. This will give the filter a chance to adjust itself slowly to the new load, and do so without creating undue stress on the biomass that is already in the tank. If you do not follow these recommendations you will find that you will have a difficult time keeping nitrite to a maximum of 0.1 mg per liter in your tank on a continuous basis. You will stress the fish, and the risk that diseases will take hold becomes greater.

It does not pay to make water changes when you first cycle a filter, or tank. Indeed in doing so, you remove the elements that the bacteria need for growth and maturation of the filter. Making such water changes will result in your cycling time being slower than normal, as each time that you change water, you inhibit the bacterial growth by removing pollutants (=food). The balance between the amount of pollution due to the biomass now present in the tank, and size of the filter required to handle that amount is therefore not achieved. Bacteria only grow if the food they require is present, and by removing it artificially, you are preventing a number of bacteria from growing.

You must cycle your filter in such a way, that enough bacteria are naturally present, to deal effectively with the amount of pollution in the water. Read how to set up your aquarium for biological filtration in another book, in detail, and follow the instructions as best as you can.

We know, you are impatient and you would like to put more Invertebrates and Fish in your reef tank. For the long term stability of that tank however, you need to go as slowly as possible in the beginning, and only gradually build up the biomass, thereby allowing the filter to adjust itself each time to the new amounts of ammonium and nitrite to be treated. Nothing happens instantaneously. Cycling a filter takes time, and unfortunately there are no real shortcuts.

You can somewhat speed up the cycling period by introducing a bacterial "seeding". This can be achieved in several ways.

Take a few handfuls of substrate, or filter material, from an aquarium that has cycled already, put the substrate or filter material in a filter bag, and put the bag in the top area of the trickle filter, right where the water is flowing into it. This will transfer a seed of bacteria to the new filter. This will speed cycling of the tank up by about 6 to 8 days maximum, and is a technique frequently used.

Some commercial products are available that portend to contain "dormant" bacteria that can be added to the tank to speed up the cycling process. Controlled testing has demonstrated that some of them do indeed shave a week or so off the cycling time, and that a potent colony of bacteria develops (S.Sharon,1985). The danger is that if the old tank contains undesirable bacteria, e.g. parasites, you might transfer those too.

— take soil from your garden, from an area where you have flowers or plants growing. Put it in a jar mixed with water that does not contain chlorine or chloramine. Shake the jar after closing it properly. Open the jar and let the soil settle. Let stand for about 3 hours. Use a wide-mouth jar only, to ensure that oxygen can penetrate.

Use only the top clear water from the jar and add it to the aquarium water. This water contains the same strain of bacteria that is required in the filter (Vanden Niewenhuyzen,1978). This should also be a cleaner seeding method than taking substrate from another tank. Add dormant bacteria, and your tank should cycle is somewhat less time than usual.

## 3.1 Traditional methods

To those of you who have kept marine tanks for a while, it should be clear that we are here referring to "Undergravel" filtration. This method, which is described in every aquarium book, has proven itself, and has enabled us to get where we are in the hobby. Spotte(1979) has written extensively on the subject, and so have many other distinguished authors. We defer you to them for details on how to set up such filters, flow rates, recommended media, sizes, their benefits drawbacks and so on.

Undergravel filtration is still the best traditional filtration method around. It can be combined with various other methods such as cannister filters, outside filters, and box filters, to maximize efficiency, and give those of you who keep heavy loads in their tanks more filtration. This may be needed to cope with additional amounts of pollution present in the aquarium due to the heavy biomass populating such tanks.

Since this method has been described in detail in so many books, we will not cover it here. Let us just say that undergravel filters require cleaning to make them work efficiently . Indeed, areas that clog, due to detritus accumulating in the substrate, restrict the water flow, and as a result, inhibit the growth of the desirable bacteria that break down ammonia and nitrite. Moreover, such areas might result in anaerobic (no oxygen) activity, which is especially detrimental to Invertebrates and needs to be avoided at all cost.

Although well maintained filters should no clog (Spotte, in Seawater Aquariums) and can be kept running for long periods of time, it is our experience that this is not so. Invariably, because of the high rates of water pulled through the substrate, detritus is trapped. As the amount of this trapped material increases, it clogs certain areas, restricting the amount of oxygen that can reach the detritus, since less or no water goes through that area anymore. This creates anaerobic activity after a while. This is potentially very dangerous to invertebrate life forms because of the small amounts of Hydrogen sulfide that can be created in the process.

Kipper (1987) also indicates that the flow through an undergravel filter is very uneven. Certain areas, where less substrate is present, restrict the water flow less, and more of the water passes through them as a result. Water indeed finds the path of least resistance. This happens for instance too in the areas where you place rocks, and push them down into the substrate. Around the base of those rocks, the layer of substrate is much thinner than in other areas, and consequently more water will flow through those spots. This in itself is not the problem. The danger is that since your pump moves only so much water, other areas will have less water going through them, less water meaning less oxygen, and again the possibility looms of anaerobic activity.

Kipper demonstrated that his findings are correct by using dyes, and watching how the colored water was coming through the undergravel filter.

Besides the traditional Undergravel Filters, reverse flow undergravel filters are nowadays also advocated, and portrayed to give better results. Providing the water that is forcefully pushed through the gravel, from underneath is clean, meaning mechanically prefiltered, these filters seem to perform slightly better than the regular flow ones. This was evidenced in research done by Sharon Sascha in Germany last year, using the Eheim reverse flow undergravel system, and by the results obtained, and seen by the author, in a 220 gallon aquarium maintained by John Sadowsky of Florida.

We refer those who are interested in this particular approach, to other literature dealing with this excellent filtration method. Several magazines have published articles on the efficiency of these filters and how to operate them. You should therefore have no problem finding sufficient sources of information if you wish to know more about reserve undergravel filters.

With regard to undergravel filtration in general, Stephen Spotte, in his book : "Seawater Aquariums, The Captive Environment" has described the process, and results to be expected, in great detail. The book is published by Wiley Interscience and is widely available.

When using undergravel filters, you will require either so-called power heads, or a good air pump, to initiate  and maintain the water flow through the substrate. Since water needs to be able to flow unrestricted through the gravel or whatever substrate is used, it is important to use the right kind of material, not too thick and not too thin, the correct size recommended is usually around 2 to 5 mm grains.

Keep in mind that one of the drawbacks of an undergravel filter is that whenever it is cleaned, either using a commercially sold gravel cleaner, or doing it the old fashioned way, by hand,the biological filter is strongly disturbed. This is obviously not desirable, as it requires the filter to rebuild itself to full potential after each cleaning. During that interim period, ammonia and nitrite will be present in the tank, and this will stress the Fish.

This is exactly what one needs to try to avoid. The less stress, meaning the stabler the conditions in the aquarium are, the better off the biomass in the tank is. Keeping such conditions stable is one of the goals of modern aquarium keeping, and it can be achieved, as will be clear to you, once you have read through this book, and applied the techniques suggested.

If one does not wish to install advanced and more intricate filtration, such as the one we will discuss later, the undergravel filter is still the best filter around.

Contrary to belief, and to information often found in articles, the lift tubes, powered by air, do not significantly increase the amount of oxygen in the water. Therefore stronger flow through stronger aeration, does not increase the dissolved oxygen level in any dramatic way. Oxygen is absorbed at the air - water interface. Agitating the surface is therefore beneficial, as it brings water layers with less oxygen to the top, where while exposed to the surrounding air, which contains more oxygen, it absorbs O2.

And of course in a marine aquarium high dissolved oxygen levels are very desirable, putting less stress on the Fish, and reducing the frequency of parasitic infestations and diseases.

Additionally, as we will see later, higher levels of dissolved oxygen correspond to higher Redox potential levels, or said differently water of better chemistry. High Redox levels also promote the disappearance of micro-algae, those undesirable forms of algae that many an aquarist has had to deal with. This is because these micro-algae do not survive in the high oxidation reduction levels associated with high redox potentials.

Keep in mind that an aquarium is an isolated mass of water, where the degree of pollution is always much higher than in the ocean, especially in areas around Reefs. Our Fish and Invertebrates therefore have to cope with water quality conditions that are far from what they are normally accustomed to.

The better filtration and water purifying methods we use therefore, the better an environment we are creating.

Most of the pollution comes from the uneaten and not completely digested food that breaks down in the water. Whatever care in feeding we take, a certain amount of food drops to the bottom and does not get eaten. Moreover, if we feed to often, fish will excrete an amount of not completely digested food. Their digestion is slow.

Overfed fish, or fish that are fed too often, create the same deleterious conditions in the aquarium : organic overload, and the resulting ammonia and nitrites plus other breakdown products. These include but are not limited to : catabolic breakdown products of protein, trimethylamine oxide, urea, uric acid, albumin, creatine, creatinine, amino acids, fish tissue breakdown products and so on (deGraaf,1979) (Thiel,1981).

The amount of nitrogen in various forms excreted by Fish and In- vertebrates is quite large, to the extent of 50 mg N per 100 gram of weight per day (Saeki, 1964). It was estimated that 25 to 50 percent of this is in the form of ammonium. This is an enormous amount for a small milieu such as an aquarium to eliminate, unless of course the filtration used is of superior quality and efficiency and sized correctly.

The latter illustrates the need to use the right medium and a sufficient quantity of it.

Fortunately, such efficient filtration can be achieved, as will become evident in the next few sections on Filtration.

Modern Aquarium with Corner overflow box, and holes in the bottom
Photo : Dupla Aquaristik Gmbh and Nollmann Aquaristik

## 3.2 Newer Methods

### 3.2.1 Cannister Filters

Cannister filters can be used in conjunction with other types of filters such as the "undergravel" filter, or just as stand alone filters, as is often done in marine tanks. Cannister filters are more recent, and have greatly been improved in the last years. The appearance on the market of brands such as Eheim and Magnum, PEP, Lifeguard and others, now allow the aquarist to not only use these types of filters as mechanical water purifiers, but also as combination units of biological, chemical and mechanical filtration, a major technological advance.

In our experience these units offer superior filtration, especially when sized correctly for both flow and capacity, according to the manufacturer's recommendations.

These cannister filters also come in handy when one has a tank that is carrying a high load, and is in need of additional biological filtration, or even additional chemical and/or mechanical filtration. This could be the case, for instance while going on vacation, when no water changes can be done; or if additional fish and invertebrates are placed in the aquarium for a brief period of time, when another tank is being modified.

One of the most important recommendations when it comes to cannister filters, and any other filter for that matter, is to clean them as regularly as possible. This will prevent detritus from accumulating inside the filter, decay, remove dissolved oxygen from the water, and maybe even start anaerobic processes. This could lead to the produc- tion of hydrogen sulfide.

Thiel(1981) observes that the easier it is to reach the filters, the more often they are likely to be cleaned. Keep that in mind when setting up your aquarium. It is also much easier to do things right the first time around, when you initially set up your tank, than after the tanks has been running for months, when suddenly complications start showing up.

This might take a little more time and planning, but the effort will pay off in the long run in both money and survival of the biomass.

Get expert advice if you are not sure of exactly what you need, or read a few more articles or refer to a few more books. Talk to store personnel and ask as many questions as need to be asked until you are satisfied you have all the answers that you feel you need to do things right. Select a store that has tanks that look healthy and in good condition, and where the type of equipment that you are interested in is being used of course.

Box and Cannister Filters of various recent makes.
Both types have been used successfully for many years
Photo Dupla Aquaristik Gmbh

Carefully select the materials you put inside your cannister, make sure they are of superior quality. For instance it is important that you select materials that do not leach any substances in the water that could harm the Fish and Invertebrates, especially the Invertebrates, which are in general much more sensitive than the Fish you keep.

Carbon is perhaps the one item where you need to pay particular attention, as there are so many varieties of inferior quality being sold. Buy carbon that carries a reliable brand name, rinse it in tepid water, and let it sit in water for about an hour or two. Superior grade carbons usually do not give off a lot of dust, meaning when you rinse them the water running off is not black. Keep that in mind the next time you need to buy carbon.

Lately products that contain both carbon and resins have appeared on the market. They offer the advantages of both carbon and another material that removes noxious materials from the water. Change them regularly, as there is no way to determine when the carbon and or resin is/are "exhausted", meaning that they cannot remove such elements from the water anymore. Dupla, a German company even features a carbon "efficiency" test. This is a simple plastic test card that allows you to determine based on color perception, whether your carbon is still active, or whether is has outlived its useful life, and needs changing. We explained earlier how you can make such a test yourself if you wish to do so.

When it comes to selecting a cannister filter, do not skimp on the quality, indeed the life of your Fish and Invertebrates might depend on it.

We have already addressed the need to clean filters in the section on undergravel filters. This is also the case with cannisters. Unfortunately, doing so reduces the biological filter efficiency drastically, as most bacteria are killed off during the cleaning process. Some hobbyists use two filters to circumvent this problem.

This is a much better way especially since the cleaning of the cannisters can be alternated between the two. This leaves at least one cannister with a mature filter in operation, and this method is certainly desirable over just running one cannister.

Cannister filters are often used in combination with undergravel filters, to provide additional biological filtration, combining it with both chemical and mechanical media. When used in such a fashion, these filters are a definite plus. When used alone, the amount of surface area they provide for bacteria to grow is rather limited, and the use of larger than normal, or several cannisters is therefore recommended in Reef tanks. A definite advantage of these filters is that they provide good water circulation, in addition to their filtering ability. Regular maintenance is paramount however, otherwise cannister filters will quickly start depleting the dissolved oxygen levels.

Decay inside the filter starts occurring if they are left running without servicing for long periods of time. One major drawback of both these and the undergravel filter is that both have a short life if electricity falls out due to a power loss, or if they stop due to mechanical failure of the pump.

Should this happen while you are absent, and should the electricity come back on, say after 4 or 5 hours, these filters can kill off the whole tank, by pushing water full of noxious elements back into the aquarium. This can only be avoided by using a trip switch in line, where once the pump stops, e.g. due to electrical failure, it can only be restarted manually. But this is of no help when the power failure is of only short time, and no harm was in fact done to the biological filter. A no win situation it would appear. Such switches will however save fish and invertebrate lives, and it is highly recommended that you install one or more of them on your filter(s).

Some hobbyists fill their cannister filters with broken coral and other such material, to enhance the carbonate hardness and maintain a stabler pH. Kipper(1987) indicates that these materials only dissolve at pH levels below 7, which is not the case in our aquarium. It would therefore appear that doing so does not actually result in an improved KH level.

Only the addition of carbon dioxide can create such an effect, by lowering the pH in the filter, in a small mass of water and as a result dissolving some of the Calcium and Magnesium carbonates and bi-carbonates, thus building up the buffer and maintaining a more constant pH. This entails the usage of a $CO_2$ reactor, which is explained elsewhere in this book.

## 3.2.2 Box filters or outside filters

Such filters have been available for quite some time, and make excellent additions to existing filtration methods such as undergravel filters. They could for instance be added to heavily loaded tanks to provide that additional amount of filtration that is required.

Using them on reef systems, as the main source of filtration does not seem appropriate however, as these filters where not really developed with the kind of bio-loads in mind typically found in a reef system.

Many models exist, and we refer those of you who are interested to books that deal more in detail with them.

No reference material has been found, nor do we have experience with using these filters in reef-like systems.

The filter described next does have a lot in common though with such filters. But the biological surface area is much greater and that is of course exactly what we should be interested in.

## 3.2.3 Bio-mesh filters

This is one of the newer types of filtration, introduced in Germany a few years ago, and only sold in the United States by Dupla Exclusiv, as far as we know at the time of printing.

These filters look very similar to the traditional box filters that we all know, but the plates through which the water has to flow, -and depending on the size of the filter, this number varies from 2 to 5-, are made of a special fiber that will let the water through quite easily, but traps the dirt and suspended detritus.

The first of the plates is the only one that needs cleaning, - this is the one that stops detritus from going through, acting as a mechanical filter -, the other plates act as a growing area for the bacteria that break down the ammonia and the nitrite to nitrate. These filters can sustain heavy water flows. The larger models easily over 1400 gallons per hour if needed.

An interesting feature of these filters, is that they can be placed in -side, on the side, in the back, or underneath the aquarium. The only changes to be made are the way in which the PVC plumbing is eff -ected. The better models have a special openings where electrodes for pH, Redox potential and such, can be inserted, thus not cluttering up the Reef aquarium.

Bio-mesh filters, because of the very high surface area that they accord for bacterial growth, represent a definite step up from the undergravel filter. It has been calculated (Jung,1986) that 1 square foot of the mesh used in the filters sold by Dupla, offers 24.4 square feet of submersed surface area for bacteria to grow in an oxygen-rich conditions.

The area is rich in oxygen because high flow rates are easily achieved, and because the individual plate layers are so thin, albeit large.

Bio-mesh filters require surprisingly little maintenance. The first plate is the one that needs to be cleaned regularly, indeed it gets quite dirty after a few days, as it picks up the detritus and cleans the aquarium water mechanically. It is removed by lifting it out, rinsing it a few times in tepid water, until gross particulate matter that was stuck to it is removed. The other plates remain untouched. They harbor the bacteria which we do not wish to disturb

# Bio-Mesh  Filters

Bio-Mesh Filters, are a new type of filter
recently introduced in the United States

Water flows in through compartment A and
overflows into B, where a filter basket
retains gross particulate matter

From B the water passes into the D
compartments which are the mesh plates
through which the water has to go
to be able to get back to the aquarium
from compartment E

A small to medium pump can run these filters  which
are designed for tanks up to 180 gallons

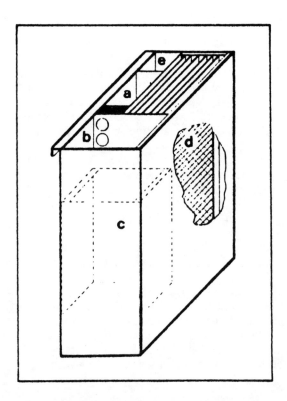

to ensure and maintain high levels of biological filtration. The filtering capacity of the first plate can be changed by switching filter plates.

Several mesh sizes can indeed be used. When newly set up in a Reef that has lots of detritus that needs to be removed, once can use a finer mesh. When the tank has been running on such a filter for several weeks, a medium type mesh can be used instead. This still picks up the large enough materials that need to be removed, to keep the Reef water clean, but will not need to be cleaned as frequently.

Flow levels through these filters are similar to the recommendations for other filters, e.g. undergravel ones. As a guide, multiply the actual water content of the aquarium by 5 or 6. Look for a pump delivering that true output, not just the quantity the pump is rated for as back pressure will reduce the pump's true output. Back pressure occurs from both the height against which the pump has to push to reach the filter or aquarium, and also as a result of the fittings and valves that you have to use to guide the water back and control its flow.

Bio-mesh filters could for instance be used as add-ons to an existing system that already has a filter, but needs more biological filtration because the tank is overloaded. Because these filters are relatively inexpensive, they are an ideal way to cope with such a situation rapidly and without great expense.

Of course an aquarium can be run on nothing but such a filter. They exist in various sizes and can therefore be matched to any type of marine tank that you might have. We have seen two models that are standard. Model 55-90, will handle tanks of 55 to 90 gallons, and Model 110-150 will handle reef tanks up to 150 gallons.

Custom size bio-mesh filters can also be ordered from Dupla, allowing you to match their size up to the specific aquarium you have in mind, and allowing you to influence the shape of the filter to some degree, to fit it into the space you have available.

Bio-mesh filters have multiple plates of a rather large size, 18 x 18 inches in the larger model that we have seen. Thanks to this size the total amount of water that flows through the filter, moves slowly but evenly through the various layers. This promotes superior filtration, both mechanically and biologically. Because in such set ups there is hardly any head pressure to deal with the pump needed to run bio-mesh filters is usually smaller than the one needed to run other type of filters.

The second plate may be cleaned if need be. This should not be the case, however in extremely dirty tanks this may need to be done. The other plates

1. Bio-Mesh Filter plates, the holes at the top ensure throughflow should the plate clog
2. View of a plate and how it will look after bacteria have settled on it for a while
3. Different type fine filter, by Nollmann - Dupla, that sits in the bottom of the trickle filter and ensures that no dirt gets into the water when it is removed for cleaning

Photos Horst E. Kipper and M. Prashun

should be left alone. The brownish color that develops on these plates is in fact your bacteria layer.

Since these filters have many "plates", removing one when cleaning is needed, is only marginally affecting the biological filtration, as the other untouched plates can continue to function while the new or cleaned plate builds up bacteria again. This is a major advantage over cannister and under-gravel filters of course. Selzle(1987) even claims that removing the plate for cleaning, does not affect the biological capacity of the filter at all, since so large a biological filter exists that the bacteria that are destroyed when cleaning the first plate , does not upset the filtration capability at all.

We have run a 180 gallon reef tank on such a filter for over two years and can report that the water quality is superior to that obtained with undergravel filtration, that redox levels are in the 390 mv range at noontime, and that all life in the aquarium is holding up extremely well. Oxygen levels are at saturation levels at noontime, and increase to slightly over saturation by late afternoon.

Bio-mesh filters are a major improvement in biological filtration, they are potent, do an excellent biological filtration job, and are not expensive to acquire and install.

This is of course a new technique, and hopefully we will see some more reports from aquarists who have used them, and are able to give us more insight in their experiences.

## 3.2.4 Corner overflow - filters

These are in reality not filters at all, but a means of bringing water to trickle filters positioned underneath the aquarium, by means of surface skimming and overflow principles. They consist of 1 or 2 pieces of glass or acrylic material, glued or bonded to the actual tank drawing. Their size is directly related to the size of the aquarium, or better to the amount of water that they have to process.

The top of the partitions is serrated, like a comb, to prevent Fish from being flushed into the actual cavity. At the bottom of the "corner box" water flows to the trickle or other type of filter, through a hole drilled in the tank. A bulkhead or tank fitting and pipe or tubing, guides the water to the top of the actual filtering unit.

The corner box can be set up to act as a mechanical filter as well, by filling it with appropriate material. This is desirable to prevent detritus of large size from entering the trickle or wet dry filter. Keep in mind however that this area will need very regular cleaning to prevent decay, reduction of dissolved oxygen levels, anaerobic activity etc.

To prevent the floss, or sponge or other material used as pre-filter from being sucked into the hole at the bottom of the corner box, a ledge in the form of a plate, with holes drilled in it, should be placed at the bottom of the corner box at about 3 inches above the water intake that leads to the filter underneath the aquarium. Many variations on how to set up this overflow to the filter exist. We cannot describe them all of course. Let it suffice to say that as long as the overflow can handle the quantity of water you plan to push through it, and as long as it pre-filters the water adequately, the rest is not important. Some people use the so-called Efimech from Eheim, or Biomech from Kordon to pre-filter the water. This is an excellent material, as it does trap dirt of all sizes. It requires frequent cleaning however to prevent clogging and anaerobic activity.

As the name implies " Efi Mech" is an efficient mechanical filter medium.

Besides floss and sponge, other materials such as broken pieces of coral or other calcium and magnesium containing materials are used. This is done in an effort to buffer the water by means of ionic exchanges. It should be clear however that as the medium gets dirtier, the ionic exchange between it and the water will be severely restricted, if not halted altogether. Regular cleaning is again the answer, and preferably in an acid type bath such as water and a little vinegar. This will remove slime and other materials that have coated the medium.

If no overflow box is used to provide water to the filter, the alternative is to use a syphon that takes water out of the tank and guides it down to the trickle filter. Syphons however can be problematic.

Indeed should the pump that pushes the water back to the aquarium fail, or should a simple and even just a short power failure occur, the system will not work any longer.

As the syphon brings water down, and hopefully it has been set up so that it can only bring back as much water as the bottom of the filter can hold, the syphon will eventually break since no water is coming back to the aquarium. Once the pump restarts, when power comes back, it will empty the sump of the filter and run dry and burn out, unless protected by a float switch. The filtration however is stopped until human intervention restarts the syphon. A very undesirable situation.

Automatic syphons are now available, which restart the water flow downwards automatically, once the pump itself restarts. These units are obviously the only ones you should use on your reef aquarium. Anything else is too unreliable and will eventually endanger the lifeforms you keep in your tank. Since several such models are being made available shortly, as far as we understand, you should have no problem finding one that fits your budget. We have already pointed out the one made by Summit Aquatics which as far as we have been able to determine can handle large water flows and does restart automatically.

Of course corner boxes are the better way to go, and they are easily installed when first setting up your tank. Retro-fitting, however,is a problem. The only way is to empty the tank, drill the hole(s) and build the corner box. Not everyone wants to do so and therefore the automatic syphon is the only viable alternative. Make sure however that the syphon used can handle the kind of water flow rates that your pump is going to deliver, and which you should have established based on the size of the tank.

Five to six times the content of the tank is usually acceptable as a true output, not as a rated output at zero feet of head. Indeed as the pump deals with back pressure its output is reduced. You should therefore acquire a pump that gives a higher output than what you are really in need of. Usually an extra 25 percent will do the job. E.g. if you need 600 gallons of output, buy a pump that has a rating of 800 to 900 gallons per hour. In this way you will be sure to have the water flow rates required for your reef tank. Remember, if the output ends up being too strong, which is unlikely, you can always regualte it by means of a ball valve, or re-direct some of the flow directly to the aquarium, rather than to the top of the trickle filter, by means of a T-fitting and some extra pipe. This results in the same amount of water re-circulting, but not all of it is going to the tank, some is re-directed to the top of the trickle filter.

## 3.3 Trickle Filtration and Trickle Filters

If biological filtration is as important as we have indicated so far, then surely we want to use a type of filter that will maximize filtration efficiency, and do so on a continuous basis. We do, therefore, not want to use some arcane device, that has not proven itself for some time, but that has the benefit of being inexpensive. Rather we want a proven filter, containing a proven medium, to which we can entrust the life and growth of the biomass we maintain.

Nobody. we repeat nobody in the aquarium hobby can lay claim to having "invented" the trickle filter, sometimes also called a wet dry filter -a misnomer we feel, as no section of the filter is meant to be dry-, or an ammonia tower. The reason we are so adamant about this, is because we want to give

The trickle filter
1  Water inlet
2  Pre-filter material
3  Sieve to distribute water evenly
4  Bioball filter material
5  Air inlet for optimum $O_2$ availability
6  Separation plate
7  Fine filter box
8  Pre-filter to protect pump
9  Pump

In the front right corner one can also see the
float switch to prevent pump from running
dry, and control the water level in the
bottom part of the trickle filter.

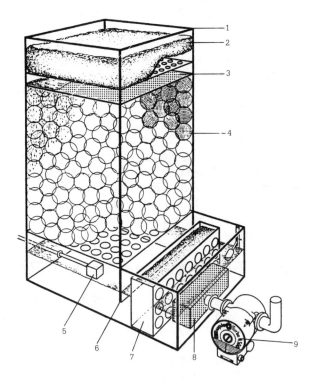

Perhaps not the most advanced trickle filter but surely
one that is easy to build and maintain
Notice the fine filtering at both the top of the filter and also before the
water can return to the aquarium

Drawing Dupla Aquaristik Gmbh

credit to a German, foresighted aquarist and manufacturer, Horst E. Kipper, who knowing about the existence of these types of filters, had the courage to test it to see if it could be used with benefit in the hobby. Having determined that this was so, he then incorporated the filter in a much more complex aquarium set up that his company markets in Europe, the USA, Australia and several South East Asian countries and Japan.

Ammonia towers have been around for decades, in particular in water sewage treatment. They are therefore not only "not" new, but have proven their efficiency under rough conditions for many years. Surely, if they can handle the kind of sewage found in industrialized countries, these filters must be able to handle the pollution normally found in a closed aquarium environment. The answer Horst Kipper found was an unqualified yes, if these filters were set up correctly.

A trickle filter then, consists of two main parts. An area through which the aquarium water can flow over a medium where bacteria can grow, and that medium itself. Both are important in terms of correctly setting up the filter, and both will require your special attention. There are also a few other items that you will need to pay attention to, as you will find out while reading the rest of this section.

### 3.3.1 The Filter itself :

The filter can be round or rectangular or square, or really any shape you wish, as long as you can fill it up with a certain quantity of a medium where biological filtration will be promoted.

It can be made out of glass, or acrylic material, or pvc sheet or pipe, or even other materials treated so that they are salt water resistant and safe. For instance, we could conceivably build a filter out of wood that has been coated with several layers of polyurethane, or we could use a stainless steel vat, as long as the stainless steel is of the saltwater resistant kind (usually referred to as 316SS).

Practically speaking however, most aquarists will want to either buy or build a filter that is made out of glass or acrylic material. Because of the ease of building and ease of assembly the filter is usually square or rectangular. The size is determined by the amount of media that it needs to hold, using the formula given elsewhere in this chapter with regard to media amounts used for reef tanks. Provision is made for good water distribution over the medium by using either a drip plate, or a spray bar type assembly. Both have their merits, as described elsewhere. Since the water that flows over the medium, needs to be returned to the aquarium, so we can maintain a continuous process, we need to let it collect in an area at the bottom, the sump, and from there, with a pump sized to fit the type of aquarium that you have, pump it back to the tank.

The biological filtration process being an aerobic one, we need to provide sufficient quantities of oxygen in the filter. To do so we use a standard air pump available in any pet store, and blow a continuous stream of air inside the area where the medium is located.

In essence that is all there is to it. The diagram below shows you how such a filter can look, and what type of constraints are put on it.

Building such a filter is not easy if you wish to have a unit that will work for long periods of time, without fail, and give the efficiency that you need to maintain a healthy reef like tank. It can be done, but if you have no previous experience with glass or acrylic material, the type of glues and bonds required and how to apply them, we strongly suggest that you acquire one of the many models that are now available on the market, especially since most of those models incorporate a few of the advanced features that are described later in this chapter.

With the advent of the many so-called "reef" systems, a multitude of trickle filters are available through ads in magazines, and or in pet stores. One error frequently made however is to mix elements from different filters and combine them to come up with a hybrid type filter, this is not advisable. Every manufacturer tries to build a filter that is as complete as he feels it needs to be. Adding elements that come from other filters might detract from the efficiency of the filter you end up with. Keep that in mind when making modifications to your own.

A few of the trickle filter features that are important to understand are :

since you will have to rely on your pump 24 hours a day, it is a good idea to protect it from running dry, overheating and shutting itself off. This is done with the use of a float switch, placed in line with the pump electric supply. The switch operates very much like a light switch, as long as it is in the on position the pump will run. When in the off position the pump stops. The latter occurs when the water level in the sump becomes too low. Should you not have such a switch, the pump would suck air, dry lock, run hot and shut off permanently, until you did something about it. By then your reef could have died off...

The only thing that you need to do, is install the float switch at the desired level, by making its horizontal level, about 1.5 inches higher than the top of the water intake. This will prevent both the pump from running dry, and also the sucking in of air because of a small whirlpool right above the water

# A Basic Trickle Filter

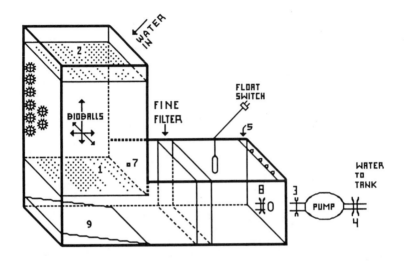

A Basic and easy to build trickle filter. Many improvements are still possible.
1, 2 : plates holding fine filter media and trickle filter media
3, 4, 8 : Ball valves and Check valve (8)
9 : slanted plate, makes detritus come forward for easy cleaning
Only one compartment for fine filtering is provided. This can also be used for carbon
Drawing A. Thiel

# Float switch assembly

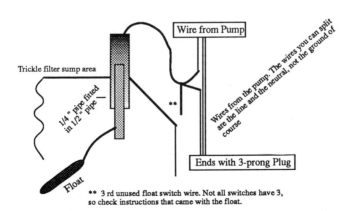

** 3 rd unused float switch wire. Not all switches have 3,
so check instructions that came with the float.

# TYPICAL TRICKLE FILTER WITH ADD-ONS

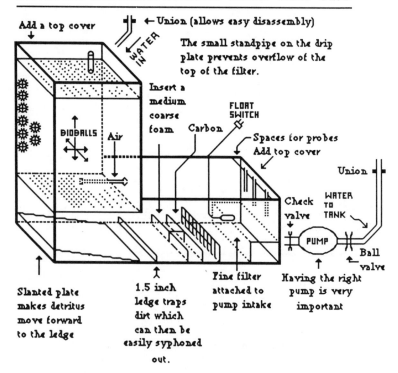

Add a top cover

← Union (allows easy disassembly)

WATER IN

The small standpipe on the drip plate prevents overflow of the top of the filter.

Insert a medium coarse foam    Carbon

FLOAT SWITCH

BIOBALLS    Air

Spaces for probes
Add top cover

Union

Check valve

WATER TO TANK

PUMP

Ball valve

Slanted plate makes detritus move forward to the ledge

1.5 inch ledge traps dirt which can then be easily syphoned out.

Fine filter attached to pump intake

Having the right pump is very important

Certain trickle filters now have removable media compartments. This is of course a major advantage, making cleaning of the sump very easy.

The foam compartment is doubled. This allows for one pad to be removed and cleaned while the other one is still used for slow throughflow and denitrification intake, which would also make the pump heat up and stop eventually.

There are various types of float switches. They are described in ano- ther chapter. As indicated mercury switches are a little more expensive, but are more reliable in the long run. When buying such a switch make sure that it can handle the amperage generated by the pump you use -amp rating- or the float switch will stick after a number of hours of use, either in the open or in the closed position. If this happens you have a defective float switch and will need to acquire a new one.

Once installed the float switch will regulate the working of the pump by shutting it off when not enough water is in the sump, and switching it back on when that same water level rises again. The float switch goes up and down with the water level in the sump, as its name implies.

Why does the water level rise in the sump? Either because you added water, or because the overflow filter in the aquarium let more water come down, this while the pump was off, which obviously results in the sump level rising. Water will always continue to come down from the aquarium into the filter, even after the pump stops, because of the way the overflow box is made, at least the top of it, which should be like a comb-like piece of acrylic or such material. If you cannot buy one in a pet store, you can easily manufacture one if you have an electric handsaw. Take a strip of acrylic, or such, that is about 3 inches wide, and long enough the cover all top parts of the overflow. If you made the overflow box square or rectangular you will obviously need two pieces, and if you made it triangular you will need only one.

## 3.3.2. Installing a Check Valve

The pump returns water to the aquarium. The pipe or tubing by means of which this is done, is in most cases beneath the water level. In the event of pump failure, or main power failure, this piping can act as a syphon, in the downwards direction. Depending on how deep that same pipe is beneath the water level, this could cause the sump to overflow. And as we all know from past experience, salt water does a considerable amount of damage. Installing a check valve, in line, will prevent such an overflow from happening.

However, check valves need cleaning once in a while, indeed if dirt builds up inside they might let a trickle of water through, negating their purpose. In our experience, it is a good idea to clean this valve once a month. You should therefore buy a valve that can be opened, and such a type is usually referred to a true-union valve. It should be of the same pipe size as the rest of the system. If you return water to the aquarium with 3/4 inch pipe then that should be the check valve size too.

We have found however that in most cases the better type pumps, have 1 inch fittings, so you will be using one inch pipe or flexible tubing to return the water, and your check valve should therefore be one inch.

One can also use what is called a Y-check valve. They are pricier than regular check valves but have the advantage of reducing the flow of the water less.

Also make sure that whichever valve you acquire, that it is salt water safe. This means that it cannot have any metal on the inside, not even small screws that are sometimes used to hold some of the parts together.

Y-check valves made by Hayward, are made 100 percent out of PVC, even the spring inside that acts as the check mechanism.

The check valve can be installed between the pump and the trickle filter, inside the trickle filter, or between the pump and the tank. It does not make a difference in its workings. However, since you will need to clean it, you should place it either inside the sump, or between the sump and the pump.

Check valves prevent the backflow of water, which is their purpose. They however also prevent air from escaping from the piping, and as a result, when you first start up your filtration, you will need to make sure the pump is primed, meaning that no air is trapped inside of it. To do this is really easy. Push a long piece of rigid plastic tubing, the one used in undergravel filter up-lift tubes, and push against the ball in the check valve. This will let water and air flow back and prime the pump. Of course, do not forget to remove the piece of tubing.

### 3.3.3 Types of Valves used

Besides a check valve, two more valves are required when building or setting up a trickle filter. They are called ball valves, and their purpose is to allow you to regulate the flow back to the aquarium on one hand, and close this same water line off if need be, on the other. Why?

There are several reasons. If you are using a strong pump, you might wish to regulate the exact water flow back to the aquarium, and set it at the level that you are happy with. This is done by means of a valve placed between the pump and the aquarium, and only by that valve. Do not restrict output on the intake side of a pump, it might lead to the creation of cavitation, a situation where the impeller of the pump breaks up the too little water, and chases the dissolved gasses out. This can be observed by the presence of tiny air and other gas bubbles coming into the aquarium at the outflow pipe.

Again you will need to clean that valve once in a while, therefore use true-union ball valve, they cost a little more, but they will save you a great deal of aggravation later. Believe me, I have seen many tanks without a true union valve, and can assure you that when cleaning or pump maintenance is necessary, great problems and a lot of "expletive deleted" type language can be heard. A second reason you require a valve is to isolate the sump of the trickle filter from the pump, so you can service the pump itself. This true-union ball valve is placed between the sump and the pump. If now you need to take the pump out of line, to either service it, or clean it, all you will need to do, is to close the two ball valves, unscrew the two unions closest to the pump, one on each valve, and remove the pump.

If you placed the check valve between the sump and the pump, then the second ball valve needs to be placed between the sump and the check valve. This will allow you to remove the check valve, after closing both valves. The only water that will flow out of the pipes in both cases discussed, either pump or check valve servicing, is the water that is in the short length of pipe between the two valves, plus the water in the pump itself. A towel placed underneath the pump will easily accommodate this quantity.

Ball valves are serviced once every 3 months or so, by opening and closing it several times, switching the pump off while closed of course, and on while open. Doing this will force the accumulated dirt out of the ball section of the valve.

## 3.3.4 Spaces for Carbon, Sponges, Foam, Electrodes and other implements

Some basic filters contain such compartments, and slots, but not all of them. Check if you can find one that does, as it makes your life easier, and also makes the water flow more efficiently over the sponge and carbon. See advanced trickle filters for more details, and for a more detailed explanation on what these various compartments do for you. Some filters even have small skimmers built into them which sometimes also allow for the addition of ozone. Many different types of Trickle Filters are advertised in the hobby magazines, and better stores might have several on display. You could also contact the manufacturers and ask them to send you a photograph or brochure with pictures.

## 3.3.5 The Filter Medium

We know that we require bacteria to grow in the filter we have just built or acquired. That was explained in detail in the beginning of this chapter. We

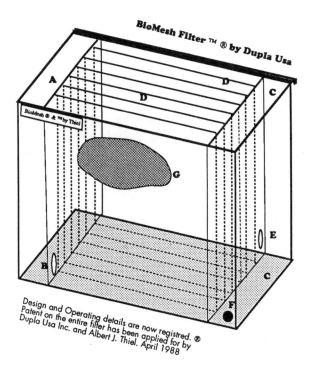

also know that these bacteria function optimally in an aerobic (oxygen rich) environment, and we are therefore pumping air into the area of the filter where the medium we will use is positioned, and we do so above the sump's water level.

Although some pictures we have seen, give the impression that this air inlet is below the water surface in the sump of the filter, our recommendation is to position it above that level, as its efficiency is greatly increased when you set it up in that fashion.

Since in a reef like aquarium a great deal of pollutants are created, by fish, invertebrates, micro-algae and macro-algae alike, and since we wish to keep the size of the filter we have or will buy, to one we can easily fit underneath our aquarium, and since we wish to fill it up with a cost efficient medium, selecting the latter is not going to be an easy task, unless we make some trade-offs.

Inexpensive material with little surface area, might require us to use more of it, thus needing a larger filter, whose purchase price might offset the money saved on the medium itself.

Media with a rather large surface area, but that restrict the water flow, are not acceptable, as they will trap dirt in the process of restricting the flow, will require regular cleaning, which is exactly what we do not want to do. In fact we want to avoid having to do so at all cost, as we have pointed out many times already.

Small media, with extremely high surface areas, e.g. carbon-like ma -terials, with pores - Matrix is such a material - will harbor different kinds of bacteria than we want, including anaerobic ones (bacteria requiring no oxygen), and will trap a great deal of dirt, again posing the cleaning dilemma. Additionally any anaerobic activity is dangerous, hard to control, and too little research exists to allow us to make recommendations that we can feel comfortable with.

Material such as pvc pipe cut-ups, or plastic hair curlers, might not restrict the flow, are inexpensive, but do not offer a great deal of surface area, or at least do not maximize the surface area for bacterial growth.

They also trap dirt, even large pieces of detritus and decomposing fish, and will only lead to low redox potential levels, lower dissolved oxygen levels, and other problems over time. We do not recommend that you use them.

Making the right choice is therefore not as easy as it might have appeared right at the beginning.

Our recommendation is simple : use the material that gives the best cost to surface area ratio, without flow restriction and without possible clogging over time. There are a few of them on the market, and the one we personally feel fits our recommendation, because it was developed based on a computer designed model, is the Bioball, sold by Dupla.

Our second choice would go to the Norton Ring, then the Pall ring, followed by the Jaeger Tri-packs, but of course that is only a personal choice.

Newer materials such as Bio-Beads and Matrix fit in another category. They can be used in trickle filters as well, but will trap dirt and they will require cleaning.

Destroying bacteria in the process of doing so is exactly what we are trying to avoid when we step up to trickle filtration. This does not mean that they should not be used of course. What we are saying is that there are media that are better suited for trickle filters.

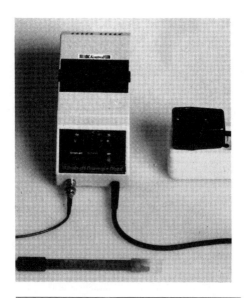

*Modern pH continuous controllers can measure the pH accurately and control the supply of $CO_2$.*

# 3.4. Advanced Trickle Filters

Advanced trickle filters are nothing more than regular trickle filters, like the ones we have looked at in the previous chapter, that have been improved by the addition of several features :

- better aeration of the media
- space built in for advanced heaters
- provision made for ozone addition
- spaces for carbon bags
- spaces for fine filters e.g. sponges
- improved drip plates with overflow and dissolved gasses return
- spray bar
- or drip plate
- provision for returning water from a protein skimmer

Filters that are able to hold a number of filter media quantities and that incorporate these features, are now sold in quite a number of pet stores and through ads in various magazines. Custom built units that will allow anyone to obtain a unit to fit the job, even if the tank is of a non standard size, and larger than the biggest of the models offered can handle, can be ordered from various sources.

As already indicated, we recommend that 10 to 15 percent of the actual water content of the tank, in equivalent volume of media be used, providing the media is a large surface media, meaning over 20 square feet per gallon of media. Increasing the amount of media is obviously not harmful, to the contrary it will only benefit the tank; on the other hand there is no need to overdo it,just remember to base the amount of media used, on its surface area.

Many media are now available, from self-made types to very sophisticated, computer generated models made into molds and then produced in quantity. Some of these include, either by generic or by brand name, often registered by their manufacturers :

- Efi-Mech by Eheim
- Biomech by Kordon
- Jaeger Tri-packs, sold as Bio-spheres
- Norton Rings
- Pall rings
- Raschig rings
- Matrix by Seachem (porous like carbon)
- Cut PVC pipe
- D.L.S. material (DLS stands for Double Layered Spiral)

- Crushed coral pieces
- Broken up pieces of dead coral rock
- Bioballs by Dupla
- Hair curlers in plastic material
- Plastic shotgun wadding
- Biopax also made by Jaeger Tri-packs
- and many other such media

Besides checking the surface area of the medium you use, you should make sure that it does not trap dirt. If it does, it will need to be cleaned regularly, meaning you will severely upset the biological filter each time you do so. And we have already indicated several times that you need to avoid that at all costs.

You may have read in some article that you can clean the filter gently without harm to the bacteria. This may be true of fresh water filters, but in marine tanks it is definitely not. Moreover, removing dirt usually means more than just a little gentle rinsing. Bacteria just do not care for such treatment, especially if the salinity of the water is changed in the process. Accumulated dirt is also mixed into the water each time the filter media is cleaned. This is unavoidable, and you must have experienced it yourself when cleaning your D.L.S. or other material.

Let us now take a look at the various extra options that can be already built into a trickle filter when you buy it, or can be added to them yourself afterwards.

## 3.4.1. Aeration

Since the biological filtration process is an aerobic one, we need to ensure that high and stable levels of oxygen are always present in the filter areas that hold the medium on which we want the bacteria to grow. This should be obvious.

Providing such oxygen levels can however only be achieved if we force air into that area, on a constant basis, using a good quality air pump that delivers a substantial amount of air. How much air is dependent on the size of tank, i.e. the filter, but should not be less than 200 liter per hour, and preferably more. In larger set-ups you should increase that amount to 400 and even 500 liters per hour. Check air pump specifications to determine which one will do the job for you. The air inlet needs to be above the water level that stands in the sump of the trickle filter. The diagram shows where to locate the inlet. An airstone is not necessary.

To spread the air evenly throughout the filter, you may wish to use a set-up

that is slightly more intricate. Cut a piece of PVC pipe length-wise in half. Use a size that is larger than the pipe used for the actual air dispersion. Glue that half pipe into a small tank fitting (one of the ones described in an earlier chapter) and thread that through the front piece of glass, where you screw it firmly into place using a the other part of the tank fitting to which a rubber or other plastic O-ring has been fitted first. The length of the piece of half-pipe is dependent on the size of the filter, but it should reach from front to back.

Now use thinner pipe that will slide through the the tank fitting and can be fitted into a smaller male adapter that can be screwed into the tank fitting. After you have drilled holes into that second piece of pipe, about one inch apart, and closed off the end of it with an end cap, you are ready to attach air hose to it and start the process going.

As the air is pushed into the thinner pipe it escapes into the filter through the smaller holes. Because you have used the tank fitting, you can unscrew the thin pipe to clean the air holes, without the media in the filter falling down and preventing you from re-inserting the air inlet. A continuous supply of air ensures that oxygen is present in sufficient quantities at all times.

## 3.4.2. Drip plate fabrication and modifications

Drip plates should do just that. Let the water drip evenly over whatever medium you have used inside the filter. An easy way to make such a plate is to take the correct inside dimensions of your filter, and buy a piece of acrylic material of that size, taking off 1/8 inch off all the measurements to ensure an easy fit. Now scribe the plate with lines equidistant by one inch. After you have done so in one direction, do the same in the other direction.

The easiest way to do this is by using a ruler that is one inch wide, and an Exacto knife or acrylic scriber.After that, drill holes 3/16 inch, where the lines intersect. Depending on the amount of water flow that you are aiming for, 3/16 inch might be too small to prevent the water from backing up too much. Should this happen, make the holes in the center 1/4 inch, and drill as many as necessary to maintain a water level on the drip plate of 1/2 to 3/4 inch at all times.

The drip plate itself needs to be siliconed around the edges to the filter, to prevent run-off of the water against the filter panes, because such water is not being efficiently brought in contact with the Nitrosomonas and Nitrobacter. Since silicone and acrylic do not really bond, the plate will always be easy to remove. The seal however will be strong enough to maintain the water level on the plate, which will ensure an even flow of water down into

# Drip Plate Fabrication - Gate Material for Overflows

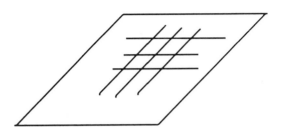

To fabricate a drip plate all you need is a piece of plexiglass or acrylic. Scribe it with equi-distant lines in both directions ( at 90 degree angle). Where the lines cross you will then need to drill  3/16 inch holes. Place it inside the top of your trickle filter, on a little ledge that you have glued into it with silicone. Once the plate is in, make it water tight around the edges by running a thin bead of silicone. This will force the water to go through the holes you have drilled. To prevent overflow, drill one large hole, say one inch, and bond a piece of Pvc pipe into to it. The height of that piece should be about 1.5 inches. Should the water now rise on the top of the drip plate, once it reaches the top of that piece of pipe, it will flow through there and prevent the filter from overflowing.

To make gate material : use a 1.5 inch piece of acrylic or pvc sheet. Cut slots, like a comb, at about 1/2 inch distance from each other, and about 1 inch deep. This can be done with a circular saw (chop saw for instance)

Of course take all necessary precautions when using such tools.

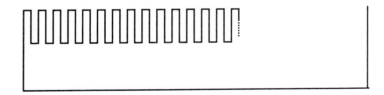

the filter and over the filter's medium.

Further improvements to the plate can be made. Some aquarists are afraid of water backing up and overflowing the filter. This could occur if the holes become plugged due to maintenance neglect. It is rare, but it could happen. To prevent this, make a hole in the plate in which you can glue a PVC coupling. Adjust the height of this fitting above the plate, to 1/4 inch below the top of the filter. If the water now rises, because it cannot flow through the smaller holes, it will flow through the much larger hole of the pvc coupling once it reaches the top of this fitting, preventing the filter overflow. Use either a 3/4 inch or 1 inch coupling, depending on your flow rates. Of course if this happens you need to determine the cause. If it is due to the plugging up of the holes, better maintenance practices need to be instituted.

If you are concerned about loss of dissolved gasses, such as $CO_2$, especially if you keep a reef with lots of macro-algae, and you are not using a system that adds $CO_2$, you may wish to adapt your drip plate somewhat more.

First, the overflow hole, if you installed one, needs to be fitted with a one way valve (check valve),to prevent air pushed into the filter from escaping that way.

Secondly, a small rigid piece of tubing needs to be pushed through one of the drip plate holes, and glued in. To the top of the 2 inch piece (one inch sticks out) attach airline tubing, preferably silicone or pvc hose, and guide it back to the tank or to the bottom of the trickle filter. Attach an airstone to it, and you are now pushing part of the dissolved gasses that escaped back into the water. This will not resolve the escaping of dissolved gasses completely, but it will reduce it considerably.

## 3.4.3. Spaces for carbon bags, sponges etc.

Although this might seem trivial, such built in spaces make a hobbyist's life quite a bit easier. Just think about how you solve the problem now, if you solve it easily at all. Built-in compartments not only hold such bags or sponges in place, but ensure that the flow of water through them is much more efficient, and is that not the name of the game?

If your filter does not have them, you may wish to add some yourself. Use acrylic and silicone. You should not have too many problems doing so, especially if you have a model that you were able to look at somewhere in a store. For sponge filters make the compartments tight, and for carbon bags make them so the water has to come in through different slots.

## 3.4.4. Built-in skimmer

Not too many trickle filters sold commercially incorporate such units. One filter deserves mention for its high quality and is manufactured by SeaKleer Reefs : it is known as the Pisces filter. At the time of this writing it would appear that a model looking very similar, but quite a bit less expensive, is also marketed, albeit through another company. We have very little info on this filter at the time of this writing but would expect that you will see ads for it in the hobby magazines in the next few weeks or months.

Although such skimmers cannot compete in efficiency with dedicated units that are installed outside the tank, their inclusion in a trickle filter is certainly a plus, especially for those aquarists who do not elect to buy separate skimmers. The Pisces models mentioned also allow the injection of ozone, which makes them very versatile. These filters also provide space for electrodes and a heater. The Summit Aquatic models have all these features as well, except for the skimmer. Our feeling on the subject is that to do things right one should install an outside and properly sized skimmer anyway, so the lack of a skimmer in a trickle filter is not a minus by any means.

Summit Aquatics in Fulton, Mo 65251, makes excellent units as well. They also manufacture a Dupla proprietory unit.

*Be very careful when adding ozone to such a skimmer. If it finds its way into the back part of the filter, you will kill off your biological filter.*

Another filter presently on the market, with a removable medium compartment, the BioPak 105, is also of excellent quality, and provides space for electrodes, a heater, a float switch, has a check-valve built in, and can be run at very high flow rates. This unit can also be obtained in 20, 30 and 40 gallon capacities. Based on the specification sheets available it is also sold at a very advantageous price.These filters are marketed by Dupla.

Although the Dupla model contains Bioballs, other packing matterials can be placed in it. These filters come from Germany, which makes them quite a bit more expensive than any other units on the market. This is unfortunate but cannot be helped, due to the negative influence of the dollar–deutsch mark exchange rates on the price.

Of all the models presently on the market, and there are dozens right now, none is really "the" one to use. They all perform the same basic function, some a little better than others perhaps, but the same biological filtration nevertheless. Which model to chose is therefore not an easy task.

Some of the important features to look for are for instance :

° quality of the bonding agents
° are paste-like bonds used rather than liquid ones
° is the thickness of the acrylic or glass at least quarter inch
° are the seams re-inforced
° is the water input large enough e.g. one inch or more
° is the water output hole at least one inch
° is space for electrodes
° and float switches
° and heaters provided
° can the sump easily be accessed, e.g. is the media compartment
  removable

Taking these criteria into consideration will reduce your choices and make your decision a little easier.

## 3.4.5. Spray Bar or Drip plate ?

The decision on whether to buy a filter using a spray bar, or a drip plate, depends on which type of tank you maintain. We feel however that in all cases drip plates have a better efficiency rate than the spray bar types. This is based on experience with both, on marine tanks that contain fish, invertebrates and lots of macro-algae. And the choice is especially important for the latter ones.

Spray bars diffuse the water evenly and continuously over the me- dium used, except in the corner areas. This is a problem when using materials that fill the filter completely, as opposed to materials such as D.L.S. and similar. Additionally it has been our experience that at higher flow rates, drip plates perform better and do not create splashing of the water. The choice however is yours. You might be used to a spray bar and have good results with it.

Drip plates distribute the water evenly over all of the filter medium, as we have seen earlier. Flow rates are not a problem, as by increasing the size of the holes in the plate, we can easily raise the permitted pump output to very high levels. We have installed such a system that handles 4500 gallons per hour, for an 1800 gallon Reef at the Hyatt Regency in Atlanta, Georgia. A sizeable aquarium indeed, built on the premises by Tropi-quarium of Atlanta.

Moreover, and this is a major difference, drip plates contain the escaping dissolved gasses much better than spray bars. This is important in aquariums that contain a lot of macro-algae, which require $CO_2$, a gas which escapes easily into the air, if not trapped and redirected somehow. This can easily be done as we have already seen in this chapter.

Drip plates are also easy to make yourself, unlike spray bars, es-pecially spray bars that rotate well and for long periods of time, meaning the better quality ones.

By no means do we wish imply that spray bars cannot do the job we look for in our filters. We have however observed that drip plates result in a better water distribution, and that they contain most of the dissolved gasses, especially if we modify the plate somewhat. This is important, particularly for macro and symbiotic algae, which require the carbon dioxide which is present only in small quantities to begin with.

Containing such gasses is thus important. Of course, if you are util -izing either a manual or an automated carbon dioxide diffusion system, you will be able to compensate for this loss.

## 3.4.6. Media for Trickle filters

Of the many media sold for trickle filters, there are a few that stand out for various reasons :

- Efi-Mech and Biomech : Ceramic pieces. Both these materials are used in trickle filters and offer large surface areas for bacterial growth. Both however restrict flow and have a tendency to clog as time goes on, because both trap detritus and act a mechanical filters in addition to acting as bacterial filters. Although this is good for water quality, it is not the ideal material to use because, since as they require cleaning, it forces us to take the filter apart, rinse the ceramic pieces and thus destroy some of the bacteria. Additionally if one forgets to clean the filter, back up might occur and the unit could overflow resulting in greater problems. If however you are willing to cope with these drawbacks, then you can certainly use these materials in your trickle filters. We personally feel however that mech is better used in the corner overflow. Once a week cleaning should prevent any overflow prob-lems. With high flow rates, back up can occur much sooner, and regular cleaning becomes critical.

- Tri-packs : These spheres which are sold under several names and in differ-ent sizes are excellent. They do not restrict the flow and offer a great deal of surface area for bacterial growth. Using the small size you can obtain as much area as Bioballs, the other preferred medium , however in doing so you will have to compare the prices you pay for each carefully. Tri-packs come in three sizes and each size has a different surface area per gallon vol-ume. As the size gets smaller the surface area increases, as there are less empty spaces. The smallest size is the one we have experience with, and it has performed up to its promises. Tri-packs are one of the better media to use in your filters.

They can be obtained from certain stores and some mail order companies. Some distributors of plastic materials also sell them, however you will have to buy larger quantities.

- Bioballs from Dupla : The preferred medium for both reasons of economy and efficiency. Bioballs do not trap dirt and do not restrict the water flow, while at the same time giving maximum surface area for biological filtration. The shape was computer designed to provide both maximum through-flow and maximum surface area. The smoothness of the Bioball is an additional plus, as it prevents layers of live bacteria growing over layers of dead bacteria. Dead ones just wash off and new ones grow in their place. Developed by a major Swiss company they have been tested for over 9 years in Germany, and are used by stores and public aquariums, as well as in research projects.

Recently a modification in the mold used to make the Bioballs, has enabled the manufacturer to increase the surface area even more. One gallon of Bioballs = approximately 55 balls, as per the new instruction sheet issued by Dupla, and now provides 23 square feet of surface area.

It was also pointed out to us that certain shops or dealers indicate that Bioballs do not have the the surface area claimed. We do not know why people say such things of course.

Rest assured that unless someone has computer equipment and sophisticated algorithms available to do such calculations, no one would even know how to start calculating the surface of a Bioball, or any similar type packing material for trickle filtration for that matter.

Also keep in mind that the surface area could be expressed differently if one wanted to, as, although the surface seems smooth, if one looked at it at the microscopic level, it has a valley and mound appearance, which makes the surface area even larger of course. The reason for this is that bacteria can live on the slopes too, since they are so small. But neglecting that aspect of the surface area, there are still 23  square feet available.

How much surface area is needed for efficient biological filtration, and how much of each material needs to be used, can be determined using the recommendations that are given in this chapter.

## 3.4.7 Required Filter Medium Quantities

## 3.4.7.1 Required Minimum Biological Surface

Assuming that you do not have a trickle filter installed right now on your Reef tank, and that you are looking at acquiring or building one, several observations that will help you decide which unit to acquire or build, are appropriate :

a. Do not undersize the filter. The size of the filter will be determined by the amount of filter medium that is required to filter your tank. This amount varies with the medium used, since each one of them offers a different surface area. Determining which filter your Reef tank needs, requires therefore a few quick calculations

b. How much biological filtration surface area is required, per gallon of water? Once you have established this number you will be able to calculate the amount of filter medium to buy, and as a result to design the filter itself, or at least be able to determine which size to buy from the large choice of models now available. Many filters offered seem to fail to take into account that each tank is different, and requires a specifically sized filter.

Here then are the recommendations made by Thiel(1986), based on experiments conducted on his own tanks, and on conversations with many experienced aquarists in Germany.

These conversations took place as late as 1987, and the numbers given are therefore tested, and based on the empiric experience gained by respected Marine Hobbyists from Germany.

The numbers below are in square feet, and represent the surface area required for efficient biological filtration. They were originally in square decimeters, or square centimeters, depending on the source, and have been converted to US measurements, and rounded to the nearest 5 or 10 square footage.

To calculate how much of a medium you require, first find the surface area of the medium that you are considering. This will be per gallon, or per pound, or whatever the measurement is in which the medium is sold. Divide the recommended required surface area by that number, and you will know the volume of that given medium to buy.

For price comparisons purposes, you may wish to do this calculation for a few selected media, e.g. Tri-packs, Bioballs, Norton Rings, and others if you wish, multiplying the cost per unit of volume, by the volume you buy in each case. Then decide which one to buy, keeping in mind that the least expensive one is not necessarily the best one for you.

Refer back to the section that deals with trickle filter media to look up the relative merits of each.

The surface areas given apply to media that are not restricting the water coming down from the tank. This means that the water can flow through without the medium trapping dirt particles. We are indeed talking about biological filters, not mechanical filters.

Filters materials such as dolomite, gravel type substances, Ceramic rings and so on, are to be dealt with totally differently, as they do not fit the model. We have already indicated that we consider them to be more mechanical than biological filtering media, and we do therefore not advocate their use in trickle filters.

Of course over a period of time, anything will act as a venue for bacteria..., but what we are interested in is the concentration of such bacteria, as that is what determines the efficiency of the filter.

## *Required Biological growth surface in Reef Aquariums*

| Tank size | H | M | L |
|-----------|-----|-----|-----|
| 29 | 145 | 115 | 100 |
| 40 | 200 | 155 | 140 |
| 55 | 225 | 190 | 150 |
| 70 | 275 | 240 | 190 |
| 90 | 295 | 250 | 205 |
| 110 | 350 | 330 | 255 |
| 125 | 400 | 345 | 290 |
| 135 | 435 | 375 | 310 |
| 150 | 450 | 415 | 345 |
| 180 | 520 | 485 | 410 |
| 220 | 600 | 505 | 445 |

Based on both articles that appeared in Germany, in Aquarium Society newsletters, and on conversations the author had with many advanced aquarists. Adapted by A. Thiel for publication in this book

Once you have determined the medium, and the quantity of that medium required, you will be able to figure out how large a container, trickle filter that is, you will need to buy or build.

Make sure also that it still fits underneath the aquarium, in the cabinet, if that is where you decided to place it. Less expensive media, with less surface areas, might be economical, but they may take up so much space to achieve the required biological filtration surface area, that it is no longer practical to use them.

## 3.4.7.2 Calculating the size of the Trickle Filter

This is a simple calculation. The following example can be used by anyone wishing to build their own filter. Just substitute your quantity, and your cabinet measurements for the ones we used.

Before doing the actual calculations however, we need to establish a few basics. In addition to the column that holds the medium, you will need extra space for the sump depth, and a small area on the top where the water collects before it trickle down through the drip plate. Indeed, the drip plate should sit about 2 inches below the top of the filter. This is especially important when you run high flow rates. It allows for about a quarter to half an inch of water to collect on top of the plate at all times. This will in turn ensure that the water distribution over the medium is uniform and continuous, and that you are using as much of the surface area of the medium for actual biological filtration, as you possibly can.

Between the bottom of the media column, and the bottom of the sump, a clearance of 8 to 10 inches should exist. This is important, as it determines the quantity of water the sump can actually hold. This influences the strength at which the pump can be run, and consequently the water flow. Stronger pumps, giving high flow rates, definitely need large sumps. It is wise to make this sump a little larger than you wanted to, as this will allow you to install a stronger water pump on the tank, if you wish to do so at some time in the future, which will allow stronger water flows.

With this said, we now know that after we find the size of the compartment that will hold the filter medium, we will need to add at least 10 and possibly 12 inches to its height, and some space lengthwise for the front part of the filter, the area where you will be reaching into the sump itself, for maintenance and other chores.

The first factor that we need to deal with, is the maximum width that the filter can be, as we cannot change the size of the cabinet.

Let us assume for this example that our cabinet is 18 inches wide, 6 feet long, and 26 inches high.

We are calculating the size of the filter required for a 110 gallon tank, with medium load, using Bioballs by Dupla.

Based on the chart given above we need 330 square feet of surface area. Each gallon of Bioballs has 23 square feet of surface (as per new product sheet by the manufacturer). This means that we require 330 : 23 = 14.35 gals of the medium. We round this off to 15 gallons.

The calculation is as follows :

- multiply that quantity by 231, in our case that equals : 3465

- divide this by the width of the cabinet minus 2 inches. This is not a mandatory number, but 2 inches leaves enough space to move the unit in, and forward or sideways if necessary when installing it. In our example the result is : 216.56

- now divide this number by the maximum height that you want the filter to reach inside the cabinet, deducting first either 10 or 12 inches from that same number ( the 10 or 12 represent the 2 inches at the top, and the 8 or 10 inches height of the sump). We have taken 8 for the sump, plus 2 for the top portion above the plate, and the maximum height we want is 22 inches. This results in dividing 216.56 by 22 minus 10, which equals 12. This results in approximately 18.

We now know the measurements of our filter :

- the width is 16 inches

- the length is 18 inches for the filter, to which we still need to add the length of the sump

- the height is 22 inches

The area that holds the Bioballs is 16 x 18 x 12, an area that will hold approximately 15 gallons of Bioballs, which is exactly what we wanted to begin with.

The total measurement of the trickle filter will depend on how long you wish to make the sump. Usually 10 to 12 inches will do. Its height is determined by the number that you used previously in the calculation. If you used 8, make the sump 12 inches tall. If you used 10, make the sump 14 inches tall. These additional inches give you an extra measure of security.

### 3.4.7.3 What airflow is required ?

Use a strong pump to blow air into the column that holds the medium. To be able to grow a potent bacterial colony, good oxygenation is required.

As a guideline 35 to 40 liters of pump rating per gallon of medium is recommended. Check the instructions that come with the air pump before acquiring it, and if you decide on a used one, make sure that the diaphragm is replaced before you install it. In our example, with 15 gallons of Bioballs, we would want a pump that delivers about 600 liters

## 3.4.7.4  Denitrification

Several add-on devices that are now sold promise to reduce nitrate levels in Reef tanks. We do not question that they do, but object to the use of additives such as glucose and lactose to achieve the desired effect. We find that such is not necessary in a well run trickle filter, as such filters will stabilize the nitrate levels automatically, after a few months, if set up correctly.

What we are advocating is denitrification "the natural way" without resorting to processes that are difficult to control, dangerous if not correctly installed, and not necessarily more efficient than more traditional methods. German aquarists very seldom use these artificial denitrification units.

Too many problems have resulted with them, because of the difficulty in monitoring what exactly is happening, how to assess the quantity of fluid necessary for any given tank, and the total lack of evidence that such filters are not harmful to the tank's biomass. If you are using one now, and if you are satisfied that the system really works, you might be on to something. We have not yet discovered these benefits, and most importantly how to use these denitrators under repeatable and controlled conditions. Each experiment seems to yield different results.

We suggest the following completely safe procedure : in your trickle filter, in the sump, place a block of coarse sponge-like material that runs the entire width of the filter. Its height should be no more than 3.5 inches, and its width about 4. If a compartment where such a sponge can be placed exists in your filter, you obviously acquired one of the better models.

If it does not exist, you can easily make one, by glueing some acrylic material that has been pre-drilled with quarter inch holes that are half inch equi-distant in all directions, in the bottom of the sump. This will hold the block of material in place.

When water flows down from the tank, over the filter medium, collecting in the sump, and is drawn out by the pump, it needs to go either through or over this sponge. Obviously it will move faster above the sponge, than through the sponge itself. This will create an area inside the sponge that is low in oxygen, not anaerobic, but just low in dissolved oxygen. In this area bacteria that are referred to as facultatively aerobic-anaerobic will grow in a short matter of time. These bacteria will denitrify the water, meaning they will reduce nitrate levels and do so in a safe way, (Dr.Wolff,1986).

Nitrate levels will not be reduced to zero, but will stabilize at a safe level of around 10 to 15 mg per liter, depending on tank size and tank load. This has been demonstrated experimentally in several test aquariums at Dupla Aquaristik Gmbh in Germany, tanks which the author was able to see, and verify the nitrate levels of. Zero nitrate levels are not recommended anyway since all macro-algae require them as a nutrient.

Alternatively, if the sponge block is not used, a double fine filter, through which all the water going back to the aquarium needs to pass, can be installed in the sump. This is usually some form of round plastic material that is covered with medium coarseness type foam. The fine filters can be cleaned in rotation, always leaving one with bacteria to remove nitrates. It is suggested to clean these fine filters every 10 to 12 weeks.

Such filters are available in pet stores, and can easily be adapted to fit your particular trickle filter. Some trickle filters even come with one of them, (Dupla). For this method to work, one definitely needs a double filter. Since only one at a time is cleaned, a filter with sufficient bac-teria is always present in the sump.

It is highly likely that, as time goes on, better denitrification methods will be found. We hope that such efficient systems will be available to Reef aquarists soon, as nitrate can indeed pose serious problems to the Corals and other Inverts such reef tanks contain, when levels get excessive (over 45 mg/l)

Yet another method to reduce nitrates, but not just nitrates - phosphates are removed in this fashion as well- consists in increasing the number of macro-algae in the tank. Simpler is hardly possible. Macro-algae remove nitrates and phosphates by using them as nutrients. When doing so, you must ensure that enough carbon dioxide and enough fertilizer is available for such macro-algae however. Refer to that specific chapter for more details. Algae perform many worthwhile functions in any aquarium, but are especially important in reef tanks. When adding macro-algae, ensure that they are still healthy. Reputable pet stores should be able to provide you with a good choice.

To summarize : when denitrifying, use natural methods. They are safe, duplicate what happens in nature, and do not require additives which may do more damage than good, especially in the long run. And that is what counts. Making a tank look good for a few days is no great problem. Maintaining it in super condition requires the use of safe and proven methods.

Possibly, in the near future, better methods to denitrify will be found, besides the "natural" way. We certainly hope so, as it would make many a hobbyist's life simpler, and would make one of the problems still hard to control, much more manageable.

# A Modern Aquarium, by Nollmann Aquaristik, with overflow and water returns clearly visible
### Notice the cleanliness of the siliconing !

**Photo Credit : Dupla Aquaristik Gmbh**

# 3.5 Building or Buying ?

Decisions, decisions, decisions.

Many hobbyists have called us over the last few months, and requested information on how to build the trickle filters that we have dealt with in this book, and how to add certain features.

To assist them, and spread the information widely, we wrote an article which was subsequently published in Fresh and Marine Aquarium magazine. We felt that it would still be of help to a number of aquarists, and have therefore included it in this book, with a few modifications. The full article was published in the January 1988 issue.

The advent of newer technologies of aquarium keeping has hit the US hobbyist's market faster than anyone could have imagined, just 15 months ago. Suddenly overseas technology abounds

"Minireefs ", "Aquareefs ", "Dupla Systems ", " Carefree Reefs", "Ocean Reefs", "Sea Kleer Reefs" and variations or combinations of these, are to be found in Tropical Fish stores and Hobbyists homes all over the country.

Most of these names are trade-marked, and we wish to acknowledge that fact right here and now. Some manufacturers have also patented either their whole filters, or some portion of it.

One now reads regularly about : Wet-dry systems, trickle filters, protein skimmers or foam fractionators , denitrators, ozonization, lighting —metal halides and actinic bulb— requirements, nutrition , redox and ORP measuremnt, etc...., to an extent never seen before in the hobby.

Suddenly Invertebrate and Corals seem to overtake fish in the Hobbyist's interest.

Of course, traditional aquarium keeping is still the way the majority of aquariums are kept. Slowly however, Hobbyists are progressing toward more modern ways of trying to duplicate the environment in which the biomass ( fish an inverts) they keep in their aquariums is living.

This concerted effort to keep these fish and invertebrates alive - or should I say "grow", and look more natural - is certainly a big step forward.

So what seems to be at the basis of this " step forward " ?

## 3.5.1  Advantages

It would appear that the majority of the progress made, is in the area of water quality, meaning the chemical nature of the water in which the animal life forms are kept. This - in laymen's terms - means filtration, regardless of how filtration is achieved, whether by cannister filters, undergravel filters or some of the more modern ways such as trickle filtration or wet/dry systems, or even the latest ones available on the German market " the BioMesch " filter ( a trademark ).

In essence, we are moving from the traditional undergravel and/or cannister filter, toward a combination of wet/dry (-also called trickle filters-) and cannister filters.

The technology used is not new. It has been used in water sewage treatment plants for many years. Downsizing these techniques to the small mass of water in the aquarium however was a major feat, and is definitely new.

If filtration is the area in which modern systems are trying to improve the way we have been keeping our aquariums - it is only one of them I should add - then how can we learn from the expert methods that we read about ?

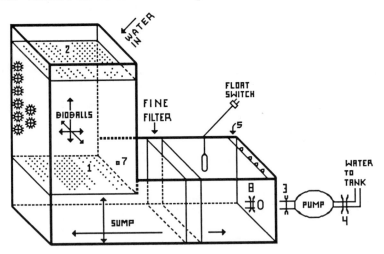

The above filter is a very basic unit. See elsewhere for more advanced models

Perhaps, and before attacking the subject of whether we should build our own or buy a commercial model, we should try to identify what these "new" filters should do for our aquariums, and what constraints we should put on them :

If we want to better the filtration methods we use, we either want, or expect, or require the filter to perform certain functions, so let's look at a few of the steps required to attain this enhanced water quality .

1. To achieve better biological filtration, we should maximize the size of the bacterial colony that actually "polishes" the water,

2. to achieve this, we should provide an as close to ideal environment for these bacteria to live in, meaning high in oxygen content,

3. we should do this in a "container" that fits under the aquarium, or if it has to be set on the side of it, can be made as inconspicuous as possible,

4. the area of biological filtration should be maintenance free, meaning that we should make it separate from the mechanical (fine) filtering, and the chemical (e.g. carbon and/or resins) filtration. Indeed, if we do so we do not need to touch (clean) the biological filter, we only need to change the material used for fine filtration and change carbon/resin. By not having to clean the biological filtration area, we do not disturb the colony as a result and do not destroy bacteria in the process,

5. we should provide enough of a growing area for the bacteria we wish to maintain, to reduce the ammonia/nitrite (which we are trying to eliminate). Eliminating nitrate is another matter altogether.

6. Maximizing growth area means using a material in the filter that provides both :
        a) maximum throughflow ( meaning that it does not restrict the water flow)
        b) maximum surface area ( meaning that it does not impede the flow of the water going through and has a very high surface area)

Combining both these constraints is obviously not as easy as it seems, so select the material you use to pack (fill up) your filter, carefully.

There are various materials available that can be placed in a trickle filter e.g. Bioballs from Dupla, Tri-Packs and Biospheres from various suppliers, DLS material, etc.. The key to which one to use remains surface area.

7. not create undesirable bacteria (e.g. anaerobic ones that might result in the production of even very low levels of Hydrogen Sulfide, which is very noxious and toxic to inverts).

8. all of this should result in a higher redox potential meaning reduction-oxidation potential of the water, or its ability to deal with the pollution that is present. More about this later in this article.

9. and, last but not least, be cost efficient.

### 3.5.2 Results

If, and when the filter used to clean the aquarium water meets , or should we say fulfills all these requirements, what can we expect :

. no ammonia
. less than 0.1 mg/l nitrite
. supersaturation levels of oxygen
. high redox
. nitrate reduction
. healthy inverts, corals and fish

Why are these results of importance to the Hobbyist ?

- Ammonia at high pH levels, which is the case in marine aquaria, is present not in the form of the ammonium ion (which is not noxious by the way) but in the form of ammonia gas, which dissolves in the water, and literally burns the gills of the fish. It should be obvious that it is totally undesirable and needs to be oxidized at all cost., (efficient filtration is required)

- Nitrite prevents hemoglobin from carrying oxygen through the bloodstream and is therefore also extremely noxious. Efficient filtration is the answer here again.

- High levels of oxygen dissolved in the water put less stress on the fish, and increase the Redox level (mv reading) of the water, which is extremely desirable when one keeps corals and inverts.

To explain Redox, in simple terms, one could say that Redox expresses the ability of the aquarium water (in our case at least) to deal with existing pollution, and the one generated by the fish and inverts we keep in our aquariums. It stands to reason that the higher the number, the better the water can deal with such pollution.

Conversely if the mv (millivolt) reading is high the water must be clean, since if it was not, the reading would be low, as all the reduction oxidation (redox) potential would have been exhausted breaking down the existing pollution.

Theories about the ideal level vary greatly. In German circles, nowadays, 350 mv and higher are the most frequently recommended number, refer to the section on redox in this book for more details.

If the trickle filter - wet/dry - is to achieve all of the above, and purify our aquarium of all noxious components, then we do certainly need quite a sophisticated piece of equipment, that should be clear by now.

So should we buy a filter or make one ourselves ?

The decision is up to you, but if you do not have experience in using the materials required ( glass or acrylic/plexiglass ) and do not have a blueprint or plan, it might pay to acquire a model that is commercially made.

### 3.5.3 Sizes of materials required

If you do wish to build your own, here are the measurements you need in either glass or acrylic to build 2 basic models ( refer to the picture in this article to determine how the various pieces fit together ).

All measurments are in inches, and the material used is one quarter inch thick. You may use glass or acrylic. The numbers in brackets represent the number of pieces of each that are required

### 3.5.3.1 Holding ten gallons of packing material :

| | | |
|---|---|---|
| Back | 15.50 x 20.00 | (1) |
| High sides | 13.00 x 20.00 | (2) |
| Low sides | 12.00 x 12.00 | (2) |
| High Front | 15.00 x 16.00 | (1) |
| Low front | 15.00 x 12.00 | (1) |
| Base | 15.50 x 25.25 | (1) |
| Front top cover | 15.50 x 12.00 | (1) |
| Back top cover | 15.50 x 13.50 | (1) |
| Top drip plate | 15.25 x 12.50 | (1) |
| Bottom plate | 15.25 x 12.50 | (1) |
| Compartments | 15.00 x 04.00 | (3) |

The original measurements in the magazine included an error in the size of the front plates, due to a typographical error. We apologize.

The three plates used to make the compartments that will hold the foam for denitrification and the carbon bag, are placed and glued or bonded in the sump. The exact location of them is not important. Space between them

depends on the amount of foam , respectively, carbon that you will place in
them.

### 3.5.3.2 Holding fifteen gallons of packing material :

Here again are the measurements for either glass or acrylic material. The
section that holds the packing material, meaning the section between the top
drip plate and the bottom plate, is sized for 15 gallons.

Remember : the measurements are based on using quarter inch material.

| | | |
|---|---|---|
| Back plate | 15.50 x 20.00 | (1) |
| High sides | 20.00 x 20.00 | (2) |
| Low sides | 12.00 x 12.00 | (2) |
| High front | 15.00 x 16.00 | (1) |
| Low front | 15.00 x 12.00 | (1) |
| Base | 15.50 x 32.25 | (1) |
| Front top cover | 15.50 x 12.25 | (1) |
| Back top cover | 15.50 x 20.50 | (1) |
| Top drip plate | 15.00 x 19.50 | (1) |
| Bottom plate | 15.00 x 19.50 | (1) |
| Compartments | 15.00 x 04.00 | (3) |

The top drip plate is, in both cases, placed 2 inches down inside the filter,
this allows for water to accummulate in that area, and "rain" down on the
packing material evenly.

The bottom plate is placed 8 inches from the bottom. This allows for a
sizeable sump, in which the packing material is not submersed.

Submersing, for instance, Bioballs, still makes them filter biologically, but
obviously to a lesser degree, because, although the surface area does not
change, less oxygen will be available to the bacteria that will grow in that
particular section.

Remember the above measurements only apply when you use quarter inch
material, glass or acrylic.

What is also important is to incorporate as many features as possible in the
filter as is feasible, e.g. if one can build or buy a filter that also performs
the skimming function, one saves a considerable amount of money. Remember however that if such a skimmer is included, you need to be very
careful if you use ozone.

Make sure that no ozone whatsoever can find its way into the back compartment, rise in the column, and kill off the biological filter.

George Bepko's contribution, who discovered that this can easily happen, is hereby acknowledged, and will hopefully help a number of aquarists.

What you need to do is take a critical look at what is offered commercially and decide for yourself. Many models, offering different features are on the market, the choice is wide.

### 3.5.4 A few pointers on "Redox" potential:

Obtaining accurate redox potential measurements, requires that a few steps be followed and that the aquarist be aware of a few caveats :

-Continuous immersion is required for at least 3 to 4 hours to get a true reading, indeed the probe reacts very slowly.

-pH levels are important when making comparisons. Do not compare a reading taken at say pH of 8.25 with one taken at a different pH ( as the pH gets lower the redox will go up ).

-what most aquarists should be concerned with, when measuring Redox is the trend. Is the mv reading going up, or down ?

- always compare measurements taken at the same time of day. Do not compare a measurement taken today at 7.00 am with one taken yesterday at noon.

Indeed as metabolism increases in the aquarium, the redox will have a tendency to go down. It stands to reason therefore that the redox will be highest early in the morning, and that it will gradually decline over the period of the day.

- do not concern yourselves with the intricate chemical processes involved, they are of no concern to us, the only thing we are interested in is the actual value and the trend.

- to get accurate readings the probe needs to be in an area with good water movement

- use a platinum/silver/silver chloride single tip prove. They have proven to be the more reliable and most accurate ones, in continuous immersion conditions.

## How can You influence the redox level ?

- use a trickle filter that is designed to super oxygenate the water
- use a protein skimmer to remove organics from the tank
- add ozone if necessary
- do not overfeed
- remove dead algae and other dead lifeforms.

You may also wish to refer to the "For what it's worth" sections of Fresh And Marine Aquarium magazines to find other ideas on how to build your own trickle filter.

**Dosing Pump to dispense trace elements and fertilizer automatically and in exact quantities at pre-determined intervals**

Photo Dupla Aquaristik Gmbh

# 4. Instrumentation

Assembling pH continuous controllers, Carbon dioxide diffusion systems, setting up Redox potential meters, carbonate hardness reactors, and other such instruments is not necessarily easy.

The steps involved in calibrating and adjusting such instruments must be meticulously followed. Moreover, many aquarists are not familiar with such devices and do not necessarily understand the reasons for which they are used, and how they allow better control of aquarium conditions leading to a more stable environment.

Most of the instrumentation discussed was developed by Dupla, Sanders, Tunze and Selzle, but the principles can be used with any other similar equipment. We are using the equipment made by these German manufacturers because all their instruments were developed speci- fically for use in Aquariums.

Some readers will be familiar with the equipment itself, others will not. We ask those who have already installed such instruments to understand that this section is intended for those who have not, and also for those who would like a review of the subject.

Often, although we would like to buy an expensive instrument, we refrain from doing so, because we are afraid that we will not understand how to operate it, how to interpret the values it gives us, or how to generally integrate such a device into the aquariums that we operate. This chapter should take the fear out of doing so forever.

The contributions that such equipment can make to Reef tanks is also often under estimated. You may not care to acquire all of it, but some instruments will definitely be a plus to your Reef.

# 4.1 Digital-Electronic pH meters

Since the pH concept itself is explained elsewhere in this book, we will limit ourselves here to the instruments and their workings.

Various pH meters are presently on the market, some in pen form, some in more sophisticated versions. Regardless of which one you decide to buy, all give a reading of the pH of the water tested with a specific accuracy, and there is the clincher. Accuracy ! The more accurate the reading, the more expensive the electrode and instrument will be.

Electrodes come in many types of function specific versions. For our purpose we need an electrode that can be immersed permanently, can withstand the water conditions of a Reef tank for extended periods of time, and is reliable in its accuracy. Such probes are not the most expensive ones, but they are also not the least expensive ones. Usually double junction, gel, non-refillable electrodes perform best in Reef aquarium conditions.

Manufacturers of pH electrodes send out catalogues that list all the electrodes that they manufacture or sell, and they usually do not charge for such catalogues. Some of the better known companies include Cole-Palmer, Fisher, and Omega. They all sell many kinds of scientific instruments, including all the ones an aquarist might be interested in.

If you decide to do away with pH testing reagents, you will do away with the inherent inaccuracy of such reagents, or said better the approximation that such reagents give, at the same time. Dry reagents are excellent to obtain a reading that is in the "general" range. The chemicals that such reagents are made up of react with the Hydrogen and Hydroxyl ions in the water ,and change color in the process.

Dry reagents however age, absorb water, and over time become more and more inaccurate. You should keep this in mind when testing your reefs, especially since the difference can be substantial, e.g. 0.2 units. Often the inaccuracy is not even due to deterioration of the reagent, but just plainly to the type of reagent used, or the combination of reagents in the test you have bought.

Example : let's assume we take a test, and the result is 8.1, this means in essence that the result could be anywhere between 7.9 and 8.3, and that is obviously not very accurate, although it does tell us that the pH is in the right range. Should the reading be 8.0 however, we cannot be too sure anymore, as the real pH could be 7.8 rather than 8.0, and that is of course too low.

If we therefore acquire a pH meter, we should buy one that does away with this approximation, in addition to doing away with the bother it usually is to use dry reagents.

Most inexpensive units have an accuracy reading of 0.2 units in either direction. Better units have an accuracy that is repeatable of maximum 0.1 units. When buying a unit look for a probe that has that specification in its descriptive material. More precise probes are available for laboratory work, but they are priced at several hundred dollars a piece.

The type of probe that we recommend can be obtained from various scientific instrument companies in the US, and should range in price from a low of 80.00 to a maximum of 250.00 dollars. Such probes are accurate to within a maximum of 0.1 units and the repeatability of the readings ensures in fact that the accuracy is in fact greater. By being able to repeat a test and come up with exactly the same result, we are able to determine that the probe is obviously highly accurate.

The specification sheets for probes usually also indicate resolution. This is usually given as 0.01, and this really means that you get a reading that is to a one hundredth of a unit, e.g. 8.17 Resolution has nothing to do with accuracy. Said differently, 0.01 means that you get a reading to 2 meaningful digits behind the decimal point.

The instrument used to read the pH, on a digital read-out, is fairly simple, and most of the ones we know of are excellent. The only thing you need to make sure, is that it gives you the same resolution as the probe you have bought or plan to buy. Basically make sure that it can give readings from a low of 2 or so, to a high of 12 or so, although most instruments will let you use probes that can go from 0 to 14.

There are several types of electrodes. Single junction, double junction, reference electrodes, refillable and gel ones, in glass or some other material, short ones, long ones, stubby or thin ones, probes for liquids and probes for semi-solids. There are in fact so many that most people get confused.

The best one to select is the double junction, gel electrode, which in our experience is excellent for continuous immersion, which is what we as aquarists want to do, and can be used in alkaline solutions.

Probes need to be calibrated. That means we need to adjust them to the instrument that we are using to read the pH with. Two calibrations are required. A low and a high is usually what is required. Dupla uses a pH 7 and a pH 9 calibration for salt water tanks. What we are in essence doing is making sure that the reading pattern, if expressed as a straight line, goes through the zero point of the x and y axis, and at exactly a 45 degree angle.

Calibrating is fairly simple. Take a test vial, put some pH 7 solution in it. Take the probe, immerse it in the liquid. Wait approximately 10 minutes. Look at the pH reading on the instrument, and if it is not 7.00, which is highly likely, adjust the reading to be exactly 7.00 by using the small adjusting buttons in the case of Dupla instruments, or the little screw or screws that certain manufacturers use instead. It is probable that when you do this adjustment, that the pH will not stay at 7.00 but will fluctuate between 6.99 and 7.01, that is normal and can be disregarded.

After the first calibration is done, you need to also calibrate for the second one. It does not matter whether you do one before the other in most cases, although some manufacturers insist that the lower one be done first.

Before undertaking the second calibration we need to make sure that no remainder of the first one is left on the probe. To do so we take a small amount of the second solution, put it in our test vial, and rinse our probe. We repeat this process three times, then we fill the vial with some more of the solution and start the calibration, this time, in the case of the Dupla system, at pH 9. We again let the probe stand in the solution for 10 minutes. Then we adjust the read-out so that it reads exactly the 9.00 that it should. Once more, the reading will probably go from 8.99 to 9.01, and again that is normal.

Some remarks about probes, also called electrodes :

– do not let the tip of the probe dry out. If you do you ,will ruin your electrode and it will give inaccurate results. You will no longer be able to calibrate it correctly.

– clean your probe regularly. Slime and algae will build up on the tip and prevent the probe from giving an accurate reading and from being adjusted, calibrated, correctly.

– do not run the wire that connects the electrode to the read-out instrument too close to an electrical wire. Interference could make the reading jump erratically. If this happens you do not need to worry, just re-arrange the wires.

– every time you clean a probe you will need to recalibrate it

– do not contaminate your reference solutions with other water, as this will result in future calibrations being incorrect.

– electrodes do wear out, so do not assume that because you have spent a hundred or more dollars, that you will be able to use it forever. If you maintain it well, and clean it regularly, it should give you at least several years of excellent service.

– do not hit the tip of the probe against any objects, especially not hard objects

– do not submerse the probe completely. Leave the top 2 inches or so out of the water. Affix it with suction cups to the glass of the aquarium, or of the filter.

– place the probe in an area that has good water circulation. This will give the best continuous read out.

– do not damage the wire that goes to the instrument in any way, as this will cause interference and give erratic readings.

– whenever you calibrate, make sure you rid yourself of static electricity first. Not doing so, will result in a read-out that is correct when you touch the instrument, but which goes way off when you move yourself away. This results in erroneous readings of the tank pH of course.

Once you have calibrated the probe, and attached it to the instrument you are ready to install it in the tank, or in the trickle filter.

If you place it in an area that has a different pH than the tank, you will get a reading that is not really the correct pH of the tank. Let us be more precise. Let's assume that you inject $CO_2$ in the aquarium, to make your macro-algae grow better, and let's assume you return that water to the bottom of the trickle filter, meaning in the sump. If you now place the probe in the sump, you will get a reading that is obviously affected by the fact that the water there contains $CO_2$, and its pH is lower than the tank water as a result. Keep that in mind.

If you return the water to the sump, place the electrode in the tank, preferably close to the overflow, where the flow of water is always good. If your $CO_2$ containing water is returned to the tank, place the electrode either in the sump, or in an area of the tank that is far away from where the water from the $CO_2$ reactor is returned.

Once the unit and probe are installed, start keeping records of the pH, preferably twice a day. Once a day is fine, twice is better, and always take the values you will compare at the same time. E.g. 7.30 am and 7.00 pm. It is also a good idea to keep the dKH (carbonate hardness) test result at the same time. This will allow for better comparisons.

Variations in both pH and carbonate hardness have causes. If you wish to maintain a well balanced reef tank, you should try to determine what these causes are, and of course eliminate them.

# 4.2 Carbon Dioxide Addition Equipment

To add carbon dioxide to a reef aquarium, one needs several pieces of equipment. There are also two main ways to add carbon dioxide : automatically and manually.

Whichever one you select is not important. If you are just starting off and you want to make sure that adding carbon dioxide is indeed something that is beneficial, it is by the way, you may wish to start with a manual system. It is much less expensive, not difficult to do, but takes a little more effort than an automatic system.

You will find an explanation on the benefits of doing so in other parts of this book.

## 4.2.1 Manual addition of CO2

This method of adding Carbon dioxide to the aquarium is discussed elsewhere in this publication, in great detail.

Let us just make one point here : if you are maintaining, or wish to maintain a healthy reef tank, you will need to monitor the levels of CO2 present in the water. This can be done using one of the several tests that are available on the market.

If you determine that your aquarium contains insufficient amounts of dissolved Carbon dioxide, you will need to find a method of adding some additional quantities.

Perhaps you do not wish to invest in a fully automated system, which runs several hundred dollars. Adding CO2 manually is then both efficient and not costly at all.

Such equipment can usually be acquired for about the same price as a good cannister filter.

Both Dennerle and Dupla manufacture such equipment. There may be other systems available in your area, which are not distributed nationally.

Assembing such carbon dioxide systems yourself, from components designed for other applications, is not recommended.

## 4.2.2 Automated addition of CO2

To add carbon dioxide automatically, we rely on the principle that CO2 and water together form carbonic acid, and that as a result, doing so will affect the pH in our reef. Since we know that by adding CO2 we will want to keep the change to a range of 0.1 to 0.2 units of pH, we can now devise a set of instruments that will allow us to do just that.

Equipment required (and some optional pieces) based on the Dupla System :

   – a cannister of CO2. The size of the cannister will depend on the size of your tank. For a 55 gallon tank we suggest a 350 gram bottle, for tanks between 55 and 110 gallons we suggest a 500 gram bottle, and for larger tanks we suggest a 1500 gram bottle. You may of course elect to use a larger bottle. The only change that will occur is that you will not need to refill the bottle as often. Larger bottles are available from welding shops or from companies that supply those same welding shops with the CO2 they sell. The thread on all bottles is the same, even on European ones, this seems to be a standard size for all bottles and will therefore not cause any difficulties with the equipment you buy.

   – a pressure valve. This indicates the pressure inside the bottle you are using and will give you advance warning when your supply is about to run out.

   – a pressure reducer, and a pressure gauge that allows you to adjust the outgoing CO2 pressure. This is required to be able to operate the solenoid that we will need.

   – a solenoid, which can be open or closed depending on the pH of the water. Do not concern yourself with why, we will explain that later

   – flexible hose to connect all pieces, preferably hose made out of silicone or pvc, as it will not wear out as quickly as most of the other tubing that is sold. Clear plastic tubing will dry out, harden and eventually crack or break, causing loss of CO2, and the resulting extra trips to have your CO2 supply refilled

   – a small check valve, preferably two small check valves. They are intended to protect your solenoid or magnetic valve. Indeed CO2 has a

## Equipment to Dispense Carbon Dioxide.

Photo Dupla Aquaristik Gmbh

tremendous pull-back force, and when the solenoid closes this results in some water being sucked into the tubing. Eventually, if you do not install the one or two check valves, this water will reach the solenoid and short it out, by making a permanent contact. Since the solenoid is much more expensive than the check valves, it is a good idea to protect that piece of equipment by installing the valves.

– a device to mix the water and the $CO_2$ as efficiently as we can, a $CO_2$ reactor as it is called in the Dupla system

– a pH Regulator and an electrode

– a connector to attach the solenoid to the pressure and pressure reducing valves. This is a small fitting with different threads on each end, and makes the connecting of the magnetic valve and the pressure gauges easier, and completely tight.

– sundry pvc pieces to bring water to the $CO_2$ reactor

How to set up the pH Regulator and Electrode is described elsewhere in the book.

The way the system operates is in essence very simple. The pH meter has a third knob that can be set at a certain pH value. We will set it at pH 8 for the purpose of this explanation. The solenoid, which is attached to the set of pressure valves, which in turn are attach to the $CO_2$ bottle, is switched on and off, by the pH regulator, based on the actual pH of the water. The latter is sensed by the probe.

Example : we set the pH regulator adjustment knob at pH 8.00

we attach all valves, the solenoid, etc. In essence we make the whole system operational (we will explain exactly how in just a bit).

The pH probe senses a pH of say 8.13, which you will be able to see on the digital read-out, the pH meter compares this with the setting you have made, which is 8.00 remember, and because the actual pH is higher than the setting, the pH regulator opens the solenoid valve, which now lets $CO_2$ through. This affects the pH of the water, brings it down somewhat, which the probe senses.

When the pH reaches 8.00 (your setting) the pH meter shuts off the magnetic valve, and no $CO_2$ now goes to the tank. This stops the lowering of the pH, in fact if your tank runs properly, and if your carbonate hardness is high, as we have suggested, the pH will have a tendency to creep up again.

The pH regulator will sense that the pH is higher again than your setting, and will re open the solenoid, which will push CO2 in the water, which will lower the pH, which will result in the solenoid being shut off, and so on. This is a continuous process.

If the pH does not go up again, the solenoid will not re open, and the only thing that happens is that no CO2 is being pushed in the water. Of course this negates the whole purpose of the exercise and you should be looking for its cause. More than likely, either your carbonate hardness is not high enough, or your tank is producing too many acids, which could occur for various reasons. The major ones are overfeeding, overcrowding and not cleaning your mechanical filters enough or not well enough. Once you have taken care of the reason for the drop, your pH will start rising again, and the CO2 dispersion system will re-start and run continuously.

Of course with an automated system you do not need to shut off the bottle at night, or do pH tests with dry reagents. The whole process is much less cumbersome and more accurate because of the fact that the pH regulator controls the whole process. The only drawback of course is that an automated system is much more expensive. However if you buy the pieces you need over a period of time, the expense becomes quite manageable.

A few more pointers on how to set up the system :

– Attach the pressure and pressure reducing valve, which comes in one piece, to the CO2 bottle. Make sure that the original O-ring is installed, and grease it somewhat if necessary.

– Attach the solenoid to the pressure valves by means of the screw that allows you to do just that. Use Teflon tape to make sure the fittings are tight. Do not over tighten, fittings are made in brass, and brass is brittle
– Attach a small length of pvc or silicone hose to the solenoid and to that length attach your first check valve. Add a few more inches of hose and attach the second check valve. Make sure you observe the flow direction of the check valve, usually indicated by an arrow

– From the second check valve run a length of hose to the top of the CO2 reactor. You may place the CO2 reactor either in the tank, against the back or side pane, or in the sump of the trickle filter

– the carbon dioxide is mixed inside the CO2 reactor by pushing water into it, and not letting the mixture out until it has gone through a circuitous route, ensuring best mixing. Our next task therefore is to bring water to the top or the side of the CO2 reactor, depending on which model you are using. Supplying this water can easily be achieved by making a T-connection on the output side of the water return,-this is between the pump and the tank-, a T-connection being the insertion of one of the fittings we described earlier in another chapter. Since we do not need a very strong flow, we will reduce the T-fitting by inserting a bushing (another fitting we described) that will bring its size down to the size of the tubing that goes to the reactor. We will then place a small airline clamp on that hose, and that clamp will allow us to regulate the water flow to the reactor.

You can of course hard-pipe the whole set-up by using the necessary bushings and fittings to reduce the pipe size to the desired diameter. Most people however seem to just use flexible tubing. To go from hard pipe ending with a T-connection to flexible, you need what is referred to as a barb, of the size that will fit inside the flexible tubing on one side, and inside the T-connector on the other side. Let's assume you are using 1 inch pipe to return the water from the sump to the aquarium.

This means that you need a one inch Tee connector, a bushing to bring one side of the Tee down to one quarter inch, a quarter inch barb, and quarter inch tubing to go to the top of the $CO_2$ reactor. The length of the tubing depends on where you place the reactor.

Not difficult to do, but not as easy to explain. As far as we know Dupla will gladly explain this over the telephone to anyone who buys their products. You can find their telephone number in the hobby magazines you read, or refer to the end to the section listing addresses and phone numbers of aquarium equipment manufacturers.

Once you have installed all the pieces, and have them in working condition, you open the bottle of $CO_2$ by turning the knob on top of the bottle. You may open the bottle completely, it does not matter, as it is not that knob that regulates the output.

Then open the side valve, on the fitting that has the pressure gauges, allowing $CO_2$ to now enter the reactor. Wait a short while and you will see bubbles entering the $CO_2$ reactor. You should set the rate of flow faster or slower depending on the size of your tank. You do not really have to worry too much as the pH regulator will close the magnetic valve, meaning shut off the output anyway, should the pH drop lower than the setting you have made, which was 8.00 in our case.

Some magnetic valves have manual overrides, which permit you to by pass the automation. Make sure the valve is set for automatic operation by referring to instruction manual that came with the valve.

Once the setting is taken care of, the system is totally operational and the only things you will have to worry about are: refilling the bottle of carbon dioxide when it is empty, testing the carbonate hardness once a week and adjusting it if necessary, making sure you clean the probe once in a while and recalibrating it. Besides that there is nothing to it.

When you are adding carbon dioxide you can increase the amount of macro-algae in the tank. Provide them with regular fertilizer as explained else-where, and make sure you are using the right kind of bulbs and enough light, and they will grow and thrive. Your corals and other inverts will also do much much better.

# 4.3 Dosing Pump, Peristaltic Pumping

Many aquarists use water additives in their aquariums. This might be fertil-izers, trace elements, water conditioners and the like.

For each of them we have a different formula for the quantity and frequency at which these need to be added.

Maintaining that frequency is in our experience always a problem, as some-times we forget, sometimes we are not at home, or in the place where the tank is, or cannot do it for some other reason. Some of us then play catch up the next time we are in a position to dispense the various additives, we sort of make up for having been unable to add them the previous time they were due to be put in.

This is obviously not a very good way of doing maintenance. Indeed, al-though some of the additives are needed all the time, they are only needed in very small quantities, on a continuous basis. We cannot put a one or two week supply in the water at once, because some of the elements, although they are very desirable in small quantities, may be noxious in larger ones. Case in point : fertilizers, some of the trace elements.

There should therefore be a better way for us to dispense these ele- ments. The constraints we wish to put on such a device are :

– we can add any amount we wish, even very small ones
– we can do so several times a day, to keep the amount of them that are dis-solved in the water, as constant as possible
– the instrument needs to be reliable, and not too conspicuous

Such instruments exist. Dupla manufactures such a "dosing" pump, and it can be highly recommended.

It consists of a small peristaltic pump, that can move minimal quantities of liquids, so small in fact that we are talking about drops. Additionally the device has a mini-timer which can be set to deliver such drops in any combination you decide on. For instance : 6 drops every 3 hours, or 4 drops every 8, or 10 drops every 4 etc. the decision on the setting you will use is entirely yours, and is determined by the size of your aquarium and the biomass you keep.

If several additives are used, a correct mixture of all of them has to be made, basing the mix on the total of each additive used per 24 hour period. After all have been mixed, add water to dilute, to prevent the fine tubing in the peristaltic pump from losing its vacuum because of the formation of crystals. The dilution factor should be 1 in 4. When you then set your dispensing unit, you must remember that each 4 drops of that solution only represents 1 drop of the real solution because you have diluted it.

Let us for clarity give an example, you can adjust the numbers afterwards and re-do the calculations as they apply to your particular situation.

We assume that per 24 hours we add the following additives :

— Duplagan (a water conditioner) 24 drops
— Fertilizer (that contains Iron) 12 drops
— Trace elements   6 drops
— Soluble vitamin mix (Dupla)  2 drops

First we want to determine how often we will refill the container that holds the solution. Let's say every 2 weeks.

This means that we need to multiply all the above numbers by 14.
We then take a bottle that will hold all those plus the water added for dilution. In our case, a 500 ml bottle will do.

We need a total of 24 times 14 + 12 times 14 + 6 times 14 + 2 times 14 which equals 616 drops. To this mixture we add the dilution, which is 3 times 616 drops or a total of 1848 drops. We thus end up with a total of 2464 drops that need to be dispensed over 14 days of 24 hours each. That equals 2464 : 14 = 176 drops per day.

We can now set our dosing pump to dispense these drops evenly over a period of 24 hours.

You could for instance use the following settings :

176 : 24 or 7 drops per hour, this would however be slightly less than we really want to dispense

176 : 12 or 15 drops every two hour, this would be slightly more than we wish to dispense

176 : 8 or 22 drops every three hours, and this would be exactly the amount you wish to dispense per 24 hour period.

The choice is really yours. Of course these numbers are only used here for our example. You will have to re-do the same calculations, using the additives that you employ and substitute the quantities that you dispense.

Using the dosing pump however lets you do these additions in such a way, that the amount of each of the additives is in pretty much the same concentration all the time, which is of course a great benefit for the stability of the tank. And remember the stabler conditions in the aquarium are, the better off you are.

Setting up a dosing pump is a matter of attaching tubing to the intake end, and running that piece of hose to your supply bottle. At the end of that hose (preferably silicone or pvc hose) attach a small fine filter that contains a little floss to filter out crystals and impurities. Additionally you need to run a piece of hose from the output end of the pump to the aquarium or to the bottom of the trickle filter. Then plug in the unit and set the timer and dispenser units you have calculated.

## 4.4 Hand held pH Meters, battery operated

These pH meters are more accurate than the pen types, because they can be fitted with better quality electrodes, are certainly a worthwhile addition to your aquarium equipment. Make sure the resolution is at least 0.01 and that the accuracy of the probe you by is at least 0.1 units.

If you have both one with a double junction gel electrode you can use the instrument in permanent immersion form. Whenever you want to check the pH, just switch on the unit and take a reading. After that switch it back off, this will make the battery last for much longer, and since the probe is immersed continuously, you will get an accurate reading every time you switch on the meter.

Calibration is also required and the principles are the same as the ones explained for the electronic pH meters elsewhere.

These meters will of course be quite a bit less expensive than the types that allow you to control a magnetic valve, by means of a relay. But if you are not dispensing CO2, or if you want a separate unit that you can use on several tanks, one after the other, it might well be worthwhile to acquire one.

# 4.5 Redox Potential Meters - Regulators

Redox potential is read in millivolts as is explained in the section on redox potential. Many types of instruments are sold by scientific instrument companies. Prices vary greatly, both with the sophistication of the unit that displays the redox potential, and with the quality of the probe used.

What is important to remember is that when buying a redox potential meter and probe, you should not skimp on quality, indeed you will need to obtain a probe that is suited for continuous immersion, and the best such probes are the platinum silver silver chloride ones.

The price in 1987 was anywhere from 85.00 to 175.00 dollars depending on the accuracy desired.

Do not buy a refillable electrode, rather get the sealed versions, they withstand continuous immersion much longer. Do not immerse the top of the probe, as recommended with pH probes. Salt solutions are very corrosive and will eventually pollute the inside of the electrode and reference liquid.

Redox meters that in addition to measuring the redox potential on a continuous basis, can also switch a relay, are much more desirable than regular meters. Indeed such units can be used to control an ozonizer.

The process to be followed is simple and as follows :

° Set up the control unit, after connecting the probe, and plug it in.

°Within a few hours you will get a meaningful measurement. Plug the ozonizer into the redox meter, and set it at the desired ozone output, (see the section on ozone for recommendations on redox potential levels).

° Now adjust the redox meter, using the set button, to switch the ozonizer off when the redox reaches 380 mv.

° Once the redox potential is that high, the unit will temporarily switch off ozone output.

° As a result, and since no ozone is going into the water anymore, the redox potential is likely to fall somewhat. This will result in

# Redox Measuring and Regulating Instrument by Selzle

Photo Dupla Aquaristik Gmbh

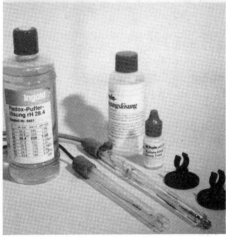

the ozonizer being switched back on, which causes the redox to rise again, and the ozonizer to be switched off again, and so on. This creates a continuous on and off cycle with the Redox potential being stabilized at the level you set it for.

Refer to the section on redox potential for further details on levels, rate of change, and other ways to influence the redox potential of your Reef.

# 4.6 Automatic Water Changers

## 4.6.1 Basics

The need to make regular water changes is not endorsed by all advanced aquarists, and certain manufacturers, as evidenced by their advertisements.

It is however clear that the amount of pollution generated , and its types, cannot be removed from the aquarium by normal filtration methods. If this is not obvious to you, we suggest that hook up a skimmer to such a tank, let it run for a few days, and then look in the cup where the foam collects. You will change your mind on water changes, and quickly.

Specifically, the following materials and pollutants appear frequently in excessive quantities in reef and other tanks :

* detritus occurring from dying off micro and macro algae
* left-over food
* dead animal life
* dead zoo and phytoplankton
* decomposition products of proteins
* phosphates
* nitrates
* sulphates
* phenols
* amines
* ketones
* skatoles
* airborne pollution
* nicotine
* pollutants entering with the water
* dust
* build up of albumin
* perfume
* tar

* amino-acids
* detritus from live rock not properly cleaned
* and still others

Some of these, as we have seen, can be removed by mechanical, biological and or chemical methods, using the filtration devices described in earlier chapters.

Evidence that not all pollutants can be removed completely, or reduced to acceptable levels however, as been found by renowned scientists and recognized experts in the field of aquarium keeping alike. To cite only a few names : Henk deGraaf, Guido Hucksteдt, Gerd Kassebeer, Jurgen Lemke-meyer, Peter Wilkens, Horst Kipper, Kaspar Horst, Graham Lundegaard, and many many others. They all recommend frequent water changes, in addition to the 3 commonly used filtration methods .

In the face of such findings one cannot but decide that water changes are indeed a must. This has also been our personal finding over the many years of involvement with marine aquaria, and more so with the ones containing invertebrates and corals.

Having established the need, there are several ways of accomplishing what we now know we have to do. Of course we need to determine frequencies and quantities. Such recommendations should be as all encompassing as possible to be of any benefit to the aquarist at large. It should be clear that, since every aquarium is a completely different eco-system, no overall recommendations can however be made. Some latitude will therefore be left for you to make individual adjustments, where required. The frequencies and amounts set forth however represent the minimum amounts to be adhered to, to improve water quality to the degree needed for keeping healthier looking reef aquariums.

## 4.6.2 Manual water changes

Most of us have been changing water in our aquariums for as long as we have had them. Whether we have been doing so regularly, and in a way that causes the least amount of stress to the biomass, is however not always certain.

Water changes should be frequent, but small. Keeping them small will not upset the water chemistry to any major degree, and will therefore not result in stress on the fish and invertebrates. Small water changes are also much easier to make than large ones. They take less time, usually do not require the setting up of hoses to evacuate the water being removed, and add the newly prepared artificial seawater; the latter should of course have been stored and aerated for some time ,to adjust its pH, remove possible traces of dissolved chlorine added by Public Water Authorities, and to give this mixture the time required to dissolve the salt and its components.

The need to have such water ready for water changes, at all times, is often not taken into account. This results in the addition to the aquarium of water that is too "raw". This will upset invertebrate and fish considerably and should therefore be abandoned. It has no place in the maintenance of Reef tanks.Letting artificial seawater stand overnight or longer, results in much more evenly dissolved salt mixes, as well as the precipitating of any gross impurities. Time will make them sink to the bottom of the vat, rather than end up in the reef tank. When you undertake the actual water change, be careful not to add them to the tank.

**Our average recommended water changes are as follows :**

**Four percent per week**
**or**
**Two percent every three days**

On a 150 gallon tank, this involves changing 6.00 gallons every week, which is not much more than one large bucket, an easily accomplished task.

Alternatively it would entail changing 3.00 gallons every 3 days, or the size of a small bucket, the kind we all have standing around anyway.

The second method appears to change more water, but that is in fact not so, because of the dilution factor. Water is diluted during the water change, and also because of the more frequent changing itself.

The water used should be of the same temperature and same salinity as the water in the aquarium. This is very important if you want to ensure that the amount of stress is minimized. Additionally use salt of superior quality, as it will ensure that the aquarium is re-supplied with a healthy quantity of trace elements.

You may increase these recommended amounts if your tank is heavily populated with fish, a fair amount of live rock, corals, anemones, and other such biomass. We have had good results with 5 percent per week in a 180 gallon reef set up that is quite populated. Nitrate levels for instance, which were stagnating at 28 mg per liter, started to slowly go down, and reached a low of around 15 mg per liter after 2 months of this treatment.Phosphates which were a 3 mg per liter, were reduced to below 1 mg per liter, with the resulting reduction in micro-algae of all types, which in itself would justify the effort, as this made the tank look more reef-like, and alive.

We have not been able to observe any lasting effect on redox potential values as a result of such water changes. Although the readings drop for about 3 hours, by 20 to 30 mv, the original redox potential values come back without any difficulty. Clean and fresh artificial salt water has a redox potential of around 240 mv, after it has been aerated for some 2 to 3 hours.

Staying on a once a week water change regimen seems to make sense. Indeed it can then be included in the program of other tasks that have to be done every week anyway, and such a schedule can be found in a later chapter. This may be contrary to what other  writers advocate. We are aware of that of course, but have found that Reef tanks do much better if water is changed regularly, and in small amounts. Try itt. We guarantee that you will not regret it.

## 4.6.3 Automatic water changing

Automating the water changing process obviously introduces an even greater factor of stability. We rely on modern instrumentation to do so, and need not bother running about with buckets, or stringing hose through the house or through the apartment. This is of course a nearly ideal situation, and is not very difficult to set up at that. It is not suggested in any of the literature that we have found, either because it involves the use of implements that are not usually sold in pet stores, or because no ones has had any specific experience with it. In Europe however, such automated water changing systems are much more common.

The following equipment is required to automate water changes :

* A reserve vat for prepared salt water
* A small, low output, water pump
* A float switch, preferably of the mercury type
* A good quality timer, e.g. Graesslin or Paragon
* Pipe and fittings, or flexible tubing
* Pvc cement and cleaner, or clamps

Based on our experience, and on the complexity of your particular application, setting up an automatic water changer, will take from half an hour to a maximum of about two.

A drain to evacuate the excess water that will accumulate in the tank, or in the trickle filter sump is also necessary. If such a drain is not available, or if it is not practical to make one, we can only automate the addition of water, not the removal of it. Of course, since we are only dealing with small quantities, removing the water should not pose a problem or create a mess.

The automatic addition still works, because after you have removed water from the aquarium - say a little every day, at feeding time -, the float switch that we will install, will sense a lower water level in the sump of the filter, and add water until it reaches the horizontal level at which the float switch was set originally.

### 4.6.3.1 Setting up an automatic water changer

First install the reserve vat in a convenient place, preferably underneath the aquarium. The vat requires an opening, fitted with a tank fitting of the same size as the pump outlet size. If you cannot, or have not drilled a hole in the vat, use a submersible pump instead. Pipe the vat to the bottom of the trickle filter, using either hard pipe or flexible tubing. Do this by using the required fittings, referring to the section on fittings and valves in this book if necessary. The size of the tubing or pipe depends on the size of the fittings of the pump.

The pump is installed so that it is between the reserve vat and the bottom of the trickle filter. A ball valve or a needle type valve should be used to regulate the water flowing to the sump when the pump is functioning.

If, on the other hand, a submersible pump is used, sink it in the vat, attach the necessary fittings, and with flexible tubing guide the output to the trickle filter. A valve should be placed, in line, to regulate the water flow. With pvc pipe this can be a ball or needle valve; if you have used flexible tubing you may wish to use some sort of clamp that you you can tighten to restrict the flow, for instance some type of C-clamp. Pet stores also sell little clamps for airline tubing that might do the job if you are using quarter inch tubing.

The pump is wired to the timer. Make sure that you are using a grounded pump, and that all wiring is according to code. The timer is wired to an outlet, preferably just a plain plug-in type electrical set-up, or if an electrician is doing the job, to a junction box. You can then set the timer to start moving water into the sump, for the length of time that you have selected.

It is recommended that you initially make the changer work while you are there, this to ensure that everything is working properly. Once you have established that all goes as you intended it, you may set the changer for any time convenient, even during the night, or early in the morning, whatever time you like. Of course make sure that excess water is automatically drained off. How to set up such a drain is explained later in this chapter.

## 4.6.4 Regulating the Water Flow

We still have to regulate the exact amount of water that is being changed, as, if we did not, the output of the pump, however small it might be, might still be larger than what you had established, as water changing quantity, based on the size of your tank. You should have calculated this beforehand, using either our recommendations, or some other formula that you are comfortable with.

**The flow can be regulated in several ways :**

* Obtain a timer that has "minute" settings, as opposed to one that only allows "hour" settings

* Start by setting the timer at the minimum on/off cycle possible, which in most cases will be 15 minutes for medium priced timers. Minute increment interval settings are usually possible on the more expensive models. Prices will vary from around 25.00 to possibly 60.00 dollars for the better types.

Depending on pump size, the amount of water selected for each water change might be pushed into the filter in a very short period of time. This will require timer adjustments. You will need to experiment with the settings, until you are satisfied with the amount of water that is moved in the time frame you set.

To determine the water quantity being moved, switch on the pump, let the water run in a bucket, as opposed to the bottom of the trickle filter, and determine how long the timer has to be set for, to dispense the amount of water you want to change. Use the valve or the clamp to make small output adjustments. This should take you perhaps 15 to 20 minutes to regulate, and is not complicated at all.

If no direct drainage is available, you must first remove the amount of water that you are changing (=new water added to the tank). If you are using an overflow to a drain, the excess water will automatically flow out, which is the purpose of it all anyway.

## 4.6.5 Installing the float switch :

We still have not installed the float switch, and we need to so, as the float switch is meant as a protection against possible overflowing of the sump of the trickle filter; this in the event the timer malfunctions, or if the pump puts out more water than intended.

None of these things are of course supposed to happen, but as Murphy says ...
(we are thinking more about visitors or children changing the settings actually).

Before explaining how to set up the float switch, let us look at how to hook up an overflow going to a drain however :
The water level in the sump is usually about half way up the height of the sump itself. This is not the result of how such filters run, but is based on the amount of water that we put in the filter when we first set it up. This leaves several inches clearance to the top, and we will use that clearance to add additional water, and make the excess flow out.

To install an overflow, you will need to be able to route the excess water to a drain that is "lower" than the bottom of the sump of the trickle filter. This can be a drain in the floor, if you have one; a sink, if one is installed in a spot lower than the trickle filter; or any area where you can make the water drain to, from where it is carried to a waste drain. This could be a sink in your cellar, or a drain in the floor of the cellar, or it could be a little more complicated than that, as we will see in the next section. Let us for the moment assume that you have such a drain.

In the side of the trickle filter, or in the bottom, you need a hole to which you can attach pipe that can be guided to that drain. Again a tank fitting will be necessary, plus some hard pipe or flexible tubing. Inside the trickle filter sump you will need to use a short piece of pipe, a 90 degree ell fitting, and another short piece of pipe, that is one inch higher than the normal level of the sump.

As the level rises, because new water is pushed into the sump, coming from the reserve vat, it will reach the top of the overflow, and start flowing out towards the drain. This is exactly what we want to achieve. New water comes in, and a mix of old and new water flows out.

If you want to minimize the amount of new water that flows out together with the old one, pipe the new water that is being added to the tank, and not to the bottom of the trickle filter. This makes the water change a little more efficient, but is not crucial in our experience. The amounts suggested earlier, cover the minimum water change requirements adequately. The dilution factor is in reality very small anyway, since the amount of water changed represents only a small portion of the water content of the aquarium.

As explained, excess water will flow away through the overflow that you have just built. But suppose it does not, because someone changed the settings, or because of mechanical failure of the timer, which as a result does not switch off. That is where the float switch, when installed, will come into play.

After building the overflow inside the trickle filter's sump, there should still be several inches left between the top of the overflow and the top of the sump.

Install the float switch in such a way, that its horizontal level is about one inch below the top of the sump, or 1.5 inches higher than the top of the overflow, whichever is easier to do, or whichever seems more adequate in your case. Mercury switches usually float on the water, rather than being in a stationary position, as some switches are. If your switch is of the latter type, you need to place the switch 's on/off level at that exact height.

Which one of the two levels you select is not really crucial, as indeed the only thing you are doing by installing the float switch, is ensuring that the float switch cuts out the pump before the sump can overflow.

This is what is called a high level control -off, when the level is too high- and the wiring for such a set up is of course different than it is for low level control. Refer to the instructions that come with the switch to determine which of the wires you need to use to control the high level.

Mercury switches usually come wired with 3 wires, of different color. Only 2 wires are used. Depending on which level control you are looking for, you need to use 2 particular wires.

Let us look at one that is available from Dupla : it has 3 wires, a blue one, a black one, and a brown one. Blue and black give low level control, meaning that the switch will cut power if the water level goes too low. Black and brown give high level control, meaning the switch will go off, when the water level goes too high. These are the two wires you would use when setting up the high level control.

The float switch is hooked up between pump and the timer, in the same way as the one hooked up to the pump that is returning the filtered water to the aquarium.

If everything works according to plan, this float switch will never have to work. If however if does, you will be very thankful that you installed it, as it will prevent the sump from overflowing.

### 4.6.5.1 How to set up the float switch when using a submersible pump

There is really no difference, providing you have the overflow installed and routed to a drain. If you have no drain, but you are removing the water by bucket or some similar means, you still install this float switch in the same way. It gives additional protection, should you forget to take water out of the tank, and the timer switches on the water changer, because as soon as the level in the sump rises too high, the float switch will shut off the pump that is pushing the new water into the sump or into the tank.

It is therefore a critical part of your set up, more so than when you have a drain, as it is easier to forget taking water out of the aquarium before the water changer timer starts, than for any of the components to fail in the other set up, where the drain automatically evacuates excess water. Keep this in mind therefore and do not set up a changer and timer, without overflow, unless you have also installed the float switch.

A drawing elsewhere in this book shows how a float switch should be hooked up to a pump. Look closely at how the wiring is done, and make sure you identify the wires correctly from the instructions that come with the switch.

### 4.6.5.2 What if you do not have drainage capability ?

You can still automate your water changes. There are however two ways to do so. One with a timer, and the other one without a timer. Both methods are explained , the second method is somewhat safer, as you will see :

### 4.6.5.2.1 With timer :

Everything is the same as in the method with overflow capability, but you have to remember to take out water before the changer starts, meaning before the timer switches the pump on, and you have to install the float switch to protect against overflow of the sump, should you forget to take the water out and the timer starts the cycle anyway. Check the previous sub chapters for exact wiring and set up details.

### 4.6.5.2.2 Without timer :

The float switch must be installed, and will start pumping water into the sump, or into the aquarium, after you have removed whatever quantity of water you decided on. Indeed removing water, will lower the level in the sump, the float switch, still set for high level control, not low, but sitting lower in the sump, will go down and start the pump. How low? At exactly the level of the of the normal level of the sump. As you remove water, the float will go down, and go out of its "off" position -the high level control-, and if it goes down enough, meaning to slightly lower than its horizontal level, it will kick in the pump that is attached to the reserve vat, and it will do so for as long as the horizontal level is not reached. How long this will take, depends on how much water you have removed manually.

## 4.6.6  Summary

As you can summarize, automatic water changing can always be set up, whether you have a drain or not, whether you use an outside pump or a submersible one. Of course the only thing that cannot be automated is the availability of salt water in the reserve vat. You will have to prepare that yourself, in a different container, let it stand for 24 or more hours, aerate it vigorously, and then transfer it to the vat from which you operate the automatic water changing. It should be obvious that the larger that vat is, the less frequently you will have to refill it.

It certainly takes the guesswork out of changing water, and relieves you of the chore of dragging buckets through the house or apartment with fresh artificial seawater. Additionally, changing water every day, in small quantities, is certainly much more beneficial than making large water changes irregularly. Last but no least, it certainly comes a lot closer that what really happens on the Coral Reefs.

# 5. Water Quality criteria

Below is a brief overview of some of the elements that can be either dissolved in the water we use, or contained in it in some other form, e.g. suspension, colloidal.

This analysis is not exhaustive, meaning not complete, but touches on the most important elements or compounds that might be present, and that could pollute the water if their concentrations become too high. If, by the way, your water is of better quality than the concentrations mentioned, the EPA considers it potable.

Before going into such an analysis however, let us take a brief look at some of the characteristics of natural sea water, in various ways

## 5.1. Natural Seawater :

Main components in ppm

| | |
|---|---|
| Oxygen 857.000 | Hydrogen 108.0 |
| Chlorine 19.000 | Sodium 10.500 |
| Magnesium 1.350 | Sulphur 885 |
| Calcium 400 | Potassium 380 |
| Bromine 65 | Carbon 28 |
| Strontium 13 | Boron 4.6 |
| Silicon 3 | |

Adapted from Brian Lundegaard (1985) Keeping Marine Fish, Blanford Press.

Besides the above elements, natural seawater also contains, as we have seen already, a number of other elements, in such minute quantities, that they are referred to as "trace elements"

Fluorine (1.5),
Nitrogen (0.5),
Lithium (0.18),
Rubidium (0.12),
Phosphorus (0.07),
Iodine (0.06),
Barium (0.03),
Aluminum (0.01),
Iron (0.01),
Molybdenum (0.01),
Zinc (0.01),
Nickel (0.0054),
Arsenic (0.003),
Copper (0.003),
Tin (0.003)
and many others, including Uranium, Manganese, Vanadium, Caesium, Silver, Yttrium, Cobalt, Selenium, Thorium, Lead, Mercury, Lanthanum, Gold, and so on.

It is in fact estimated that natural seawater contains all, or traces of all known and existing elements. Some are necessary for the biomass to survive and reproduce, others might just be present by an accident of nature, i.e. they end up in the oceans as a result of water run-offs and some forms of pollution.

Very little research exists that can definitely identify all elements that are required for reproduction and growth however. Some are known, such as nitrogen, manganese, iron, chromium and a few others. No one can however say for sure which ones are needed, without being incomplete. This certainly is an area where many discoveries can still be made.

It is also the reason why many hobbyists like to add trace elements to their tank water.

## 5.2 Artificial seawater

Besides the impurities and elements contained in the water that we use to prepare such artificial seawater, others are added and come from the salt mixtures we use. This is one of the reasons why, at the beginning of this book, we advocated using high quality salts. Most of the commercially available ones fit this picture. Of course, as in anything, there are different degrees of quality.

Tap water will, by itself, introduce a great number of impurities, as you will be able to determine from the water analysis that we recommended you obtain from your local Public Water Authorities.

Other impurities again,are the result of fish, invertebrate and plant metabolism -mainly catabolism-, and other chemical processes occurring in the Reef Aquarium on a continuous basis.

Of course airborne pollution cannot be forgotten either. Hydrocarbons from stoves and cooking, nicotine and tar from smoking, chemicals entering the water from cleaning products used in the house, pollution from the ambient air, and the same air used to power pumps and other devices e.g. skimmers and ozonizers.

The end result of all this is that, even though you might be very careful in and around the tank, there are so many different ways in which pollutants can enter the water, that it should be clear, that such pollution needs to be controlled by means of several kinds of filtration, as outlined in another chapter.

Monitoring the levels of those elements that we can easily control is therefore important and necessary.

Let us now look at some noxious elements that can appear in the reef tank :

## 5.3 Toxic and non-toxic elements

Although we are not covering every single element present in water from the mains, or in artificial seawater as prepared for your reef, several are worth looking at a little closer, as they are either toxic enough to merit attention, or necessary for life by either the fish, invertebrates, macro-algae or all.

It should also be noted that many marine algae have the ability to concentrate trace elements, and that an analysis of such levels can reveal that can reach 10, 100, 1000 times, those of surrounding water. Many studies, too numerous to mention, have demonstrated this.

We point this out, as it relates to maintenance of the reef tank. Indeed if such algae die off, they release these extremely high concentrations in the water, and such concentrations are toxic to invertebrates, and even to fish in the case of certain compounds.

Whether the infamous massive die-offs, that we probably all have experienced, can be attributed to this phenomenon is not clear yet. But caution is certainly to be recommended. Does this mean that we should avoid macro-algae altogether ?

Certainly not, indeed macro-algae, by storing some of these noxious elements perform a most valuable task for us. Without such macro-algae we could not rid the water of such elements, as techniques to do so, efficiently, are not available to the aquarist. It does however reinforce the need to provide the algae with a milieu in which they can thrive, on one hand, and remove the ones that do not look healthy, on the other hand.

## 5.3.1.  Alkalinity

The sum of all elements in the water, that will make its pH rise above 4.5 (usual definition) expressed mg per liter of Calcium Carbonate : CaCO3. Alkalinity is therefore a measure of the buffering capacity of the water. In our case this buffering ability needs to be high, as it affects the pH, the neutralization of acids of various kinds, and is required by corals and certain algae.

Depending on what you keep in your tank it should be anywhere between 12 and 18 German degrees of hardness. Good alkalinity assists in ridding the tank of excess acids, as this will result in less pH variations. During this process the buffer is slowly reduced, and the shortfall needs to be replaced. This can be done partially by water changes, but should really be taken care of through the use of products sold that do just that. Several are on the market, and can be obtained from pet stores.

Here are some materials that can affect the alkalinity : carbonates, bicarbonates also called hydrogen carbonates, phosphates and hydroxides -bases such as NaOH, sodium hydroxide, which can be bought to quick fix the pH if it goes down too much-. The buffer, while eliminating some of the acids produced, is also very effective when using the addition of $CO_2$ to the aquarium that contains lots of macro-algae. Is there a level where the alkalinity is too high ?

It is highly unlikely that this would occur naturally in your reef tank, but if you regularly add a supplement to adjust the carbonate hardness, you do need to check its level regularly, and not just rely on your "feel" for it. Too high an alkalinity would have an adverse effect on dissolved iron levels, by binding some of the soluble iron to hydroxil ions, thus creating a compound that will raise the pH on one hand, but making the iron unavailable to the plants and algae and resulting over a period of time in iron chlorosis (very frequent in fresh water tanks, rare in marine tanks, especially if the iron additive used is of the chelated type). Alkalinity would have to be higher than 650 mg per liter however for this to happen. This is equal to over 35 dKH. Some authors indicate that such high alkalinities can also pose problems for the eye fluid of fish, but we personally find that far-fetched and not something we have to concern ourselves in reef tanks.

Should you run into a situation where the alkalinity is too high, and you wish to reduce it, adding distilled water, or just water that has a much lower carbonate hardness will do the trick.

## 5.3.2  Arsenic

Arsenic enters the reef water in our tanks as an element in the salt mix, and a part of the water used to fill the tank and make water changes. Drinking water in the United States has been found to contain from 5 to 336 micrograms per liter (Kopp,1969) with a mean of 64 micrograms. Both fish and invertebrates absorb arsenic as part of the food they receive, and also from the environment. It is then excreted through feces, urine, and to a lesser extent through the skin.

Of course, and unless we make regular water changes, it can be reabsorbed, and its concentrations can slowly increase in both body tissues and the water. No test is available to the aquarist, so checking for arsenic can be done as part of a water test sent to a laboratory, or its levels in the mains water can be checked from the water analysis one can receive from the water authorities. Should you worry? If you keep fish only, it is unlikely that the levels reached in your tank will be toxic.

Some authorities report values of 31 mg per liter before Daphnia started to show signs of distress, but this was using the pentavalent form of arsenic and not the tri-valent, which itself is very toxic to invertebrates. We can therefore not rely on such reports. Tri-valent arsenic, which changes to penta-valent after some time, usually within 30 days of consumption, causes serious threats to the survival of our inverts if levels higher than 50 micrograms are maintained for long periods of time. One of the reasons is that, besides its proper noxious characteristics, fish, inverts and algae "store" forms of arsenic, and this can result in toxic levels, which will result in death. Experimental data are scarce, and the only recommendation that can be made is to adhere to the levels established for potable water, which is the maximum of 50 micrograms per liter referred to.

Ferguson(1972) points out that organically bound arsenic, as a result of the food ingested, is much less toxic.

If your mains water level Arsenic level is low, you should have no reason for concern, providing water changes are made regularly, to keep levels in check. If you keep extensive amounts of invertebrates, and if you continuously experience problems with only certain kinds of them, checking for arsenic levels, by sending a sample out, is to be recommended. We have personally experienced a situation in a friend's 300 gallon aquarium, where no anemones could be kept for any length of time due to levels of arsenic which were 3 times the recommended level, and which resulted from the high content of this element in the mains water, due to a seasonal increase in the rainy season, when water running back to the reservoir picked up the arsenic used in herbicides used for forest management. After changing great quantities of water, using a different source, the problem was remedied.

### 5.3.3  Boron

Boron does not exist as an element in nature. It usually is found as a compound mixed with sodium or calcium. It is also known that it is an essential element for plant growth, but no evidence exists that it is required by fish and invertebrates or even animals. Seawater does contain much higher levels of borate than freshwater lakes and rivers (Kopp,1967) No adverse effects have been observed even at very high levels, on aquatic life. Boron deficiency however has been shown to be detrimental to plants and macro-algae. This can be avoided by the use of a fertilizer - trace element mixture containing boron, and by regular water changes as the salt mix used contains traces of it. Spotte(1979) reports that Boron is not essential to marine life, but that it enters into the buffer capacity of seawater and can account for a sizeable amount of this buffer. Some artificial sea salts contain this element, others not. If you fit the picture of the average aquarist, you are probably using several kinds of salt. In doing so you are more than likely introducing sufficient quantities in your Reef water, and need not worry. If you are not, perhaps you are using trace element additives, and the latter usually contain boron.

### 5.3.4  Chlorine

Chlorine is extremely toxic to both fish and invertebrates, as most aquarists are aware of. What is however not always clear it that even minute concentrations can result in fish and invert death, if these levels are maintained for several hours. This is most likely to occur if water changes are made with water taken directly from the tap, to which salt is added, whereupon the mixture is added to the tank.

Although no hobbyist admits to doing this, it is our experience that the practice is much more widespread than believed. Un-attributed deaths, occurring within 96 hours of changing water, could very well be the result of minute levels of chlorine being present in the reef tank.

Chlorine levels of 10 micrograms have been shown to kill off all life in tanks if maintained on a continuous basis. This is equal to 0.01 ppm of chlorine, indeed an extremely low quantity.
To avoid mortality, or undue stress which could result in other diseases getting a foothold, all water used for the reef should therefore be free of chlorine. No exceptions.If you use distilled or such similar type water this will of course never be a problem.

One can buy mixtures that will eliminate chlorine from the water instantly. All pet stores carry several kinds. They all contain sodium thiosulfate, which we are strongly opposed to for Reef aquariums.

## 5.3.5 Copper

Everyone reading this is aware of the toxicity of copper to all invertebrates, and to fish if the concentration rises. What is not always clear is how this copper reaches the aquarium, how its concentration increases, and how this can result in massive die-offs of the biomass in the tank.

Most tap water enters the house by means of copper pipes. Water standing in these pipes for a long time, especially if it is acidic, will contain the Cu ion, which will bind with compounds in the aquarium water when it eventually is added to the tank. Our first task is therefore to reduce the danger coming from pipes, by not using water that has been in them for a while. Rather, when taking for the aquarium, let the water run for about 5 or 10 minutes, depending on whether you live in a house or an apartment building. This should eliminate if not greatly reduce the risk. After that, take the required amount of water, prepare it, aerate it and let it stand for at least 24 hours, preferably more.

Copper also enters the tank by means of the salt mix we use, although in trace concentrations of only 0.003 parts .

Additionally some of the decorations used, or some of the rocks used to "fill" the tank, might contain copper and slowly leach into the water, creating an environment that although not toxic, still contains too much copper for our invertebrates to be comfortable with.

You may think that this is all far fetched, however if you view the process over the length of time that you wish to keep your Reef Aquarium, small concentrations will gradually increase to levels that are no longer so small, and these levels will start upsetting the biomass in the aquarium. Of course macro-algae come to our assistance again, as they will remove some of the copper and store it. Inverts and fish themselves need copper, and seawater normally contains approximately 3.0 micrograms per liter (Mero,1964).

At high pH levels, copper has a tendency to precipitate, fall out, and as a result not being in solution. This will result in the tests you take not showing total copper in the tank. When the pH is changed, especially if it is lowered, some of the copper might go back in solution and stress fish and especially inverts. For no apparent reason after that, your tank just does not seem as lively as it used to be. Moreover, you probably wonder how that could be possible, since you just did a water change. The reason is not obvious, but it could very well be that copper levels have suddenly risen somewhat and are affecting the biomass, as a result of the water pH change brought about by the water change, or as a result of additional copper added to the tank from the water mains.

What should one do in such cases ? Rather than change more water, which will worsen matters, it is better to let the pH rise somewhat, by either increasing the KH, or by shutting off the CO2 for a while, or by adding NaOH if you have it available. Bring the pH back to what it was, not less and not more. This of course pre-supposes that you know what it was, either from having looked at a pH meter that you had installed, or at the notes you keep on tank conditions.

Best of all however to avoid these complications is to ensure that no copper enters the tank. The biggest danger, again, are the copper pipes that bring the water in, and the rock you use to fill the tank. Although we have no evidence that the claim is correct, J. Weissberg(1987) asserts that using lava rock has always resulted in such problems in his 300 gallon aquarium.

Your goal should be to keep the level of measurable copper to zero, that is, with the tests available in pet stores, making sure that the reagents you use are not expired or, if they do not carry an expiration date, that they do not show any signs of water absorption or discolora-tion.

Although all the negative comments on copper, it should be pointed out that copper is required in both animal and plant metabolism. Plants require it because copper is required in the production of many enzymes, and it is also necessary during photosynthesis for chlorophyll synthesis. Animals, including invertebrates, need it in the production of hemoglobin. Hemocyanin, a protein found in certain invertebrae, also contains copper.

Copper levels in waters with a high pH can be higher than in freshwater, and not as noxious, as you might have read in some literature. This is a true statement, but it is confusing at the same time, because the levels that are permissible are so low, even in salt water : 10 micrograms per liter for most species of invertebrates and corals.

## 5.3.6  Cyanide

Cyanide is one of the elements found in many compounds wherever there is industry. It is also an intermediate metabolite in many chemical processes in the animal and plant world. It is certainly a part of our reef system. Many of its compounds easily dissolve in water, e.g. Sodium Cyanide (the dreaded NaCN used in the catching of fish in certain areas). At high pH's the compound dissociates and Cyanide ion combines with hydrogen to form Hydrocyanic Acid (HCN), this is especially the case at a pH higher than 8.00 and HCN is toxic to reef life. The main danger that comes from cyanide is that it affects the oxygen metabolism. Cyanide is for instance present in the B12 vitamin cyanocobalamin an important vitamin for our reef, together with Biotin. If you are a believer in adding vitamins, do not use cyanocobalamin, but rely on hydroxocobalamin, also vitamin B12, but the latter contains no cyanide.

Although present in our aquarium from various sources, cyanide is destroyed at high reduction oxidation potentials, or by the use of ozone, chlorine, and permanganates. Of course, the latter two are of no use to us in the aquarium. Ozone is frequently used with skimmers or without them, and resolves the cyanide presence problem easily.

In tanks where no ozone is used, it is still removed in another way, through bacterial action, both aerobic and anaerobic. Train also indicates that some of the cyanide may combine with hydrogen and escape in the air, or that alternatively it is removed by photo chemical means.

Providing we keep the levels of dissolved oxygen high, with the resulting usually high redox potential values, cyanide should not concern us. Keeping redox potential levels high is discussed in another chapter. You may wish to refer to it again.

Should you ever have your water tested, a level of less than 5 micrograms per liter is considered safe.

## 5.3.7  Total dissolved gasses

Excesses of dissolved gasses, levels higher than saturation, at a given temperature and pressure, can be harmful. We know this disease as "Bubble disease", where gasses dissolved in fishes blood and system come out of solution, and form bubbles.
This seems to contradict what we have been saying about for instance oxygen, where we advocated as high as possible concentrations. Let us explain,

oxygen which is used extensively in the metabolic processes and is not to be suspected when bubble disease appears, although it extreme cases it can (Nebeker,1976). It is used up quite rapidly by the biomass in aquatic environments.

Nitrogen however, which is the major constituent of air, is much more dangerous. Measuring super saturation levels of oxygen therefore, over 110 percent, frequently around 113 percent in well run tanks, should thus not be a cause for concern. To the contrary, for many other reasons, we should try to achieve slightly higher than the saturation level, at all times, as seen in other chapters.

Super-saturation of oxygen can be achieved in several ways. Or perhaps we should say, by the combination of various techniques :

> —by making sure that enough macro algae are present in the reef
> aquarium, and that they receive adequate light and nutrients
> —and ensuring that photosynthesis can take place by providing
> —enough light
> —Carbon dioxide
> —the right kind of fertilizer
> —by using trickle filtration, with a large surface media
> —by adhering to extremely good maintenance techniques
> —by using a protein skimmer
> —and if needed an ozonizer
> —and not overcrowding the Reef.

## 5.3.8  Iron

Iron is an a essential element for both fish, invertebrates and macro-algae. We have touched upon this in the section on fertilizer and trace element mixtures that should be used in reef type aquariums. Iron is hard to keep in concentration, at high pH levels , because it has a tendency to precipitate, just like other heavy metals will do. Iron can occur in two forms, Iron 2 and Iron 3, the former one being the soluble one, and the one we are concerned with. Iron can also be present in organic or humic compounds, but again since these are bound, the iron is not available to the lifeforms in the tank, and thus they are of no interest to us here.

If Iron 2 is transformed into Iron 3, and if sulphur is present in an anaerobic area, it will form the black patches on the substrate that we equate with strong pollution, and which chemically is called FeS, ferrous sulfide. Iron can also form FeOH3 which is a hydroxide of yellowish brown color that is sometimes seen in the pipes or flexible tubing in our aquariums. If the color of the precipitate is red, then Ferric Oxide was formed Fe2O3. Of course our aim is to keep the iron we supply in solution so that it is available to the biomass. This is done by chelating the iron with for instance EDTA.

The level we wish to maintain is between 0.05 and 0.1 mg per liter, at all times. We have seen that the easiest way to do so is to use a peristaltic pump, combined with a timer, that can dispense, amongst others the iron we require in the tank.

Excesses of iron however are noxious, but will only rarely occur in our tanks because of the elevated pH of marine aquaria.

## 5.3.9 Lead

It should be clear from previous readings in other books, that besides not serving any known function in animal and plant life, lead is an extremely toxic metal that needs to be avoided at all cost. It is highly unlikely that you would encounter excessive concentrations of it in your tank, except is certain unlikely conditions exist. These include : lead leaching into the water from painted decorations placed in the tank, batteries used in the vicinity of the tank that are leaky, or feeding a contaminated food source, lead pencils dropped in the water and left there for long periods of time.

If none of these conditions exist, which we believe is likely, you should not have to worry about any danger from lead poisoning. Extremely small concentrations are lethal, and should you ever test the water, the recommended maximum level is less than 18 micrograms per liter.

## 5.3.10 Manganese

Manganese is only found in compounds with esoteric names such as pyrolusite, rhodocrocite, rhodonite, and so on. It is however a very important trace element for fish, invertebrates and algae alike. Its exact function are not completely known, but in plants lack of manganese results in chlorosis, and in animals in deformation, and loss of reproductivity.

100 micrograms is the maximum permissible limit.

It is contained in the salt mix we use, and also in the trace element mixtures that most of you add to the water, some on a more regular basis than others.

Seawater does not contain more than 2 micrograms per liter, mainly due to manganese being bio-concentrated in some forms of life, sometimes in levels 10 000times higher than the level in the surrounding water. This can be a reason for concern if a massive algae die-off should occur. It should however not lead to the conclusion that we do not want to keep macro-algae in the tank. Algae perform many vital functions in the reef tank. For more de-tails you should refer to the sec- tion on macro-algae in Chapter 15.

## 5.3.11  Mercury

Mercury has been known to be highly toxic to man and animal life for a long time. The recent discovery that microorganisms can turn inorganic mercury into organic mercury makes the situation more dramatic. Whether such life can actually survive in aquatic conditions in an aquarium has not been established. It makes any form of mercury suspicious however and def-initely to be avoided. The reason for including it into this section is because some thermometers contain mercury, and if broken, will over time ruin your tank, as it will be totally impossible to remove the running tiny beads of mercury from the water.

The only other way mercury will end up in higher concentrations in your reef, is if you do not remove dead fish, inverts and algae as the concentration in their bodies, converted by micro organisms will eventually pollute the water, usually in the form of methylmercury or mercuric chloride. This will of course not happen with one fish, but over time could cause problems.

## 5.3.12  Other dangerous chemicals

Although the chemicals mentioned hereafter are unlikely to be found in your aquarium water, in major cities, if you live in a rural and agricultural com-munity, and use well water, the cause of problems in an aquarium might be attributable to trace quantities of certain pesticides and other such chemicals used in gardens, fields, forests and the like.

If such is the case, which could only be determined by a laboratory analysis, indicating that you are suspecting such chemicals, your only alternative if you wish to keep fish is to completely change your water source, or at its worst use distilled or chemical free water only. These extremely noxious chemicals include : Malathion, Lindale, Heptachlor, Endrin, Endosulfan, Demeton, DDT, Chlorophenoxy herbicides, Chlordane, Aldrin and Dieldrin, Metoxychlor, Mirex, Parathion, PCB's, Toxaphene, and others

Many of these are not commonly used, and many are probably not even known to you, but they can leach in well water, or in other sources of potable water, and result in totally unexplained deaths.

Most are extremely noxious even at sub-microgram levels, as they all con-centrate rapidly in animal tissue, in concentrations that are quickly lethal.

Toxaphene permitted levels in aquatic environments for instance are 0.005

micrograms per liter. Mehrle(1975) found for instance that fathead minnows subjected to 0.055 microgram per liter for some time, and determined that all showed signs of retarded growth.

This should make it clear that this is the kind of pollution we cannot deal with as aquarists, and that such environmental pollution can only be dealt with by changing water supply source.

## 5.3.13  Phenol

Phenolic compounds are numerous, and a collection of chemicals of organic nature. Phenols are either mono-, di-, or polyhydric, depending on how many hydroxil groups they contain. The simplest form, phenol, has but one such group attached to the aromatic group.
We have seen that phenols appear as by-products of protein being broken down by bacteria, or by chemical oxidation. It is also known that high salinity, low oxygen levels and higher temperatures increase the toxicity of phenols. Phenols can also give water a distinctive odor, and extremely low levels are therefore recommended, 1 microgram/liter, although it would appear that no damage to fish gills occurs unless levels exceed 6 micrograms/liter (Reichenbach,1965)

As was already indicated the use of ozone strongly reduces the risk of phenolic intoxication. Moreover high quality activated carbon should be used at the same time. Of course, the use of a skimmer will remove great quantities of protein before they can decompose. You may wish to refer to the section on instruments where protein skimming is described in detail.

## 5.3.14  Phtalate esters

Phtalates are another type of undesirable organic compound, which are extremely toxic, even at very low quantities, and are found to be concentrated by fish and invertebrates in very high concentrations (Sanders,1973) Their presence in water inhibits the development of invertebrates quickly due to the up-take which very rapidly becomes toxic.

Again, there are no definitive studies that can be used to deduce what we should do in our aquariums, to keep phtalate levels low or non-existent.

Our only recommendation therefore is once more to adhere to extremely rigorous maintenance practices to ensure that potential sources of pollution are kept to a minimum, the use of a protein skimmer, and possibly to improve the latter's efficiency, an ozonizer.

Before using ozonizers, make sure that you read both the manufacturer's instructions and the chapter on ozone.

## 5.3.15  Selenium

Selenium is an element which is biologically required by both fish and invertebrates. The quantities required however are extremely small, but toxic levels are very quickly reached.

The WHO reported in 1972 that levels of 50 to 300 micrograms/l are found, usually as an oxidized form of selenium, e.g. ferric selenate, calcium selenate and so on. On the other hand ingestion of levels as low as 0.07 mg per day have been known to be toxic.

Most salt mixes contain selenium in the form of traces, which are sufficient to maintain adequate levels in reef tanks at all times, because of the water changes that regularly replenish their supply.

## 5.3.16  Hydrogen  Sulfide

This sulphur containing compound formed under anaerobic conditions, that we have all heard about, is extremely noxious, and very unpleasant in smell. It can be detected in the air in concentrations of only 0.002 ppm. The reason H2S can appear at all in the aquarium is because our tanks contain inorganic sulphates, and some organic sulphur compounds from the decomposition of protein matter.

In well aerated tanks, high in oxygen content, small amounts of hydrogen sulfide will be re-oxidized biologically to elemental sulphur which is not toxic. The lower the oxygen levels are allowed to go however the more toxic H2S becomes. pH also affects the presence of H2S, however at the pH's we run our tank, some of the H2S will always be present, although as the pH rises more and more of it is converted to HS (hydrosulfide ion), but not enough for us to be able not to worry about it.

Invertebrates are particularly at risk, because often H2S is formed in the substrate, and escapes into the layer of water right above it, where frequently one finds a lot of invertebrates.

If strong water circulation is used, as we have recommended on several occasions, this hydrogen sulfide is mixed with the rest of the aquarium water, and can then harm and stress most of the tank inhabitants. It has been demonstrated that levels of 0.3 to 0.4 mg/l are still tolerable, but that slightly higher levels will start harming the biomass (Colby,1967) It was also discovered that the higher the temperature, the more sensitive to H2S the biomass becomes.

Rather than trying to find ways to cope with existing H2S, we should rather maintain our tanks in such conditions that it does not form. This can be achieved by ensuring high dissolved oxygen levels, no dead spots in the tank, and good maintenance practices.

Of course this includes the removal of any dead material from the aquarium as soon as it is noticed. Care of any mechanical and fine filters is extremely important in this regard. Power head pumps, behind coral formations, will also greatly assist in reducing the risk of H2S formation.

## 5.3.17  Nicotine

The danger of Nicotine should not be neglected. Concentrations found in Reef tank water maintained in places where either the tank owner smokes, or visitors do, are always much higher than one would expect.

Does this mean that you should forbid people to smoke in that room, or not smoke in it yourself?

Rather than getting involved in the pros and cons of the matter, we would rather recommend that you definitely use activated carbon filtration on such tanks. Doing so will resolve the problem and keep levels at an acceptable minimal value.

## 5.3.18 Pollution in the air

Some authors suggest that the air used to drive air pumps, meaning the ambient air, contains many pollutants that should be filtered out.

Is this really necessary ? If you are really fussy, the answer is yes. In all likelihood however the amount of pollution is small enough to be neglected. If you have an air filter, or can build one, it is of course not a bad idea to use it. If you do, remember to clean it frequently. A carbon cartridge, e.g. a small piece of acrylic lift tube, filled with activated carbon, and sealed with silicone or some similar material, to which the airline intake tubing is attached, will do a fine job for you. It is also easy to make yourself.

# O₂-Reaktor

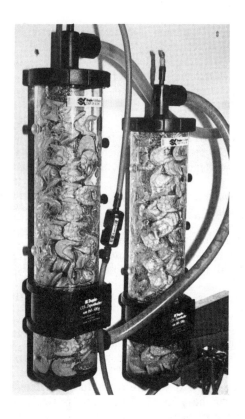

# 6. Required Water flow

We are all aware of the fact that recirculating aquarium water is of utmost importance. Authors such Spotte, Kipper, Horst, Selzle, Wilkens and many others have stressed this for many many years, indicating in their own ways, that the flow rate is even more important in marine aquariums than in freshwater ones. Numerous articles on the subject have been published, and all seem to arrive at the same conclusion.

No aquarist would disagree. We all try to circulate water as powerfully as we can, and acquire water pumps that are meant to do just that.

Do we however always end up with the desired flow rates ? The answer is a very non qualified no !

Although we set out to purchase a pump that is rated for the amount of water that we want to move, per hour, or as close to that number as is available, invariably, after a few weeks, we have the impression that we would like to increase that flow, if only we could. Sometimes we would just like to re direct the flow more evenly throughout the tank. It seems as if water is not getting to all the spots we want it to get to. It might also appear that the pump is not delivering the amount of gallons we have anticipated.

The explanation is not complicated. Most manufacturers rate their pumps for output at zero feet of head; of course no aquarist operates a pump in that fashion.

When pumps are subjected to back pressure, which is created by the need to elevate the water back to the aquarium level, by the friction that occurs because of the constriction of the pipe or tubing used, by the fittings that help guide the pipe or tubing back to the aquarium, the pump's output is reduced. The higher the back pressure, or head as it is called, the greater the output loss will be. In fact most manufacturers include a maximum head figure in their pump specification sheets. This is the pressure at which the pump will fail to push any water at all.

Mind you, although this is expressed in feet or meters, this is only a partially correct way of expressing it. You can conceivably make a pump fail, by pushing water up only a few feet, but making too many 90 degree angles, and other such connections, as they all increase the total head, or back pressure, on the pump. This will result in the actual head exceeding the maximum that is allowed for the pump used, with the result that no water is in fact reaching the aquarium. In addition, the pump is likely to heat up and start transferring that heat to the aquarium water. Exactly what we do not want to happen!

In traditional tank set ups, and in reefs, the head or back pressure is usually very manageable by the pumps we use. However the amount of head is such that we do not get the zero feet output rating that the manufacturer lists. This translates into not getting the number of gallons of output that you had expected from the pump you bought.

Common sense therefore tells us that we should always buy a pump of a higher rating than the number of gallons that we are looking for. This will account for the back pressure and fittings that we use, and ensure that after the head loss, enough output is still available to do the job.

It is also important to stick with the inlet and output pipe sizes that the manufacturer recommends or uses. If you acquire a pump that has 3/4 inch fittings, do not reduce them to 1/2 inch. This will strongly reduce the output, make the pump run warmer and much noisier, and will shorten the life of the motor. Not to mention the heat transfer already referred to.

Based on experience with various models that are available to hobbyists, we recommend that you purchase a pump with an output that is at least 20 to 25 percent higher than what you are really looking to obtain. If you wish to push 600 gallons per hour through the tank, you should buy a pump with a rated output, at zero feet, of at least 720 to 750 gallons per hour.

Of course, in reef tanks, only use pumps that are totally salt water safe. Some manufacturers use the label SC, for semi corrosive, to indicate that the pump can be used in such liquids. Other manufacturers do not provide such ratings, and you will have to decide based on the components that the pump is made out of, whether or not it can be used on your reef aquarium. Pumps with poly propylene, polyethylene, polystyrene, poly sulfone, or

316 stainless steel are completely safe. Make sure that no other materials are used inside of the pump, e.g. metal screws to hold parts in place. Seal and o rings should also be in a salt water resistant material, e.g. EPDM, Viton. Plain rubber gaskets will not hold for any length of time.

The next factor to take into account is the noise generated by the motor. If your reef is in a living room, or in a place where you spend a lot of time, this becomes very important. Pump manufacturers do normally not provide noise ratings, and you will have to talk to some fellow aquarists, members of Aquarium Societies, or a reliable pet store employee, to find out. Do not necessarily believe what you are being told. Ask for a reference, if need be and check. Pumps can be costly, and you do not want to find out, belatedly, that your pump is not of an acceptable noise level. You may in some cases wish to call the manufacturer. Since pumps vary greatly in both power and quality, we feel that we cannot recommend anyone in particular. There are several excellent models on the market however.

## 6.1 Designing the water flow

Circulating water through a reef aquarium poses totally different problems than what we are used to in conventional tanks. Indeed the type of biomass that is placed in the aquarium needs more circulation on one hand, and hinders that circulation on the other. Live rock, corals, and other large formations, make it more difficult to get an even water flow throughout the aquarium.

It is however not very difficult to solve these problems. A little ingenuity and few extra pieces of equipment will do just fine.

Since in reef tanks water movement inside the tank is very important as well, particular attention needs to be paid to how this is done. There are two different set-ups that we need to look at :

### 6.1.1 Aquariums with holes for returning water

Instead of one hole for returning water to the aquarium, it is best to have two. One on each side of the bottom plate of the aquarium. This requires that the tank be drilled and that tank fittings, or bulkhead fittings are used. What these fittings are, and where to get them is explained later in this chapter.

Returning the water from below the tank has several advantages :

* no tubing or piping is visible above or behind the aquarium
* access for cleaning all valves and pipes is much easier

* by setting up the internal directional flows in a particular fashion, one can ensure that dirt that accumulates at the bottom is stirred and ends up in the fine filter
* and at the same time eliminates dead spots, especially in the outside corners of the aquarium, and behind the rocks, live or other, that are placed in the reef tank.

You will require two bulkhead fittings, or tank fittings as they are called sometimes (see section on fittings).

Insert the tank fittings through the holes, and tighten them properly. Run the pipe from the pump to the bottom of the fitting, making sure that all required valves have been piped in. This includes ball and check valves.

On the inside of the tank, reduce the size to 1/2 inch each, by means of a reducer fitting of the proper sizing. One end of it is the same size as the pipe coming from the pump, the other end of it is half inch. Reducers are also called bushings. Although they serve the same purpose, they do look different. Insert a short piece of pipe into the tank fitting, on the inside of the tank. Then add at 45 degree angle fitting, and another short piece of half inch pipe. By short we mean 2 to 3 inches long.

The direction of the flow is determined by the direction you point the top piece of half inch towards. We recommend that this be towards the outside or side panels of the tank. In this fashion all the water that comes back in the tank, has to hit the side first and then spreads out in two directions when it comes back . This not only spreads the water more evenly, but eliminates dead spots in the corners of the aquarium, especially behind the rock placed there.

This dual return set up requires a T connector as well, as the water coming from the pump needs to be split in two directions, one to each of the holes drilled in the bottom of the aquarium. The size of the bulkheads and T connection depends on the size pipe that you are running from the tank to return the water to the tank.

You can conceivably refine this set-up to make it work alternatively from the right and from the left. This then duplicates the tidal effect.

This is done by adding a solenoid valve to each side, meaning on each water return, plus a timer. You need a double pole double throw timer for this. Indeed, you want one solenoid to open at the same time as the other one closes. This in effect makes the all the water return through one of the sides, for a period of time you determine, e.g. 6 hours, and then through the other side, for 6 hours, and so on. This is beneficial to corals and invertebrates. It is not hard to set up but does require that you know how to install solenoid valves.

You could of course have it done by an electrician or someone you know who is handy with electrical work, and has the permits required to do so in your area. If you select this type of water return, do not reduce the bulkhead fittings to 1/2 inch, but leave them of the size of the pipe coming from the pump. That way, the water return is not restricted.

Solenoid valves can be obtained from plumbing supply houses. Make sure that you get the right size, and most importantly that no metal parts are used on the inside of the valve. The Hayward company makes such a valve.

## 6.1.2 Aquariums without holes

In this particular case, since you do not have holes in the bottom, you will to either use hard pvc pipe or flexible tubing and run it along the back and over the tank. The set up is the same as described in 6.1.1, but the water now comes in from the top.

The direction should also be towards the side panes. This will stir up the bottom, and make the detritus that accumulates there end up in the fine filter. Remember to clean these regularly. You can still add the solenoids if you wish, and install these underneath the aquarium in the cabinet. The sizing of the pipe and the types of fittings used are the same.

The set up does not change, even if you use an overflow box, with a syphon, for returning the water to the filter, as opposed to an overflow box with a hole in the bottom of the aquarium.

The only real change is the fact that overflow syphon boxes usually do not allow as much flow as overflows with holes in the bottom of the tank. With newer models appearing on the market rather rapidly, we are sure that this problem will however be resolved soon.

If you decide to use this alternative, affix the pvc pipe or flexible tubing properly to the back of the tank. This will avoid noise, and slipping of the pipe. Special clamps can be obtained from your fittings supplier, in pvc or some other material.

## 6.1.3 Hard piping, or using Flexible Tubing ?

There is no particular rationale for selecting one over the other, except for the fact that hard piping will look better and more professionally finished than flexible hose. Additionally with flexible tubing you will need different fittings, e.g. barbs.

It might look a little messier, but from an efficiency standpoint there is no difference. You decide !

When using pvc pipe, try to obtain the grey type in what is called schedule 40. It looks much nicer than the standard off white color. The "schedule" is a technical reference that determines the safe pressure and temperature ratings of the pipe. It is not important to us, as we run open systems, at temperatures that do not require higher schedule ratings.

## 6.1.4 More on recommended Flow rates

Reef tanks require more flow than regular tanks. Being able to alternate the side from which the water comes back into the tank is an advantage, but not a necessity or requirement however.

Reef tanks additionally require a lot of internal circulation. It is therefore recommended to sink a power head in the back of the tank, on each side corner, and direct the flow at a 45 degree angel towards the front. This will ensure good circulation behind all the rocks and live rock that you have placed in the aquarium.

This may seem trivial, but it is not. Dead spots will often occur and will result in a lowering of the redox potential, which is undesirable at best.

Remember to clean the intakes of the power heads regularly, so the intake does not get clogged. This should be done at least every two weeks, preferably more often.

Use powerful types, that displace several hundred gallons per hour, that are easy to clean, and that are safe. Do not skimp on the expense of them, get good quality ones. Remember they run on full electrical current, and no one wants to get "zapped".

## 6.1.5 Flow rates

We recommend that you install a pump that will give you a flow rate that is at least 4 times the content of the aquarium in a moderately populated tank. For tanks that are heavy in live rock, it is recommended to go up to 6 times the water content. Just about everyone should be able to achieve the desired flows with a pump that displaces anywhere from 600 gallons per hour for small tanks, to around 1000 gallons per hour for larger tanks e.g. 150 gallon ones.

Remember when buying a pump, that the biomass in your reef tank depends on its performance for "life"; that the pump has to run 24 hours a day; and that you therefore need a very reliable piece of equipment. There are several such units on the market, March, Little Giant, Teal, and the pumps manufactured for Dupla, with capacities of up to 2300 gallons per hour.

Also ensure that spare parts are easily available, and again that the pump does not contain any internal pieces that are not suited for use in marine aquariums.

Since the kind of pump you are likely to acquire, or already have, might have cost somewhat more than you had expected, it is a good idea to protect it with a float switch. The latter will prevent the pump from running dry in the event that the level in the trickle filter sump becomes too low.

Such a switch is easily installed, and not a great expense either. Switches of the mercury type last for the longest periods of time, and are extremely reliable.

# The aim:

The aquarium must be cleaned
and freed on a continous basis of
waste and metabolic breakdown
products from fish and plants. This
should occur through biological
filtration, i. e. by using a suitable
material on which bacteria can
easily grow and regenerate the
water. Dirty prefilters should be
avoided, as this inevita leads to
great loss of oxygen in the water.

# The Dupla-Bioball

The Dupla Bioball prevents such
dangers right from the beginning.
The Dupla Bioball is a filtration
material with a particular large
surface area. It is made in such a
way that large colonies of bacteria
can grow on it without reducing
the amount of filtering surface,
which is what occurs if one uses
porous materials, as bacteria
grow on top of other bacteria.
Since the material is not porous no
anaerobic areas can form. The
Dupla Bioball can be used in both
submerged and trickle filters.
Required amount: 5 to 10 percent
of the water content of the aquarium. The Bioball will work without
attention or change and will last
forever if a suitable prefilter is used.

# 7.Common Fittings and Valves

Although it would seem odd to include a section on plumbing fittings in a Reef tank book, it is felt that such fittings are used so often in Reef set ups, and that so many hobbyists are confused by the many names and types, that it would be helpful to describe the types that are commonly needed to complete the tank.

If you are familiar with pvc and fittings and valves, you can of course elect to skip this section.

## 7.1 Fittings

There are many more fittings than the ones described here. This list however includes the most commonly used ones in setting up reef-like aquariums, especially when using the hard pipe method.

### 7.1.1 Coupling

a fitting used to connect two pieces of pipe of the same size. The pipe slides in the coupling, on each side, and is usually glued in with pvc cement, after having used pvc cleaner on all pieces that will be bonded.

This last remark applies to all fittings, and will not be repeated. It is important to do so with every fitting and pipe that is cemented into a fitting, to ensure the integrity of the bond and prevent leaks.

Couplings come in threaded and non threaded versions. Threaded ones obviously need a fitting that has the reverse type of thread if you plan to connect them to some other piece of pipe.

### 7.1.2 Ell or 90 degree angled fitting :

used to pipe at a 90 degree angle. Pipes slips in on both sides. The result is a 90 degree turn in the piping direction. These fittings come both threaded and un threaded. Most frequently you will use the un threaded version. This is a fitting that you will more than likely use frequently if you "hard" pipe your system.

The threaded version comes in handy sometimes when you need to make a 90 degree angle right at the output of a device that ends with a female fitting.

### 7.1.3 Ell 45 degree angled fitting :

same as above, except that the angle is only 45 degrees. The fittings allow you to make unusual 90 degree turns, by using 2 of them, and connecting them with a very short piece of pipe. The shortest you can go in this case, is the length of the slip in times two. How far pipe can slip into a fitting depends on the size of the fitting. In 3/4 inch this is usually 3/4 inch.

### 7.1.4 T-connector :

a fitting that has three openings. Looks like a T, and is used to add an additional water line, at 90 degrees to the existing one. It takes pipe from 3 sides. This fitting is used to make a by pass on the water line, e.g. to direct water to the second water return hole in the bottom of the aquarium. It can also be used to direct water to the $CO_2$ reactor, or any other device that needs water to run.

Do not use it to run a skimmer however. The reason for this is simple: when the pump stops, due to the action of the float switch or some other reason, no water will go to the skimmer for a brief moment, or at least until the pump restarts. This makes it very difficult to adjust the skimmer to a correct water flow level.

To direct water to a protein skimmer you should use a dedicated pump.

### 7.1.5 Female adapter :

looks like a coupling, but has an inside thread on one side. Such a fitting is needed to connect pipe to, for instance, a pump that ends with a male fitting. It is also used to connect pipe to another piece of pipe that ends with a male thread. Other uses include connecting pipe to a male threaded barb (hose to pipe adapter)

## 7.1.6  Male adapter :

looks like a coupling but has thread on the outside on one end. Pipe can be inserted on one side, and the threaded end needs to be connected to a fitting that has a female, meaning inside thread. Used on pumps that end with a female threaded fitting.

## 7.1.7  Bushing :

a piece that can be fitted inside another fitting to reduce its inside diameter. Needed if e.g. you are using one inch pipe, and you want to connect smaller pipe to it. What you would do is first attach a coupling of one inch size to the one inch pipe. Secondly you would insert a bushing into the other end of the coupling, and then insert your smaller pipe inside that now reduced coupling. Bushings come in all sizes, and can also be obtained in threaded version. You would use the latter if you wanted to reduce a female adapter. Bushings are also sometimes called reducers. They look different, but perform the same basic function : connecting pipe of different sizes.

## 7.1.8  Barb :

a fitting that can be either male, or female, threaded on one end, or just plain, and that is used to connect hose to pvc pipe. One end is sized to take flexible tubing of the size that the fitting is for, the other end takes pvc or similar pipe. This is used if you switch from hard pipe to flexible in certain sections or for a certain purpose. It is also used when you pipe your set up completely with flexible tubing. On the side where the hose is fit on, or where you attach the flexible tubing, a clamp is usually added to ensure that the hose respectively the flexible tubing, cannot slide off, especially when it is under pressure. These fittings can be found in hardware stores or plumbing supply houses. Most of you are probably familiar with them as they are frequently used with garden hoses as well.

## 7.1.9  Nipple :

a fitting with a male thread on both sides, that can be used to make a male fitting out of a female one, by screwing one side of the nipple into the female fitting. A general remark about screwing fittings together : make sure you put Teflon or similar tape around the male side, to ensure water tightness. This has the advantage that the fittings can always be unscrewed later.

Four to five layers of Teflon are recommended. Nipples can also be used as short connectors between to fittings. Other uses include making a male ending valve, out of one that is female threaded. Nipple fittings can be obtained in several different lengths, depending on their function.

# 7.2 Valves

Valves are used for a variety of purposes. Most often to regulate or stop the water from flowing. Other uses include preventing back flow, creating pressure in a bypass line etc. Good quality valves are not inexpensive. They last longer however and save a lot of trouble.
Installing valves requires pre-planning. So think through the way you are piping your aquarium. Retro-fitting valves is of course possible, but is it more complicated and time consuming.

Some of the better known manufacturers include : Hayward, G+F, Nibco and Chemtrol, as well as Asahi.

## 7.2.1 Ball valves :

a valve used to control flow. It has a hollow ball on its inside, which when turned by means of the handle, restricts and therefore reduces the water flow. Ball valves come in several forms : true union, half union, plain, and can be had threaded and un threaded in all these versions. We recommend that you use True union types, as they are easy to remove, and re usable. The plain versions, also called throw away types, are cheaper but are also harder to fine tune. They save a few dollars but will not give you the flexibility that you can get from the true union types.

## 7.2.2 Check valve :

a valve that only permits water to go through in one direction. This can prevent backflow of water from the aquarium, if installed in that water return line (to the aquarium), and is important, as it will prevent your trickle filter from overflowing should the power go out, or your pump fail. Check valves should also be obtained in the true union type, as this will allow easy dismantling when they need to be cleaned. Cleaning them is important, to ensure that they keep doing what they are supposed to do, prevent water from flowing back, even in a small continuous trickle. Check valves are an important safety feature, so buy the better ones. Since they also somewhat restrict the flow, you may wish to acquire the Y check type, which works with a spring made out of PVC, rather than a ball, as the traditional ones. Check valves have saved a lot of carpets and parquets... believe us.

## 7.2.3 Flow valve :

a valve that has a float on the inside, usually spring loaded, which is pushed backed when the water flows through. The outside of the valve has markings, which indicate how much water is going through at anytime. This tells you how much water is circulating. If you acquire one, make sure that it does not contain any metal parts. Nice to have, but not a requirement. Plumbing supply houses usually do not carry them. Scientific supply houses usually do. Cost: around 50.00 dollars for a good quality one. Alternatively, Flow "meters" are available. They perform the same function, perhaps with more precision, but their price is much higher. Unless you really need extremely accurate measurements we do not feel that you need to consider them

### 7.2.4 Needle valve :

a valve which regulates flow by means of a needle pointed internal mechanism, which can be lowered or raised, by turning a knob on the outside. This allows for easier adjustment of flows than a ball valve. It is preferred in situations where flow needs to be controlled more carefully, as for instance the amount of water that goes to a $CO_2$ reactor, to an oxygen reactor, or any other such purpose where minimal or very exact amounts of water are required. When moving and controlling large quantities of water, you should use a good ball valve, when controlling small amounts and more accurate restriction is required, needle valves will do a better job. You may wish to use this type of valve to adjust the water going to the protein skimmer for instance. Highly accurate amounts can then be regulated.

### 7.2.5 Gate valve :

uses the same principle as the ball valve, but even less precise adjustment. Good when just open and closed situations occur. Not often used in the hobby, except in very large set-ups.

### 7.2.6 Foot valve :

Usually a check valve that has been fitted with a screen on one side. This valve is for instance installed inside the trickle filter, and prevents large dirt particles from entering the pump. Not necessary but a good addition to the trickle filter as it will reduce pump cleaning frequency. Foot valves do however not perform the way fine filters do. They will however prevent large particulate matter from getting into the pump. We have only used them on set ups that are 240 gallons and up.

### 7.2.7 Butterfly valve :

Another type of water flow control valve, not recommended in Reef aquariums smaller than 300 gallons. It is in fact used mostly to just open or close the flow. Unless you are running a multiple tank system it is unlikely that you will require this type of valve.

## 7.2.8 Unions :

Although technically not "valves", these fittings , when placed in line, allow you to disconnect lengths of pipe without having to cut.

They can be used in locations where it is likely that you will have to remove the pipe for some purpose or another. They are similar to what pet stores sell as "quick disconnects". They are however not as expensive, and will do the job.

Unions are also very helpful in making connections that obstruct some part of the system, or filter, that you will need to get to later. E.g. a pipe running over the filter, will be in the way whenever you wish to access the sump of the filter. By placing two unions in line, the piece at fault can be removed and re fitted when the job is done.

## 7.2.9 Solenoid valves

Solenoid valves are not really valves, but on off devices. They come in two versions. Normally closed or normally open depending on the use. A normally closed valve does not let the water through (or some other liquid or gas) unless it is electrically triggered to open.

This could be the case if a float switch was in line with it, and the float switch sensed for instance that the water in a vat is too low. This would open the solenoid, which, if attached to a pressurized water source, would let the water through. The float switch would rise, and shut the solenoid again. Alternatively if you used a normally open solenoid, it would let water through unless electrically triggered not to.

An example is : a vat is being filled. The float switch senses that the level has reached the pre determined height, and shuts off the solenoid. Another application would occur if you have two water returns to the tank and you want to alternate where the water comes from. For instance 6 hours from one return, then 6 hours from the other one. Two solenoid and a timer are installed. The timer opens one valve and closes the other one every six hours. To do this you need to use both a normally open and a normally closed solenoid. This will reverse the direction the water is going from one return to the other one.

# 7.3 Summary

You have probably not used valves and fittings on your regular aquariums, by which we mean aquariums not set up as Reefs. If you have, probably not to the extent described in this section.

Although they are not an absolute requirement to operate a Reef aquarium, they make the aquarist's life a lot easier, and allow for a number of tasks to be performed without having to undertake major changes first, and give the possibility to control the water flow in ways not otherwise possible.

They will also allow you to disconnect pipes easily, without water spillage, if properly installed, when maintenance tasks require that such be done. And since we have stressed the need for maintenance many times already, you may as well take care of your tank with the least amount of difficulties as possible.

We strongly recommend that you include them in your tank set ups.

# Carbon Dioxide Diffusion : Components for small and large tanks

Photo Dupla Aquaristik Gmbh

## Components for small to large aquariums

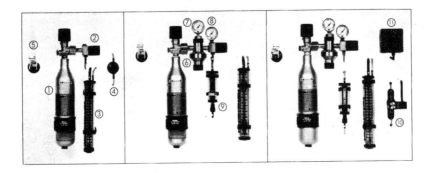

| 1st stage manual | 1st extension stage | Further extension partially automatic | Next extension fully automatic |
|---|---|---|---|
| ① $CO_2$ Bottle<br>② Ventil 1000<br>③ Reactor 400<br>④ Check Valve<br>⑤ $CO_2$ Test | ⑥ Pressure Reducer S<br>⑦ Manometer V<br>⑧ Manometer N (or: Fitting S)<br>⑨ Bubble Counter | ⑩ Magnetic Valve<br>⑪ Timer | ⑫ Dupla-pH-Continuous Controller<br>⑬ pH Electrode |

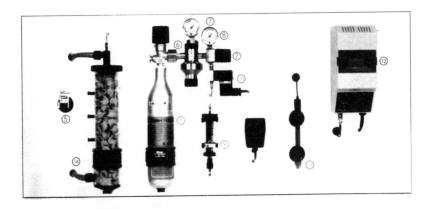

# 8. Water Analysis

## 8.1 Criteria and General Observations

We are all aware of the importance of testing Aquarium water. At least we should be.

Merely performing tests, and not knowing what the results obtained really mean is not productive and is not efficient. The same applies to understanding the tests themselves, and being able to interpret the values obtained. Only this knowledge will enable you to determine whether the situation needs to be corrected.

These remarks might seem obvious, but it is our experience, unfortunately, that often aquarists do not possess this knowledge. And even if they do, fail to be able to decide on what corrective measures need to be taken, to improve a problematic situation, or preventing one from deteriorating further. Perhaps one of the main reasons for this is the fact that meager literature is available on a regular basis that deals in depth with testing and interpreting values.

In this chapter we will review such tests, and attempt to make recommendations to improve conditions where ever possible. This does not mean that such recommendations are the last word on the subject. As we all know, ideal conditions at which to run a reef tank do not really exist. Every tank is somewhat different in content, filtration, and efficiency. These parameters would affect the values of certain tests, and the levels at which they should be maintained.

There are however levels that can be considered safe, or should we say safer, for the long term stability of the aquarium. Those are the values that we advocate. They are not necessarily based on lengthy scientific experiments, conducted under the most stringent conditions, ensuring that they are repeatable. They are based on personal experience, and the group experience of many German aquarists, and the findings that they have shared with and reported to us. We trust these people, they are aquarists like us, and have over the years accumulated a breadth of knowledge that is hard to challenge.

Some of the tests we will discuss may be new to you, or you may question the need for them. Do not get alarmed or do not be discouraged, as you read on, if not already, you will understand why they are being performed, and you will come to better understand the inner workings of your Reef tank.

Since we cannot give ideal values that absolutely need to be adhered to, for the reasons already explained, we will give recommended levels. Our recommendations might differ from those of other authors however. Let that not confuse you.

Try what we recommend, and if you are not satisfied with these recommendations, you can always go back to your old habits. But we do believe that what we advocate will suit your reef, not because we say so, but because these values are based on the experiences of so many other hobbyists, especially German ones.

Some of the tests are widely available, others are not. You may have to call around to find out who carries the particular ones that you need. If you try hard enough you will find them all. And this applies to hobbyists both in the United States and Canada.

Most problem tanks can be brought back under control with nothing more than better maintenance techniques, others will require the acquisition of additional equipment. You will have to decide yourself, based on your situation, which category you are in.

A little perseverance will help you manage conditions much more efficiently, often without the need to spend great amounts of money.

The latter is only the case if you decide that you would like to automate a number of aquarium functions. In such a case you need to buy the equipment to do so, and some can be pricey. However when you invest in such instruments, you are in reality buying scientific grade equipment, meant to last, and to give highly accurate results. Remember also that such equipment is delicate and that it needs to be treated as such.

When problems are found, and solutions are at hand, the only missing item is the aquarist's time to undertake whatever is necessary to correct the situation. And time we all have. At least, if we wish to keep a healthy reef, we should.

## 8.2 Carbon dioxide

Carbon dioxide is required for plant and algal metabolism. It enables plants and algae, especially the macro algae types - the ones we are most interested in anyway - to gain access to the nutrients required for growth, through a process called photo synthesis. This process requires a fair amount of light, as can be seen in the chapter on that topic. Reef life requires high levels of light, usually much more than one used to provide anyway.

Different plants and macro-algae require different amounts of light. Not all invertebrates and corals need strong light either. Some however need very strong light. For instance, Caulerpa species algae, which are usually readily available in pet stores, or through the mail, require intensities of 16.500 Lux. Only under those conditions will they grow for extended periods of time, and send off runners, which is the typical propagation method used by those algae.

Light is not the nutrient, but the catalyst that set off the photo-synthesis by which nutrients are absorbed. One of these is carbon dioxide.

Carbon dioxide is always present in the water. The amounts found in marine water are always much smaller than what is normally found in well maintained fresh water tanks. The reason for this is the high pH, the salinity, and the fact that a chemical process regulates the presence of 3 elements that we have already touched upon briefly in various sections.

Chemically there exists a balance between dissolved $CO_2$, the pH and the carbonate hardness of the water. This is not something that occurs in the aquarium only, it is a chemical process in water.

Since there is a balance, it is possible to influence any one of the three by making changes in the two others. In our case, we would want to influence the amount of $CO_2$ dissolved in the water. We want to increase it, to make more of it available to the algae and invertebrates that harbor symbiotic algae. We do this because algae perform many functions in the aquarium, and because symbiotic algae enable invertebrate hosts to live longer and generally do better. This ultimately results in a better looking reef.

Although carbon dioxide is present in the water, at all times, the amount found is usually very low, and is reduced when strong water movement occurs.

Charts giving dissolved carbon dioxide levels in seawater are not common. Few authors have investigated the subject thoroughly. Kipper has done some research on the matter and reported results in his book " Das Optimale Meerwasser Aquarium ", which unfortunately only exists in German.

Typically the following values apply :

| pH  | dKH | $CO_2$ mg/l |
|-----|-----|-------------|
| 8.0 | 5   | 1.18        |
| 8.0 | 10  | 3.00        |
| 8.0 | 15  | 4.40        |
| 8.0 | 20  | 5.90        |

Adapted from Kipper(1987) in various publications.

What does this tell us ? At a pH level in the general range of what we keep our aquariums at, higher levels of carbonate hardness enable the water to hold more carbon dioxide.

You will probably say that your tank does not run at a pH of 8.0, and we of course realize that. Be reminded however that over the course of a 24 hour period the pH fluctuates greatly, especially in an aquarium that contains different biomass forms, including macro algae (Thiel,1986).

This fluctuation can exceed 0.5 pH degrees. You may not notice it, more than likely because you do not really check the pH in the middle of the night or the early morning hours, and perhaps also not to the degree of accuracy necessary to determine these changes. But it does.

The point however was to demonstrate that the control of the carbonate hardness is one way to ensure that the water can maintain higher levels of dissolved $CO_2$.

This carbon dioxide is then available to both macro algae and to symbiotic algae. If $CO_2$ is freely available, it does not have to be extracted from carbonates and bi carbonates that make up the buffer of the water, and help maintain a stable pH. If $CO_2$ is in short supply, algae and symbiotic algae will over a period of time reduce the buffer, and this will lead to a drop of the pH. Carbonates indeed neutralize organic and other acids, and in doing so assure that we are not faced with continuous pH drops, or acid fall as it is sometimes referred to.

Please realize that this is a simplified explanation for a much more complicated chemical process that occurs, as one of many such chemical processes, in the reef tank.

Since we know that carbon dioxide is required, and since we already identified one way to affect its level, what other ways can we look at :

Carbon dioxide is also produced as a by product of fish respiration, of plant metabolism during the night (or more correctly : when the lights are off and the room is dark), as a by product of biological filtration the latter especially while the filter is being matured and from changes that naturally occur in the bi carbonate buffering system.

Often however the levels necessary to prevent algae from reducing the buffer, in their search for carbon dioxide, are not present in the tank. This can be measured by using a CO2 test. Several are available on the market. Dupla in particular makes one that allows for the measurement of a mg per liter value. When not enough carbon dioxide is present, several things can happen :

°macro algae do not grow and die off slowly, with the resulting pollution.

°symbiotic algae cannot perform their function within invertebrates, and our tank does not look alive, or the inverts die.

°this results in the filters having to perform at much higher levels than we had probably designed them for, which leads to pollution that is not removed and stress on the biomass.

°if this happens, intermediate protein breakdown products might reach concentrations that are harmful to invertebrates. Such compounds include : tryptophane and indole (Hueckstedt,1968). Normally these have to be broken down into melamines and other such related compounds. The interruption of this process results in an unexplained "just not looking so well" tank.

Since we cannot, as aquarists, test for such and other intermediate breakdown products, we are at loss to explain what happened, and start looking for miracle cures. Such cures do not exist.

Understanding the principle and the function of CO2 in the tank however, might enable us to at least ensure that fish and invertebrate losses cannot be attributed to this particular cause.

If not enough carbon dioxide is present in your tank, adding it by means of an outside source might be the solution to one possible cause of problems with your reef. This can be done manually or with an automated system. Both are described in this book, using methods and equipment available from Dupla, the only company, to our knowledge who distributes both a manual and an automated system in the United States and Canada.

Incidentally, adding Carbon dioxide to the water, in small quantities, will produce carbonic acid, which will in turn result in a small, and controllable drop in the pH, (see manual and automatic addition of carbon dioxide for more details). This small drop will result in a resulting small increase in the redox potential of the water.

One can usually also determine whether enough carbon dioxide is present in a rather simplistic way : visually; not very accurate of course, but nevertheless a method that can be used.

If enough carbon dioxide is present, macro algae will photo synthesize properly, and will give off small bubbles of oxygen during the day time. This does not happen immediately after the lights have been turned on, but a few hours later. These bubbles will rise in small strings towards the surface.

Some of this oxygen is also absorbed by the aquarium water. This particular type of oxygen is 3 times more dissolvable in water than atmospheric oxygen. A boon, and another example of one of the beneficial functions that macro algae perform in the reef tank, providing they are given proper care and the necessary amount of nutrients.

DeGraaf also indicates that ozone can affect the amount of carbon dioxide present slightly upwards, however more research is necessary in this area. Kipper(1987) in his book"Das Optimale Aquarium" strongly advo cates the use of carbon dioxide addition equipment and explains va rious methods of doing so.

Testing for CO2, in mg/l is therefore advocated. How to perform such a test is explained in Appendix 1.

We personally strive to maintain between 3.5 and 3.75 mg per liter, at a pH of 8.05 to 8.1, a carbonate hardness of 15 dKH, and a temperature of 25 degrees Celcius.

If you are presently not adding carbon dioxide to the tank, you will need to start doing so slowly. Remember stability and slow changes prevent a lot of unhappy experiences in Reef tanks.

## 8.2.1 The manual Addition of CO2

Few items are needed to add carbon dioxide manually to the tank. Here are the ones required to put a simple system into place in reef set-up of up to 150 gallons :

° a cannister of carbon dioxide, the size is determined by the contents of the tank. Indeed small cannisters will run out too quickly and need to be refilled too frequently. This is not always easy, as pet stores are not equipped to do so. One usually needs to go to a welding supply place, as all of them carry $CO_2$

° a valve controlling the cannister's output (Dupla or Scuba shops carry such valves)

° silicone or pvc flexible tubing

° a diffuser to reduce the $CO_2$ into very fine bubbles, so they will mix in a more efficient way with the water in the aquarium

° a carbonate hardness test

° a pH test of the high range type

° carbonate hardness generator (Dupla, Seachem or Kordon) to allow you to increase the carbonate hardness should it be necessary.

The first thing that you need to do to do is to take an accurate pH and carbonate hardness test and record the numbers. The dKH needs to be at least 12, and preferably higher. We adjust the dKH in our tanks to read 15 at least, using the Dupla carbonate hardness test.

The output valve is connected to the carbon dioxide bottle, the silicone or pvc hose to the diffuser. The latter is placed in the aquarium, as low as you can place it, but still in a visible location. This will allow you to adjust the carbon dioxide output easily, since you will be able to see the bubbles rise, and the rate at which they rise inside the diffuser.

After all the connections have been made, open the carbon dioxide bottle by turning the knob at its top, watch the $CO_2$ enter the diffuser, and count how many bubbles you can see going up in 15 seconds.

When you open the $CO_2$ bottle, do so very slowly, and only open it slightly at first. Now adjust the output to a maximum of 10 bubbles per minute, meaning one bubble approximately every 6 seconds. Let $CO_2$ go into the aquarium for about 10 minutes, and take another pH test. Stop the carbon dioxide supply by closing the bottle again. Of course if you have a pH meter, you can immerse the probe permanently in the water, and observe what effect the carbon dioxide produces.

Since we know that $CO_2$ added to water will lower the pH, because it forms carbonic acid, we can use this chemical phenomenon as a yardstick for the quantity we will add. This can be done, because we only want to lower the pH in the tank by 0.1 to 0.2 units; e.g. from 8.21 to 8.10, or for those who do not have a unit that gives a digital read out, but use powdered reagents, from 8.2 to 8.1. In essence what you want to do, is lower the pH by such an amount using the original test result as the reference number.

Do not make these adjustments however if the pH is too low to start with. If your pH is below 8.0 before starting this procedure, you should not add carbon dioxide until you have increased it to an acceptable level, of at least 8.2. To do so you will need to look for the cause why it was so low to begin with, and eliminate that cause.

If after doing the second pH test we find that the pH has not been lowered by the desired amount, turn up the output of CO2 slightly, to say 15 bubbles per minute, or one bubble every 4 seconds. Wait another ten minutes and take another pH test.

If the desired reduction has been obtained leave the CO2 output where it is. If the reduction is higher than 0.2 lower the output to an intermediate amount, e.g. 12 bubbles or 13 bubbles. If on the other hand the reduction is still not enough, increase the output further and keep testing the pH.

The idea is to dose exactly the amount needed to bring the pH down by 0.1 to maximum 0.2 units, while dispensing CO2 continuously.

Once you have determined that amount, take a KH test, a carbonate hardness test, and write the value down somewhere where you will be able to find it when you need it again, which will be in 24 hours.

Indeed as carbon dioxide is added, and carbonic acid formed, the buffer is being reduced slightly, and you will need to monitor how fast this happens in your tank.

The buffer is the sum total of the carbonates and bi carbonates in the water. These constitute the buffering capacity of the water, also called acid binding capacity. This is in essence the ability of the water to deal with the continuous production of acids of all kinds, including of course, the carbonic acid generated by the addition of carbon dioxide. Should this buffering capacity become too low, the pH will start falling, and the fall is the more pronounced, the lower the buffer, or carbonate hardness, is. It is therefore quite important, for safety reasons, to check the carbonate hardness and maintain it at the proper level.

The size of the carbonate hardness level is a matter of controversy. Kipper(1987) recommends maintaining it at a dKH of 15 , on the basis that on the reefs the dKH is usually between 7 and 9, and that a reserve is needed. Selzle(1986) recommends higher levels, to ensure that the dKH cannot fall too low, and to promote growth of both corals and calcareous algae such as Halimeda species.

Thiel(1987) suggests levels of 15 - 18 dKH with 15 as a minimum in reef tanks that contain many corals and other such life forms. This is the level that we recommend you maintain. Checking once a week, as part of your regular maintenance routine should do.

After 24 hours, and for a few days in a row, take a KH test and determine at what rate the KH in your reef tanks falls. Once you have a good idea of this number, you are ready to take corrective action and establish the number of KH building tablets, or other compound you might have acquired, that you need to add to the tank to maintain a stable KH, at the level you have decided upon.

A brief note : most KH generators contain colloidal matter that will make protein skimmers work much more efficiently, meaning there will be more wet type. This could easily make your skimmer overflow.

If you have one in operation, and you plan to use a KH builder, make sure you watch the effect the KH generator has, and turn the skimmer down appropriately to prevent the beaker from overflowing.

This colloidal matter is not harmful. It is used to prevent the compounds that generate the higher carbonate hardness, from clouding your reef's water.

Once you have determined the exact output rate of carbon dioxide, and once you know the dKH adjustment to be made, the addition of $CO_2$ will not pose any dangers, or cause any problems.

Leave the whole set up running during the day, when the lights are on, when photosynthesis takes place that is, and turn it off, I repeat turn it off, at night. This is done by closing the knob that controls the bottle or cannister.

Do not touch the output setting knob, as if you do, you will have to start your whole output adjustment again. In the morning, when the lights are turned on again, you re open the $CO_2$ bottle and the supply and addition will re start.

Of course, you might ask what if my pH is already low, say 8.0 ? In that case, something is probably wrong with your carbonate buffer to begin with. You should test,and adjust the dKH.

At the same time, make sure your mechanical filters are clean. Do not over-feed and do not overload your tank, as all these factors will result in a lowering of the pH due to the presence of excess acids of many kinds. Before adding $CO_2$, you will need to address those problems and resolve them.

If your system is set up correctly, and if enough light is provided , you will be able to observe, after as little a one week, small tiny strings of bubbles rising to the surface. This is nascent oxygen! It dissolves extremely well in water and will ensure full or super  saturation of oxygen in your reef tank.

Check the output on a regular basis, and have the bottle of carbon dioxide refilled whenever it is empty. It helps to have a spare, full, bottle around that you can hook up to the reef, while the empty bottle is being filled.

# 8.3 Phosphates :

Phosphates occur in the aquarium as by  products of food and feces de-composition, algal die  off and other such reasons. Few aquarists ever test for their presence however.

Phosphates might also be brought into the aquarium when they are con-tained in the water used to fill the aquarium, and do water changes. As indi-cated earlier in this book such water should also be tested, and results kept. It was even suggested to check with the local water supply company to ob-tain a free (most of the time) copy of a rather complete water analysis.

In open seas and around the reef, phosphate is present in minimal quantities only, e.g. 0.01 mg per liter. In our tanks, closed systems, phosphate levels can easily rise to several milligrams per liter, with the ensuing problems.

Excess phosphates, levels over 1 to maximum 2 mg per liter will give rise to outbreaks of micro  algae, slimy types, and other such undesirable micro algae, often seen in not well maintained aquariums.

Lack of maintenance, and overfeeding, are often the cause. Not removing dying  off algae, or not checking the water supply, can be other reasons.

Definitely keep phosphate levels to a minimum. Preferably below 1 mg per liter.

Several tests are available that give quite accurate results. So accurate in fact that it is very important not to touch the water being tested with fingers and hands, or not using test cylinders or vials that are not totally clean. Indeed, some phosphate is always present on our fingers and skin, and if transferred to the water that we are testing, this would falsify the test's results enough to make us believe that our water is overloaded.

With proper running filtration and a good amount of macro algae growth in the tank, it is possible to maintain phosphate levels to practically zero. Indeed phosphate is a preferred food source for all algae.

Should your tank contain too much phosphate, several methods are available to reduce their levels : the most obvious one is to make several water changes, over a period of a week or so, changing 5 to 6 percent of the water each time, a quantity small enough not to upset the water chemistry balance too much, making sure that the water that is being used does not contain too much phosphates to begin with. If the latter is the case, you will have to look for another water source. In the worst of all cases, this might involve buying chemical free water from a local supermarket, or some other supplier. This can however be costly after a while.

IIt is usually much better look for another water supply source, e.g. well water or rain water, or water taken from another aquarist's house. You might have to be a little resourceful if your case is one of unfit water from the water mains. Another option is to use distilled or chemical free water, or as these are sometimes called : de ionized water.

Another way of dealing with phosphates is to strongly increase the amount of macro algae Since few pet stores carry adequate quantities, you may need to browse through some hobby magazines, and order by mail from supply houses in Florida or California or Hawaii. There are several , and based on our experience, the quality of the algae they sell is excellent in most cases. This is also a way to obtain a wider choice.

Combining reduced feeding and increased amounts of macro algae, usually will slowly take care of the excess phosphate problem.

Yet another method is to plainly and simply reduce the biomass in the aquarium. This means doing exactly what no aquarist likes to do : reducing the amount of fish and invertebrates in the tank.

Alternatively this is perhaps the time to consider switching to a bigger aquarium.

If that is not possible, there still is another method which will give excellent results. This consists in making the quantity of water in the system larger. To do this, a vat, or another aquarium needs to be hooked up, connected through pipe or flexible tubing to the main water mass, and made to circulate. Such a vat can be connected for instance to the sump of your trickle filter.

This will result in less fish per gallon, and combined with one or more of the other methods, will result in a reduction of the amount of phosphates in the water. The latter method, although perhaps not the easiest to make, is certainly very cost effective and makes quite a bit of sense in a tank that is either already overloaded, or on the verge of being.

Adding such a vat to a trickle filter requires very little. Space, either underneath or beside the aquarium, and a few tank fittings, and some pipe will more than likely be all you need. Talking to a few other hobbyists while designing how you plan to do this will certainly not hurt either.

To maximize the efficiency of the vat you will use, make the pipe connections from high in the new vat, to low in the filter. Make the water from the tank overflow run into the new vat. When the water in the new vat reaches the holes drilled high up, the water will start overflowing into the filter, from where it is sucked up by the pump, and pushed back to the aquarium.

The water should come in the new vat on one end, and should flow out on the other end. This ensures good flow and continuous change of waster in the vat. The piping for this set up can be done with either hard or flexible pipe of course.

# 8.4 Ozone and ozonizers

We have already indicated that using excessive amounts of ozone is dangerous. It is also counter productive, because it results in more damage than good. Testing for ozone can be done in various ways. Chemically speaking the better method would be to use a compound called O Tolidine (ortho). This is however a chemical that is not easy for an aquarist to obtain, and can only be bought in quantity from chemical supply houses. It is a chemical that is no safe for aquarists to use, and therefore not to be recommended. It is now classified as a carcinogen. Stay away from it therefore unless you are trained in doing scientific testing.

Alternatively, sodium thiosulfate may be used. If residual ozone is present in the water being tested, it will turn yellow. Test by using a clean glass, some aquarium water, and add sodium thiosulfate crystals to the rate of 5 gr per liter. The yellowing if any should occur within 15 to 60 seconds, depending on the quantity. This does not allow for quantitative measurements, but at least it could be used for a qualitative test.

Then again, in most cases, carbon and whether or not one can smell ozone, should suffice for our purposes. Ozone being very pungent, minute quantities can be sensed immediately. If this occurs, reduce the quantity being dispensed, and or look for the cause of the ozone escaping into the air. If output reduction does not solve the problem, the ozonizer should be turned off until the situation has been corrected.

Frequently the cause is a ruptured hose, or bad connections somewhere in the line between the ozonizer and the skimmer. Make sure that you use ozone resistant fittings and hose, for all such connections.

Prevention is always the best way to choose in this case. It is also simple to achieve. Flow the water coming from the skimmer over highly activated carbon before returning it to the aquarium, and make sure all fittings and connections are tight and regularly checked.

Excess ozone in the air is noxious. If one can smell ozone the cause has to be found, and the ozonizer turned off, or its output reduced.

Since ozone, over time, increases the redox potential of the water, and providing good maintenance practices are followed, one should be able to reduce the amount used as time goes on. In this respect, check the section on redox potential for more details.

An important remark : if fish die in an aquarium where no ozone is used, the hobbyist finds all sorts of reasons for this occurrence, e.g. nitrite went up too high, fish came in sick, pH dropped too much and legion others. If this happens however in an aquarium in which ozone is being used, the aquarist immediately blames ozone poisoning for the loss of fish. Both are incorrect interpretations of a condition that can indeed have many causes, and without "proof" no single reason can be isolated. Tests have to be made, results looked at, and compared with recommended levels, and through a process of elimination the real reason has to be found. Just blaming ozone for all of one's problems is not fair, as usually it is not the case. One of the reasons is that the devices used to produce ozone for aquariums are so rudimentary, and of such little output and often even reduced efficiency that more than likely the reason lies elsewhere.

The exception to this rule is however sometimes obvious, and the result of an aquarist's lack of knowledge of quantities of ozone that should be used in small tanks.

Small tanks in this case means an aquariums that is 55 gallons or less. Certainly, we cannot use devices that put out 250 mg per hour on such a small amount of water. If our recommendations are followed such disasters will not happen. They have in the past, and as a result ozone has become the scapegoat for many fish and invert deaths, that cannot be attributed to some other "real" cause. Please keep this in mind, especially when talking to friends who are also in the hobby, and want to impress you with their knowledge of the dangers of ozone.

Because ozone is such a strong oxidizer, it breaks down protein and releases ammonium quickly. If this happens in an aquarium with an undersized filter, this will lead to suddenly increased levels of ammonia, This stresses and kills fish, for the simple reason that the filter is not able to deal with such a sudden increase, and not as rapidly as it is being produced.

For this reason we recommend that in aquariums where no ozone is used, one should introduce it slowly at first, and take at least 10 days to bring it up to the desired level.

Of course, the safest way to use ozone is to do so in conjunction with a properly sized skimmer, using a redox potential regulator, set at a certain value redox potential value. When that value is reached, the ozonizer is automatically shut off. See the section on redox potential for more details and recommended values.

Very frequently one will find that, as time goes by, less and less ozone is required to maintain a desired redox potential value. The obvious reason is that as the water becomes purer, smaller amounts of ozone, have a greater effect. This leads in the long run to the unit that one has acquired, probably being stronger than is required. This can not be avoided unfortunately, as in the beginning such a strong unit is a must to "polish" the water by removing excess organics.

## 8.5 Copper

No reef aquarium can be treated with copper. Copper is extremely noxious to invertebrates and will destroy your reef set-up in no time at all. Levels measured should therefore be zero or trace level. Some traces of copper will of course always be present, but we repeat traces only, as they are part of the trace elements in the artificial seawater mix. These traces are necessary, as they are required by all life in the aquarium.

Many tests for copper are available on the market. All are simple to use. No one should have any problems in this respect.

It is important to realize that copper can be present in the aquarium in various chemical compound forms. Some of these are not soluble at high pH levels, however as this level changes, some of the non  dissolved copper might go into solution and create problems. It is therefore important to remember that one should never use dead coral, or other forms of decoration, that came from an aquarium that was previously treated.

Copper that had precipitated might, at some point, go back in solution, with all the disastrous consequences. In case of doubt, abstain from using such rock.

Should copper levels be detected, e.g. 0.1 mg per liter and up, immediate remedial action needs to be taken. Water changes, with water that does not contain copper  check it to be safe  , needs to be undertaken. More than one change will be necessary to achieve the desired result. This is due to undissolved copper going into solution as water is being changed. Where the copper came from originally is of course not possible to determine from our vantage point, however since it is present it needs to be removed at all cost.

Besides water changes, new ,meaning fresh from the package, activated carbon of superior quality may be used. This will however also temporarily lower your oxygen levels, and your redox potential. This can however be dealt with later, as your predicament at this stage is to remove the copper.

Some liquids that remove or reduce copper in the aquarium are sold in many pet stores. They are fine in freshwater aquariums but should not be used in marine tanks. Most of them in fact do not remove copper as such from the water, they just bind it and make it fall out of solution. This does not resolve our problem, as that precipitated copper can go back into solution when pH fluctuations occur.

Using such products would in essence give you a false sense of security, but you are in reality flirting with disaster.

Besides these products, and water changes, you may also use filter media that perform like carbon in removing noxious heavy metals such as copper. They come in pads, or sometimes they come in the form of a resin. Resins are excellent as they are made to perform a specific task. Many of them however will leach phenols in the water, which we have seen in the chapter on filtration, is not desirable. One can also not measure, not easily that is, when they have exhausted their ab  , adsorption capacity. Although we do not suggest you avoid them, we feel that until more research is available, and until tests can be bought to measure their efficiency and effectiveness, you should use care when using them.

As a related topic, be careful when using water additives. Check their content very carefully before adding them to the tank. If no content is listed, call the manufacturer and ask the following question to a technical person : does your product contain any copper or other heavy metals at all? If the answer is yes, or if you do not get a categoric no, do not use it. Experience has shown that so called miracle cures for all sorts of diseases often contain copper in some form. Since manufacturers do not like to give away the composition of their products, for obvious reasons, caution is recommended. Moreover, many of these products were developed before the Reef concept was practiced by aquarists, and as such the presence of copper or other heavy metals, did not pose the problem that it does nowadays. Manufacturers will have to change such products to conform to the requirements of Reef aquariums, lest they are not interested in that part of the hobby. This is however unlikely , since reef type tanks are here to stay, we believe.

It should be clear also than any alloys that contain copper can not be used, a typical example is of course brass.

## 8.6 Other heavy metals

Everything that has been said about copper applies to all other heavy metals as well.

This is particularly so for zinc, lead, mercury, tin etc. No such metals should be used in a marine reef tank. Under normal conditions such heavy metals will not find their way into the reef. Make sure that any decorations, instrumentation, fittings and such, do not contain any metals. There are a few exceptions, for instance precious metals such as gold, platinum or silver. The latter however is not recommended either.

Pumps and other such devices may contain inside parts that are metallic. Check and be sure, rather than taking risks. A steel referred to as 316 stainless steel can be used as it has extremely high resistance.

Silver is a special case however, as it has bactericidal qualities as well. Little research in that area seems to exist that can be applied to our hobby and we should therefore avoid products containing this element.

## 8.7 General hardness

Because the hardness of seawater is always over 300 dKH, and because this permanent hardness is rarely affected by any of the processes occurring in the aquarium, we should not concern ourselves with this particular measurement unduly.

In fact to our knowledge no one makes a general hardness test for use in the marine hobby. If you tried to use a general hardness test, e.g. Tetra or Dupla, you may find that you would probably exhaust the test reagent, before you actually came up with a value.

# 8.8 Carbonate Hardness

We have stressed the importance of the carbonate hardness on various occasions in this book already. We have recommended values of dKH 15 to 18, and indicated that some authors suggest even higher levels. What seems to be uniformly accepted though is the fact that carbonate hardness needs to be monitored and maintained at levels that are higher than what is normally found on the reef.

No drawbacks to this practice have been identified, unless levels are raised to over dKH 35, which is most unlikely to happen in a Reef tank.

If one finds that the dKH is too low, remedial action should be taken, by adding a product that is intended specifically for marine tanks, such as for instance the KH generator sold by Dupla. This product is available in two sizes of tablets, and in several container sizes.

Adding these products needs to be done slowly. The binders required to ensure that the product will not cloud the water, will make skimmers work more efficiently and can cause the beaker of such skimmers to fill up rather quickly. Add only one or maximum two tablets at a time, and wait approximately 3 hours between applications.

Example : you determined that the KH in your aquarium is 11 dKH, using a reliable test kit.

You wish to raise the carbonate hardness to 15. Your tank contains 100 gallons of water  it is a 110, but with the rock etc, you figure the net water content is 100  .

This means that you need to raise the dKH by 4 degrees. Using the large Dupla tablets, which raise 50 gallons one dKH degree. A simple calculation tells us that you will need 2 (50 gallons x 2) times 4 ( for 4 degrees) to bring the dKH to 15.

Add these tablets slowly, 2 at a time over a period of 12 hours. Watch the skimmer if you use one.

Approximately 2 hours after the last tablets were added, take another KH test to ensure that you have reached the 15 dKH level.

Substitute whatever numbers apply to; our particular reef tank, find the required number of tablets, and you will be able to re  adjust the level to its proper value, 15 dKH . Test for KH hardness once a week, and adjust as required. If you are using carbon dioxide equipment on your tank, you will use slightly more KH tablets.

Remember the reason for high carbonate levels are multiple, one of the main ones being the water buffer, which regulates the amount of carbon dioxide the water can contain, and ensures a stabler pH.

# 8.9 Dissolved Oxygen Level-Organic Load

As already indicated on several occasions, it is extremely important to monitor dissolved oxygen levels - DOL - on a regular basis. Indeed higher levels benefit all the biomass in our aquariums.

Water cannot, for physical reasons, contain as much oxygen as air.

The specific amount depends on the temperature and the quality of the water. DOL is temperature dependent. This relationship is inverse, meaning that, as the temperature goes up, the amount of dissolved oxygen DO goes down. For any given temperature there is a maximum amount of DO water can contain. For each temperature level, a corresponding saturation level exists.

That is the level we should aim to achieve in our reef aquarium, or better, slightly higher than this maximum. This, in itself might, sound like a contradiction, but is in fact not so. Super saturation most always exists on the reef, especially during times of peak photosynthesis.

**How then is this achieved ?**

Algae produce oxygen, in a form much more dissolvable in water than atmospheric oxygen, three times more dissolvable in fact, some sources have even put this number at five.

Since excesses produced beyond the saturation level will escape into the atmosphere, water achieves its maximum saturation level, by taking up as much oxygen as possible, and by releasing any excess into the atmosphere.

When the reef is photosynthesizing at its peak, in the early afternoon, when the sun is at its highest, the over pressure of oxygen produced, cannot escape fast enough, and for a few hours the sea water on the reef can actually show dissolved oxygen levels of 110 to 120 percent of saturation. This is called super saturation. Of course as the day progresses, and as photosynthesis decreases, dissolved oxygen levels will go back down to 100 percent.

At night when no photosynthesis occurs  no light  the levels will go below saturation as macro and other algae, as well as fish and invertebrate, use the oxygen present in the water for their metabolism.

Our aim is to attempt to re  create these conditions in our reef tank. This is not an easy task, and is complicated by the fact that our tanks are closed systems. This is very unlike the seas around the reef, where the water is continually changing, and in fact never really carries any significant amount of pollution that would reduce DO levels. In our tanks such occurs all the time. Our task therefore is to keep these pollutant levels as low as possible, to avoid unnecessary depletion of DOL.

At high levels of dissolved oxygen, redox potential is high, which is desirable. German aquarists and researchers have advocated such high levels for several years now.

Measuring oxygen levels is not more complicated than any of the other tests that we normally perform. Several such tests are available in pet stores, e.g. Lamott and Dupla.

Compare the result of your test with a saturation level chart, and see what the difference is. This difference is called the oxygen deficit. Such a deficit can occur when you are not adhering to your maintenance program, and when you are not using the methods available nowadays to increase levels of dissolved oxygen.

Maintenance requires that you clean all mechanical and chemical filters on a regular schedule; that you remove dead or dying algae; and that any decomposing fish, invert or plant material be removed at once, meaning as soon as discovered. Since good maintenance includes checking, or at least taking a careful look at your tank every day, a dead fish should never be present in your tank for longer than 24 hours

Besides cleaning your aquarium, we mentioned other modern techniques that will raise the levels quickly and with certainty. The trickle filter, as described in this book, is one of them. The addition of ozone, and the use of a protein skimmer are two other ones.

We have described the trickle filtration principles in great detail and have outlined their benefits. You should be able to install such a filter without too much a do. Because you are blowing air in the filter column inside which the water trickles down, this same water can absorb oxygen from the surrounding air that is being pumped into it. The latter contains much more oxygen than the droplets, or small streams, of water that come down inside the filter. These drops will absorb some of this oxygen, and increase that water's dissolved oxygen level.

Adding a skimmer and an ozonizer increases dissolved oxygen levels in an indirect way.  As both these instruments "polish" the water over a period of time  remember nothing happens immediately, making it purer, they reduce the biological oxygen demand of the water.

This means that they reduce the amount of pollutants that lower the DOL, since these products are now no longer present, or if they still are, at least they have been greatly diminished in quantity. Purer water maintains higher levels of DO.

Using a well designed water circulation system, also increases dissolved oxygen levels, since layers with less oxygen can be made to come to the surface, where such water can then absorb oxygen from the surrounding air.

Contrary to common belief, lift tubes used to operate undergravel filters, with air pumps, only increase oxygen levels marginally.

Ozone itself does not add significantly to the amount of dissolved oxygen either. Most of it is used in the breakdown of proteinous matter, and in other such chemical processes.

Using enriched air  a mixture that contains more oxygen than ambient air could be a quick way to raise such D.O. levels. However this would prove to be a costly, and not very reliable process. Additionally one would have to be very careful where to inject this enriched air. Certainly not in the filter, as the high oxidation capability of such enriched air would be lethal to a great number of bacteria in the filter. This latter remark of course also applies to ozone, if it were pumped directly into the biological media column, or if the water coming out of the skimmer were directed back to the top of the trickle filter. The simple reason is that this water might still contain small amounts of ozone .

This is important to remember, as some aquarists, in good faith, believe that flowing more water through the filter is beneficial. This is of course correct, except not in the cases where ozone is mixed into the air that drives the protein skimmer.

Macro  algae, during the day, in a well balanced aquarium will exude oxygen which is of a type that is highly absorbable. Maintaining a fair amount of such algae is therefore beneficial too, besides being aesthetic as well.

Hanns Selzle(1986) and Horst Kipper(1987) describe a device called the "Oxygen Reactor", which can safely be used to inject air, under pressure, in the water. This reactor is relatively easy to install, but not easy to build yourself.

A cylindrical container, usually made of acrylic material, is filled with Bioballs and sealed at the top and the bottom. The top has three inlets. One for air, one for water entering the reactor, and one for the outcoming water. The last opening is in fact a pipe that runs from the top to about half an inch from the bottom.

Air is pumped into this reactor at the same time as water. In the Selzle model, an artificial internal over pressure is maintained, literally forcing the water and the air together. Since, because of the over pressure, the water cannot rise very much inside the cylinder, it is forced out through a pvc pipe, in the middle of the cylinder, and directed back to the aquarium.

This is a very efficient way of increasing the DOL, but it is not a unit that is recommended for beginners. Regulating the amount of air that enters the cylinder, on a constant basis, in such a way that the water in the cylinder only rises about 3 inches from the bottom, can be tricky.

Frequent adjustments of the water pump output are necessary, at least until such time as you have determined both the correct amount of air and water to inject into the reactor. It is best anyway to install a pressure gauge on the whole unit to visually determine what such pressure is. As the water flows in the cylinder, from the top, it hits a drip plate, similar to the one found in trickle filters. The water then runs down over the Bioballs, and on its way there absorb oxygen from the surrounding pressurized air. It reaches the bottom, and is forced back to the aquarium by the air over pressure that is maintained inside the cylinder.

In the Kipper model, no back pressure is used as such, but water is pumped into two much smaller cylinders that are inter connected, and that lead back to the aquarium, or the sump of the trickle filter. A small amount of air is pumped into the first of the two cylinders. Since it has no way of escaping, it can only mix with the water, which travels from the first reactor to the second one, and then back to the main aquarium water. After regulating the output for a while, one can adjust the air pump in such a way that only as much air is pumped in, as can mix with the water, without bubbles coming out of the tubing that is used to guide the water back to either the tank, or the bottom of the trickle filter. Kipper suggests using two of Dupla's Reactor S models to set up such a reactor. It would appear from the test results done at Dupla that this particular method is easier to manage than the cylinder type model described earlier.

Adding additional macro algae to the aquarium is usually one of the better ways to raise the DO level. This can however only be done when all other conditions for algae growth and photosynthesis are taken care of first as well. Indeed if these are not met, the macro algae will not grow, but die off and result in DOL being reduced, rather than increased, unless of course such dying off algae are removed as soon as they are noticed.

Huckstedt(1969) suggests the use of hydrogen peroxide to deal with oxygen deficiency quickly and efficiently. His recommendation is to add 1 centiliter of H2O2 per 20 liters of water. The hydrogen peroxide has to be the 15 percent kind, not the 3 percent sold in drugstores. He also states that even double that amount is harmless, but unnecessary.

You must be very careful when using such chemicals. Hydrogen peroxide at the levels recommended for this therapy, needs to be handled with great care.

We are personally opposed to such treatments and recommend that you stay away from them, unless you are a chemist and know how to handle such compounds.

## 8.10 Ammonia - Ammonium  Ion

You are all familiar with testing for ammonia and we will therefore not go into this any further. Appendix 1 describes how to use the Dupla NH4 test in detail.

That test is different from most others inasmuch as it tests for NH4, a simple conversion chart allows you to then determine what percentage of this NH4 is toxic, depending on the pH level of your tank.

Kipper(1986) states that 1 to 2 mg per liter of ammonia NH3 are toxic.

What is perhaps less known about ammonium, is how it behaves in an aqueous environment. At low pH levels, e.g. in fresh water tanks, most of the Ammonia N is present in the non toxic ionic form. As the pH rises, more of this ionic ammonium is converted to ammonia, a gas which is extremely toxic. In marine tanks, because of the high pH, ammonium will turn to ammonia. Ammonium is therefore a much greater threat to life in marine tanks. As the pH is lowered less ammonium is converted to ammonia gas.

It would therefore be wise not the run the reef at too high pH's to at least protect the biomass from possible ammonia intoxication.

Of course we cannot lower the pH indiscriminately, but need to maintain it in the right range. Meant is that it would be better to run the aquarium at a pH of 8.1 than 8.3

Of the total amount of ammonium measured, following percentages are
converted into ammonia gas at various pH levels

| pH  | % Ammonia |
|-----|-----------|
| 7.8 | 4.5       |
| 8.0 | 7.0       |
| 8.2 | 10        |
| 8.4 | 15        |

Adapted from Kipper,1987

If excess ammonium/ammonia is present, one needs to determine the cause.
Overcrowding, the use of medication, filters that are too small, or the wrong
material in the trickle filter, can all be causes. Do not forget that overfeeding
is usually one of the main causes of problems in any tank, and that you
should take a good look at your own feeding habits.

Isolate the one that seems to create your problem and change whatever is required to eliminate that cause.

If your filter is properly sized and contains the right medium, and if you
follow directions relating to feeding, fish population, number of inverts and
so on, you will not run into an ammonium problem.

We have dealt with ways to change aquarium set ups earlier and we refer you
back to that text. Water changing can solve the problem in the immediate,
but is of course not the solution. You need to determine the exact cause of
your problem, and not use "patch" techniques

## 8.11 Nitrite

This test is covered in every aquarium book you have read, and we will
therefore not spend much time on this particular subject. Suffice it to say
that nitrite is very noxious, should be held at minimum quantities at all
times, through superior biological filtration, and that testing for nitrite
should be part of regular maintenance, e.g. once every week.

The level should not exceed 0.1 mg per liter in a tank that is not overloaded,
and that has a mature filter. If excess nitrite is found during a test, one
should look for the cause(s) immediately.

For instance biological filtration might not be able to cope with an overload
in the aquarium, the latter being due to too many fish, or due to algae die

off, or decomposing fish matter that has not been noticed, because it is stuck behind a piece of coral. Check carefully therefore to ensure that any dead material is removed at once.

Nitrite can also occur as a result of the denitrification process that is not running its normal course. Removal of nitrate, through denitrification, is a very delicate process, and can indeed produce excess levels of nitrite, if the filter itself is sized too exactly for the reef in question, meaning it is not able to deal with any excesses produced through denitrification.

Other reasons for excessive nitrites include just plain overfeeding, and too many fish and inverts in the tank. More information on denitrification can be found elsewhere in the book.

The type of remedial action is dependent on the cause. In the event of overload it is of course relatively easy to deal with, one just lowers the biomass of the aquarium, or as explained earlier, increases the amount of water that is part of the system, by adding an additional vat connected to the filter.

We have shown that this is not as difficult a task as it might appear at first, and that the results can make the difference between a tank that runs properly, or one where continuous problems plague the hobbyist. Seriously consider this solution.

Alternatively the filter itself needs to be enlarged. If space is available, more filter media can be added to provide growth area for more bacteria. If such space is not available, one can try to add a small space above the existing filter in which more media can be placed, or if that is not possible either, the submersed area of the filter can be filled with media.

Although this does not provide as efficient a filter as in the non submersed area, it still does increase the biological filter and can solve the problem. A simple way of adding to the top of the filter, is to build a square or rectangular tray, fill it with media, drill holes in the bottom of the tray, place a dispersal plate on the top, and position this addition on the top of the existing filter.

Still another way would be, and we have found this to be a solution in many a case, to change the media being used to a medium that has more surface area than the one presently in the filter.

One might remove Biopax or Tri packs, and fill the filter with Bioballs instead, thus raising the area considerably especially if medium sized Tri packs were being used. If some other type of medium is used, the resulting difference might be even more dramatic. This is especially so if no particular medium is used but if the filter now contains D.L.S. (Double Layered Spiral) material or similar materials.

We wish to make one point very clear : when referring to area, we mean the area that is effectively, and efficiently, being used by aerobic bacteria for nitrogen breakdown products removal, not total surface area of products. If the latter were the case, D.L.S. or Matrix, or carbon, has a larger "total" area. Only part of the area these media provide is used by aerobic bacteria, and those are the only bacteria that we are interested in when talking about nitrite removal.

These materials obviously provide surface for biological filtration. The key is however not the total surface but the surface actually used by Nitrosomonas and Nitrobacter type bacteria (See also Spotte, Seawater Aquariums).

In other cases, temporarily raising the ozone output, without this resulting in excess ozone being added, will resolve the problem. Indeed ozone turns nitrite into nitrate rather quickly, and we can certainly attempt to use this fact to our benefit. Again use caution when raising ozone output. Keep it at safe levels. You should certainly not be able to smell ozone in the room where the tank is placed.

One of the reasons ozone cannot be used on a new aquarium, until after the filter has completely matured, is therefore also explained. Should you use ozone right away it will take several weeks longer for the filter to cycle, and it will cycle at a lower level of activity than the one you need in your tank, because ozone in essence interferes with the normal growth of the bacteria and the filter. This results in higher ammonium levels. Refer to the section on ozone again if you need more information on when, and how to use this strong oxidizer.

Nitrite is noxious because it inhibits the oxygen carrying ability of hemoglobin in the bloodstream. This stresses the fish considerably, and if left unchecked will lead to death of the biomass.

The importance of having a mature filter, of the proper size, to remove these noxious compounds from the water can therefore not be stressed enough.

## 8.12 Nitrate

Nitrates are a problem for many aquarists, so are phosphates. Every article and every book, stresses the fact that nitrate is not harmful. If your experience is the same as ours, you will have found that invertebrates just do not do well in an aquarium where excessive amounts of nitrate are present.

This has been observed over and over again in both small and very large aquariums. As long as only fish are kept, nitrates do not seem to pose any problem, even at such high levels as for instance 80 or more mg per liter.

Much lower levels though, already create difficulties for inverts, even in the best filtered and best maintained tanks. Of course, on the reef, hardly any nitrate is present.

What levels then should we strive for ? And what should we do, if the levels we find in our tanks are higher ?

Nitrate, in its many forms and compounds, is present in the Reef tank, as the end breakdown product of protein breakdown. Sometimes, in areas where the mains water is of bad quality, aquarists increase its level each time a water change is done, as nitrate comes in with that same water. The first step to take is therefore to check mains water for nitrates. If high levels are found, eliminate that water as a source of water changes. Alternatively, dilute it with distilled or chemical free water to reduce the influence of the nitrates it contains.

The levels we recommend that you strive for are very low : a maximum of 15 mg per liter.

How do we achieve such low levels :

— increase the amount of macro algae in the tank, making sure that they receive proper nutrition and light. Inverts use some nitrates too, but since they re circulate a lot of the nutrients they take up, as metabolic output, increasing their number does not really result in a significant enough drop in nitrates. On the contrary.

— check the mains water to ensure you are not introducing nitrates when making water changes. Or use distilled or chemical free water. Alternatively use resins or reverse osmosis filters  see later in this chapter for details Both methods will give you extremely clean water. Resins might not be easy to obtain, but reverse osmosis filters are being advertised regularly in may magazines.

— remove all dying or dead algal material immediately.

— adhere to a strict maintenance program as recommended by this author.

— use trickle filtration on your aquarium.

— inside the sump of the trickle filter, install either one foam pad through which the water flows slowly. This should be a medium coarseness pad. Such foam pads can be obtained from pet stores or from places that repair chairs, they use it to cushion the seating area, or

— install 2 fine filters, as described elsewhere, and clean only one at a time, alternating the cleaning.

— reduce the amount of food given to the fish and inverts. Do not overfeed, and pay attention to the type of food that you use. Liquid foods are excellent, but create a lot of waste and the resulting extra pollution. They should be used outside of the aquarium. Not in the aquarium.

You could force feed some of your inverts by transferring them, say once a week, to a smaller tank, and soak them, literally soak them, in water with a high amount of liquid food. Leave them in there for about one hour, and then replace them in the aquarium and dispense with the water in the small aquarium.

— monitor the organic load of the tank, using the oxygen test, and if necessary look for the causes of this organic load, and eliminate them.

— use a skimmer, and an ozonizer if you are willing to go all the way in combatting nitrate, the resulting droopiness of corals and inverts, and the micro algae growth usually associated with excess levels of nitrate and phosphates.

This is a tough program to follow! We know so! If however you want to be successful, you need to make the time and take the energy to put these recommendations to effect.

You will of course ask : what about denitrating filters to which carbohydrates are added ?

Although we are not against them per se, we do not advocate their use. We find that the method is too new; that not enough evidence exists that such is not harmful to invertebrates; that the exact long term effect on the combined biomass in an aquarium has not been established; and that similar results can be obtained by "natural" methods. Perhaps this will prove to be "the" way to go, sometime in the future, but until this has been established we would rather stick with a more natural way of taking care of nitrate problems.

If the above recommendations are followed, and if the trickle filter is installed properly, nitrate levels will decrease slowly, over a period of time. This could take from 2.5 to 4 months, but the effects of these steps, combined with other recommendations made, will pay off.

Nothing happens instantly and patience is necessary. Do not get dis-appointed if, after 3 or 4 weeks, you do not see results yet. Stay with it.

Of course, you could always do more water changes. That would reduce ni-trates too. But it is laborious and seems like overkill.

## 8.13 Conductivity

Conductivity can be used to determine the salinity of our reef tank. The units used are referred to as micro siemens.

The meter, which looks like a multimeter type instrument, needs to have a range however that will enable you to read numbers higher than 50 000 mi-cro siemens. The temperature is also a factor.

When comparing numbers make sure that they were taken at the same tem-perature, as conductivity increases with temperature, and falls with it as well.

This is a relatively new method of measuring salinity, and we would like to see more data before recommending that this technique be used at the hobbyist's level.

Additionally it requires buying yet another instrument.

## 8.14 Salinity

As already indicated, this number expresses the amount of salts dissolved in the water. As hobbyists, we do not frequently use it however, as we more than likely prefer the specific gravity measurement, for which instrumenta-tion that is accurate enough for our purposes and not very expensive can be found easily. This number expresses, in pro mille, the amount of such salts that are dissolved. The arithmetic behind it is pretty simple. One kilo = 1000 grams. If 35 grams of salts are dissolved in the water, we have a salinity of 35 in 1000 or 35 pro mille.

Specific gravity is very temperature dependent, salinity is not. But on the other hand, the s.g. we can get with the instrumentation we use, is accurate enough for our purposes.

For those interested in the effect of temperature on specific gravity, Martin Moe, in his book : The Marine Aquarium Handbook, has published a handy chart that allows quick conversion of the numbers. Stephen Spotte in his book : Seawater Aquariums, publishes similar reference tables.

# 8.15 The Use of Activated Carbon

Should you or should you not use Carbon ? And if you do, how much carbon is required.

It is known that activated carbon of good quality, preferably a research grade or a medical grade type, has been known to remove organics and other elements from the water for a long time.

Aquarists have traditionally used carbon to remove the yellowing from the water. We have seen that this is due to the presence of products such as albumin, phenol, and others.

Activated carbon also removes many other elements, small enough to be adsorbed onto the carbon. This includes many forms of airborne pollution and many impurities generated by the animal life in our tank, and many by products returned to the water by the macro algae.

It is therefore very important to use carbon, if not all the time, at least intermittently.

Carbon has been blamed for many ills. For instance it is often stated that carbon removes oxygen from the water. This is true of carbon that is not first prepared correctly, and true only when fresh carbon is introduced. The levels return to normal within a few hours and should therefore not be a reason for concern, or result in a decision not to use carbon. It is also said that, when introduced, carbon starts reducing the redox potential of the water, sometimes by as much as 45–55 mv. This is correct, but again these values return to·their normal levels within a matter of hours.

Carbon should be used on the marine aquarium. It is the third form of filtration that is definitely recommended. Mechanical filtration and biological filtration cannot remove all impurities. Chemical filtration can however remove several other impurities that can stress our reef tank biomass. We have indicated that organics and phenol are two important ones. This water detoxification is very valuable and we should not forego this simple means of improving water quality.

Carbon should always be "active", meaning still able to adsorb these impurities and not become exhausted, while when this happens, it no longer filters, and starts harboring detritus, which could lead to anaerobic activity within the carbon bag.

Which brings us to how to install the carbon filter : traditional bags are to small. What we need is a bag that is large and can be flattened to a maximum height of 1 inch once the it is filled with carbon. Place this bag in such a way that all the water that comes from the trickle filter needs to go through it. This can easily be done in a tray type filter. In newer filters, that do not have such trays, place the carbon in one of the compartments, in the sump of the filter, in such a way that the water needs to go through the carbon before being able to return to the aquarium. If you use a sponge type pad in that same sump, the carbon is installed right after that sponge. Keep the bag clean of detritus and slime. Slime is generated by the bacteria in the filter  refer to Spotte, Seawater Aquariums, for an explanation of how this slime, also called matrix, is generated and what its function is  and by the body slime of the fish that is shed.

Use a test to verify that your carbon is still detoxifying every other week. Check the section on Tests for instructions on how to use this test.

## How much carbon should be used ?

We have experimented in a 180 gallon aquarium for a period of 6 months, using varying amounts of carbon. The following levels were measured :

dissolved oxygen, redox potential, temperature, pH, salinity, organic load, using oxygen demand over 48 hours as a yardstick, carbon dioxide in mg/l and have found that the best results are obtained by using 34 ounces per 50 gallons of water. Using the carbon efficiency test we determined as well that the carbon needed replacement approximately every 26 days.

This is probably more than the quantities that you have been using. We found however that reducing the amount and making more frequent changes did not add up to the same results.

The test tank had a photo  period of 12 hours, using 2 150 watt Osram metal halide HQI TS type bulbs, contained a mixture of fish, invertebrates and micro and macro  algae. Feeding took place every other day. Food quantities were carefully controlled to ensure test accuracy.

Of course one cannot make a recommendation that applies to all tanks in all conditions and you will therefore have to experiment. The point we wished to make however is that you will more than likely require more activated carbon than you presently use, and you may need to improve the quality of such carbon, as such quality greatly influences any testing you might undertake yourself.

Does carbon remove trace elements and is it therefore to be avoided ? The answer is no. Whatever trace elements are removed, are replaced when you make water changes, and this fact can therefore, for our purposes, be neglected. Carbon removes Fe from solution, fertilizer levels for macro algae and symbiotic algae should therefore be monitored more frequently and adjusted. The recommended iron level is between 0.05 and 0.1 mg per liter.

Can carbon be used efficiently if it is only used intermittently ? Certainly. In this case you may wish to place carbon bags in the filter every 7 or 8 days, for a period of 24 to 36 hours. Adjust all fertilizer concentrations after the carbon is removed. If you are using a Dosing pump, check whether the additive levels you are dispensing now are sufficient to deal with the addition of carbon, and whether the mix that you prepared is made up with enough chelated iron containing fertilizers.

## 8.16 Ion Exchangers

Certain forms of carbon are sold mixed with resins, which act as ion exchangers in the water.

Resins can also be bought separately, and used for water purification. As long as these resins do not give off phenolic matter in the process, we see no reason why they should not be used. Products such as Lewatit have been used for that purpose in Germany for a while. They are however not used "in" the aquarium or in the trickle filters. They are only used to filter the water before it is actually adjusted for salinity and added to the aquarium. Whether the cost justifies their use has yet to be demonstrated. For aquarists living in areas where the mains water quality is particular low, such resins might be a viable option.

The difficulty is not in using them, but in obtaining them in quantities small enough that fit the hobbyist's needs. Then again if you want extra pure water for water changes and top offs, you may wish to use this approach. It is of course much simpler to just buy distilled water.

Resins, in cation and anion exchangers, are used to remove silicic acid from mains water. German aquarists report that such acid is one of the causes of stress on invertebrates, and causes outbreaks of algae. Kipper(1987) supports this theory and recommends that any water used for the reef aquarium should therefore be de ionized.

## 8.17 Reverse Osmosis

Lately, a rather sophisticated method of purifying the mains water has appeared in aquarist's magazines. Reverse osmosis, or RO, is indeed a very efficient way of cleaning the water of even the tiniest impurities and undesirable compounds.

These filters work on the principle of membrane exchanges. The type of membrane determines the micron level of impurities removed.

They are an option to be considered by those aquarists wishing extremely pure water, and not ready to buy distilled or chemical free water from an outside supplier.

Reverse osmosis is slow. But if you have the time, that should not be a factor. Once the filter runs, it will prepare a certain number of gallons for you to use, whenever you do your next water change. Depending on the type of unit that you acquire, more or less water per hour, or per day will be filtered.

This is not a filter used "on" the aquarium or trickle filter, but an outside unit, operating totally independently from the tank. You could use the RO filter on the aquarium, but because of the amount of pollution, this would become expensive and time consuming.

We are in favor of anything that improves the quality of the water used to make both water changes, and top off the aquarium, and suggest that if you do not wish to buy distilled water, in quantities, that you consider this method.

# 9. Redox Potential

## 9.1 Overview

Articles dealing with Redox potential, Redox for short, or Oxidation Reduction potential, ORP, as it is known in Europe, have recently appeared more and more frequently in trade and hobby publications. The reason is that Redox potential is being advocated more often as a relative measurement of the quality of the water. And a "good" measurement value at that.

Based on the information that is available, and the discussions on Redox potential that have been published, it would appear however that the Redox potential concept is far from understood.

Redox potential is explained in many different ways, not all of them clear enough for aquarists to understand, and often not explained in a way hobbyists can relate to, and from which they can understand how Redox potential measurements apply to Reef Tanks.

This is of course not contributing to a good understanding of the matter and confuses rather than educates many a hobbyist.

It has unfortunately also resulted in many aquarists spending hundreds of dollars on equipment that may not be adequate for continuous measurements, or it may not be the right kind for the type of water found in Reef Aquariums. By not right in this case, we mean that the electrode used is not suitable for salt water, loaded with organics, in continuous immersion use.

This leads to inaccurate readings, and perhaps even premature wear-out of an expensive piece of equipment. As Redox potential is, however, an important value to monitor in Reef Tanks, Hobbyists should take time to better understand this concept, and apply the information it supplies to Tank conditions.

Redox potential is measured in millivolt values. An electrode transmits current to a digital read-out instrument, which converts the current intensity into a number, which then appears on the display. The display-conversion unit is separate from the electrode.

Many different probes or electrodes are marketed. Most are "job specific", meaning that they are made for a particular type of application, with a specific type of sensitivity. Using probes, made for one type of application, for a totally different one,  will not give the best result. What concerns us most, is that hobbyists have been using probes that are not meant to be immersed continuously, and as a result these probes wear out very quickly, and do not give accurate values, even after a short period of time.

To add to the confusion that already exists, few people understand the Redox potential concept itself; what it represents, and how to correct readings that are deemed not adequate for Reef  Aquarium conditions.

It is also not clear to hobbyists that  the true Redox potential is not the number given by the display, but that it needs to be adjusted, based on the type of electrode used, referring to a table usually provided by the electrode manufacturer. On the other hand, once we know and understand that concept, using just the display number, especially in comparing Redox potential values taken on the same Reef Tank, at different times, is acceptable, since when we compare, we are looking more for a tendency than for an absolute value.

The reason that the electrode does not indicate the true Redox potential has to do with the reference liquids used inside the probe. However for our Reef Aquarium  purposes we will disregard that differential. It becomes important only if the true Redox potential needs to be known, which is not really the case in our situation; or if one is comparing Redox potential measurements taken with two different types of probes. This would be the case if you were comparing values found in one of your Tanks, with the ones a fellow Hobbyist has, when that Hobbyist is using a different type of probe.

In such a case, if each add the numbers given by the manufacturer,  to the reading obtained, they would have values that can be compared. Of course, this is not all that needs to be said. A few other factors also have to be compared, e.g. time of day, pH, and for instance temperature. But you will see the reason for this as you read on.
The most frequently  found probes, ranked in terms of cost and accuracy are :

-The Calomel (Kalomel) or Mercury(I) chloride. Three type of such electrode exist. Each has a different reference liquid, viz. 0.1M, 1.0M and saturated KCl, Potassium chloride.

-The Silver, Silver chloride electrode, and

-The Platinum, silver, silver chloride electrode

Which of these probes then should you acquire?

Our own experience with all of them, makes us recommend the latter one, as it seems to give the best long term accuracy and repeatability of the measurements made. Platinum, silver, silver chloride probes are easy to maintain and perform particularly well in organically tainted salt Reef Tank water.

Repeatability in this case means that after taking a redox value potential once, the same value comes up on the display again after the probe has been taken out of the Reef tank, placed in a different water mass for a few minutes, and then placed back in the same Reef Aquarium.

## 9. 2  Measuring  Redox  Potential

As you might by now have guessed, measuring Redox potential values is not as straight forward as it might have appeared to you initially.

Different types of electrodes, and different uses for such electrodes, complicate the picture somewhat.

Having recommended the use of the Platinum.silver.silver chloride probe, all measurements, and all values given later in this chapter were taken with such an electrode. Our electrode is cleaned every 4 weeks, and is checked, using the reference liquids supplied by the manufacturer. We do not use these reference liquids more than once, to prevent the solution from being contaminated, over time

Redox potential measurements are time sensitive. This means that one cannot compare a value taken at one time of day, with one taken at a totally different time of day. The reason for this is that the Redox potential in a Reef Tank fluctuates during the course of the day. It will be highest in the morning, before the lights go on, and lowest at night before the lights go off. This has to do with the increased metabolic processes that occur in the tank, due for the majority to photosynthesis and feeding.

While photosynthesis is low, the Redox potential of the Reef water increases; as metabolism speeds up, and waste is produced as a by-product, the Redox potential will start going down.

Photosynthesis increases when the lights are turned on, and decreases when they are off. More fish, invert and algal activity generates more pollution and therefore reduces the Redox potential value of the aquarium water.

To meaningfully compare Redox potential values therefore, one needs to compare values taken on different days, but at the same time of day. It is good practice to take at least two measurements per day. Our own reef tanks are checked at 7.30 am and at 10.00 pm.

Of course, this also implies that you have not changed the stocking of your Reef tank. Changing the biomass will affect the amount of breakdown materials present in the water, and will affect the redox potential value (RPV) value.

To be able to judge what is happening to the Aquarium over a period of time, you should keep notes. If you have not done so yet, you should start an Aquarium diary in which you can record the values of all the tests that you regularly make. This does not have to be a fancy diary, but something in which you can write down the date, the time, the pH, temperature, carbonate hardness, iron content, dissolved oxygen levels, copper, nitrite, nitrate, phosphate, and carbon dioxide test values, and a few remarks about Tank looks and condition. This will prove to be very helpful when things go wrong, and you are trying to determine why. And as you well know, things do go wrong, sometimes.

Besides being time sensitive, Redox potential is inversely related to pH. As the pH goes up the Redox potential goes down, and as the pH goes down the RPV will go up. When comparing values therefore, make sure that you are comparing Redox potential values taken in tanks that have the same pH. We do not mean exactly the same, as such a situation is unlikely anyway, but close to each other. For instance readings taken on tanks that have respectively pH levels of 8.10 and 8.15 can still meaningfully be compared.

Redox potential is also temperature sensitive. Again it is inversely related to temperature. With increasing temperatures the Redox potential of the same mass of water will show a decline. And vice-versa.

We indicated that as pollution increases, the Redox potential goes down. This is of course the case when you feed, as some of the food does not get eaten. Redox potential levels will typically go down by 40 to 50 mv within

15 to 20 minutes after feeding, and should return to their normal levels within 60 to 75 minutes.

Using liquid foods will cause the Redox potential to drop more, and the time it takes to regain its normal level will also be lengthened. We can not give you exact values and times, as this will depend on the quantity and the quality of the liquid food used, and how much of that food does not actually get eaten. Using liquid foods directly in a reef tank is not a good idea to begin with, as too much of it never gets eaten or absorbed. Such foods can however be used in small aquariums in which corals and inverts can literally be soaked in the food solution.

Redox potential electrodes need cleaning too. Once every 6 to 8 weeks or so, should be fine. We clean ours a little more frequently because of the accuracy that we require. This enables us to keep notes on aquarium conditions, report on them, while being sure that they have been taken with excellent equipment and with all precautions required.

Clean both the tip and the outside of the probe. Slime and micro-algae build up over time, and reduce the accuracy of the measurement. Do not be alarmed if, while cleaning the probe, you notice a very rapid decline in the reading. This is normal, even if the number goes to a negative value. Place the probe back in the aquarium, and be patient.

Redox potential probes react much slower to water chemistry conditions than for instance pH probes. Accurate measurements therefore cannot be taken in a few minutes. The best way to get a true reading is to place the probe in the tank at night and take the reading in the morning. If you wish to get a faster reading, place the probe in the water, wait at least 60 minutes before taking a reading. If you use the probe immediately after it has been cleaned, the time required to get an accurate reading is much longer. Perhaps 3 to 4 hours.

The Redox potential probe needs to be placed in a section of the aquarium where good water circulation exists. It is not a good idea to place it in the sump of the trickle filter. The values obtained there are influenced by several factors, many of which will give you a much higher reading than you really have in the Aquarium water :

- higher dissolved oxygen levels in the water coming from the trickle area,
- incidence of carbon dioxide, if used, and if the reactor is placed in the sump,
- effect of residual ozone, if used, and when the water from the skimmer is guided back to the sump of the trickle filter. This is by the way the best area to return the water to.

Truer readings are obtained by placing the probe in the Reef Tank, close to where the overflow to the trickle filter is. The water that passes over the probe in that location is a good representative mixture of the aquarium water, and the flow close to the overflow is always strong and constant.

# 9. 3 What Lowers Redox potential ?

We could define Redox potential as the ability of the Reef tank water to deal with the pollution that exists in the Reef tank. This is scientifically not correct, but it is a definition that is accurate enough, as it applies to our Reef Tanks, and is also a definition that is easy to understand.

The higher this Redox potential value number is, the better the water is able to do so, and the less pollution actually is present, as if pollution were present, the number would not be that high to begin with.

Given the above, we can also define it as a relative measure of the purity of the water. Indeed, if the Redox potential is high, there can be little pollution, because if there was pollution, the water would have tried to oxidize and reduce it, and the Redox potential would have been affected downwards by this chemical process .

Conversely, if excess pollution is present, meaning pollution that the water cannot deal with, it obviously cannot have a high Redox potential.

It should be clear therefore that low Redox potentials indicate waters that cannot deal with the pollution that is present, water that is of bad quality, and thus not adequate for our Reef Aquariums. Typically such tanks are full of undesirable micro-algae, look unappealing, and are out of balance. Redox levels in such tanks are in the general 200 to 250 mv range. Sometimes even lower.

Water with a high Redox potential on the other hand, must be purer, because if pollution were present, it would not have such a high ability to deal with that pollution.

In a closed water mass, our Aquarium the following can be said

dealing with high levels of pollution
"and"
high pollution
cannot exist at the same time.

Our goal then, is to keep the Redox potential at a high level, by eliminating all potential sources of pollution. And there are many ! Here are just a few :

- Overfeeding
- Dead or decaying fish
- Dead and decaying algae
- Filter material that is dirty
- Dead or decaying inverts
- Portions of inverts decaying
- Clogged undergravel areas
- Dirty pre-filters
- Dirty floss or such material
- Dirty ceramic rings
- Spent Activated Carbon
- Dirty sponge material
- Dead small animal life
- Sump that needs cleaning
- Unclean corner overflows
- and any other source of pollution that might exist in your particular Reef Tank.

There are plenty of possibilities as you can see.

One of the primary means to higher Redox potential levels, is eliminating all these sources of pollution. In view of this, regular and complete maintenance of the reef tank, takes on a different meaning indeed.

Let us assume that your tank has a low Redox potential level, that you start cleaning all areas that need to be cleaned, that you remove any dead material that you can see, looking behind the rocks as well, that you do not overfeed any longer, and do whatever is required to keep the Redox potential high. How long will it take to see any results from your better maintenance? We cannot give you a definite time frame, because pollution levels differ, and Redox potential values can take on quite a range. What is sure is that it will take at least 3 to 4 weeks before you actually see a meaningful increase.

Incidentally, freshly mixed salt water has a Redox potential of 230 to 240 millivolt. Adding such water to your Aquarium will therefore lower the Redox potential, if the latter had a higher Redox potential to begin with. However this is only a very temporary situation and the normal level will be re-achieved within a matter of 3 to 4 hours. This level will usually be slightly higher than the one you had before the water change.

Of course, if your water's Redox potential was lower, the overall result will be that water changes will increase the Redox potential.

Small, regular water changes are therefore beneficial in redox potential management, as they eliminate accumulated sources of several kinds of potentially noxious elements on one hand, and affect the redox potential of the water body in the aquarium upwards on the other.

Fresh un-used activated carbon will initially reduce the Redox potential level. This should however not be of concern, as the magnitude of the decrease is small and well acceptable. Depending on the quality and the type of carbon used, this can be expressed as anywhere from 40 to 75 mv, for about 48 hours (Thiel, 1986) In this respect, you should always immerse the carbon in tepid water before using it. This will enable the trapped gasses from escaping. This process can in fact by obserbed.

# 9. 4   Increasing your Redox

## 9.4.1  Maintenance

Good maintenance practices will help you maintain a healthy Redox potential level, especially if combined with good biological and good mechanical filtration.

This includes the use of a trickle filter, packed with the right kind of media, and correctly sized. The latter is important because if the filter is too small, polluting material will accumulate and lower Redox potential levels. Choose a medium that does not need to be cleaned. It will cost you less money in the long run.

There are a number of other methods available to you to increase the Redox potential, as some of you have probably already experienced. Some you may wish to use, others you may wish to stay away from, as one of them in particular is  complicated to handle accurately in a Reef Tank environment.

## 9.4.2.  Protein  Skimmers

The most frequently used method is the addition of a Protein Skimmer. This skimmer needs to be sized properly, and  good water flow through the skimmer needs to be constantly achieved to maximize the water air-bubble contact time. Skimmers will typically raise the Redox potential by anywhere from 75 to 100 mv, (Pieters,1985).

Installing a skimmer does not give immediate results. It may take as much as 14 to 20 days before the full effect of the skimmer addition can be measured. G. Bepko(1987) reports that on a 70 gallon tank he was experimenting with, the redox level reacted positively only after he had managed to determine the right amount of ozone to be used on this aquarium. This process took him over a week. Redox potential then kept rising until it reached morning levels of close to 500 mv. The ozonizer was then turned lower and the redox regulated at 450 mv.

When using a skimmer, the increase in Redox potential is very gradual, and occurs as a result of sources of pollution, mainly organic ones, slowly being skimmed out. If you were not sure whether your water was dirty, just take a good look, and smell if you have the courage, at the color and consistency of the liquid that collects in the skimmer cup !

Skimmers will only be efficient if they are of the right size for your aquarium. Moreover, depending on the type of skimmer, the amount of water that needs to be moved will vary as well. You will therefore have to follow the manufacturers recommendations closely.

Bubble size is critical and greatly increases the efficiency of the skimming effect (Spotte,1979), (Hueckstedt,1974).

Check the section on protein skimmers again if you need be.

## 9.4.3 Potassium Permanganate

Another method sometimes used but -not- recommended is the use of KMnO4, Potassium Permanganate. These purple and hygroscopic crystals will temporarily, and very quickly, raise the Redox potential several 100 mv.

We do not recommend their use. The process is difficult to control in an Aquarium environment, and it is very easy to add too many crystals. Excessive quantities have very negative effects on invertebrates and fish alike.

Potassium permanganate should only be used by those of you who wish to see its effects, and only in a Tank that has no life in it. Its availability is quite restricted, and the purity of the chemical is sometimes hard to determine.

Since crystals come in may sizes, it is not possible to give any quantitative recommendations either. Let it suffice to say that only a few crystals can raise the Redox potential 100 mv or more, in a matter of seconds. The exact effect of such a sudden increase on invertebrate life is obviously dangerous, and difficult to gauge. Once more, stay away from it unless you are a trained chemist, and know what you are doing.

Besides this, KMnO4 first turns the water purple. This gradually changes to brown, as it oxidizes organic and other compounds in the water. If used in conjunction with a skimmer this will appear as a brown sludge in the skimmer cup. If no skimmer is used, the sludge is hard to remove and makes the tank look very unsightly.

Potassium permanganate does have medicinal uses as well. This is due to its extremely high reduction oxidation potential, which kills bacteria and parasites. Conceivably one could therefore use it to treat fish that are struck with any of the commonly occurring diseases that we all have to cope with once in a while. Before attempting such treatments however, you should refer to a textbook that gives you more detailed information, and mg per liter quantities, that can safely be used.

We have seen commercially available, strongly diluted, mixtures of potassium permanganate in pet shops. If the manufacturers instructions are followed they are of course safe to use. These products are unfortunately often too long on the shelves to be of any value.

## 9.4.4  Ozone

Ozone is also frequently used in marine Tanks in conjunction with a protein skimmer. Of course ozone can be used without a skimmer, but the most efficient use and best results are obtained when the gas is injected, mixed with air, in a protein skimmer.

How much ozone should you use and how much will it raise the Redox potential ?

There really is not "one" answer to these questions. It "depends", as one often hears.

The more ozone you use, the more the Redox potential is affected, within limits, as for the ozone to be able to increase the Redox potential, there first has to be something that ozone removes in the process of building up the water quality.

If too much ozone is used, it will escape in the ambient air, and you will not fail to notice it, as ozone is a very pungent gas.

The more polluted the water is, the more ozone will be required to clean it up. As the water quality improves, smaller quantities of ozone will give more sizeable Redox potential level increases. This is one of the reasons that when one first sets up an ozonizer, it needs to be run at a fairly high level, and as time goes on, smaller quantities of ozone will keep the same Tank at the same Redox potential level.

Since the use of ozone is discussed elsewhere in this book, we will not go into any further depth here.

Besides the typical smell which is noticeable when too much ozone is being dispensed, residual ozone will be found in your water. This can be removed, to some extent, with good quality activated carbon. Make sure that you do so, as invertebrates react negatively to too high levels of ozonization. So do fish.

As a rule of thumb, if you can smell the ozone above the water surface, you are using too much of it, and need to adjust your ozonizer's output.

Oddly, often the unit used will become to powerful for our tank, as indeed, once the water quality is up to the level that you wish it to be, very little ozone may be required to keep it here.

There is unfortunately no way around this, as in the initial stages, when we are polishing the water, these high levels of ozone are required, and can only be attained by the use of a strong unit. In our experience the best units are those made by Sanders of West Germany, available from good pet stores everywhere in both the United States and Canada

## 9.5 Suggested Redox Potential Levels

We now know how to influence the Redox level itself. We still have not decided however at what level we wish the Redox potential to be in a reef-like tank.

Theories here vary greatly. Some authors recommend levels in the 350 to 380 mv range, and others indicate that much higher levels are desirable, frequently in the high 400 mv ranges.

We will not try to be the judge, but rather let you decide what is best for your own tank. You may therefore wish to experiment, and run your aquarium at different Redox levels levels for a while. An experiment is only meaningful and conclusive, if you continue it for some time. A few weeks is therefore not enough. We would suggest that, if you plan to undertake this experiment, you do not constrain it, and that you only make a judgmental value based on at least 5 to 6 months of experience with a particular redox potential level. Longer would even be better.

Perhaps you may wish to run two tanks, one at the lower level, and one at the higher one, and record how they both evolve over time. To be able to judge what is really happening, it is good practice to make some photographs, as this will give you a piece of reference. It is difficult to remember what a tank looked like three months ago.

What we can however say is that you need to run the tank at levels that are higher than 350 mv, and that the tendency of the Redox potential has to be towards the increase. We can also state that the Redox potential value should be able to rebuild itself to its original level in a matter of less than an hour after feeding. This indicates a good trend of the water chemistry.Values taken early in the morning should be over 385 mv, and should not vary by more than 60 to a maximum of 75 mv during the day. Less variation is even better. The evening reading recommended in most German circles is around 335 mv or better. More progressive circles advocate levels that are in excess of 450 mv in the morning and around 390 mv or better during the day.

As you can see there is no real consistency. Our personal experience is illustrated in an example that follows later in this chapter. We are personally in favor of levels that stay in the higher ranges, as we have found two very interesting phenomena to happen when the Redox potential levels are high :

1. fish that are known picky eaters, seem to behave rather differently in better water quality -meaning higher Redox potential levels-and we had no problem feeding them. This includes fish such Euxiphipops navarchus and E. xantometophon, Parachaetodontoplus conspicullatus and the like. Since we were able to repeat this experiment several times, with with other fish in similar conditions, we can lend some credibility to the fact that better water quality definitely improves the feeding habits of fish, even with fish that are normally not as easy to feed on frozen foods and granular foods.

2. at higher Redox potential levels the varieties of algae found in the Aquarium change over a period of as little as five weeks. This is not particularly evident with macro-algae, but is noticeably so with micro-algae. As Redox potential levels increase, over 320 mv, first, red , then brown algae disappear.

This process happens faster if the tank is outfitted with a protein skimmer, and slower if no skimmer is used. Around 345 mv the small hairlike algae become less numerous, and their quantity keeps diminishing as the Redox potential level increases further. Tanks that run at reduction oxidation levels of around 400 mv, and in which phosphate levels are below 1 mg per liter, have not given us any problems whatsoever with hair algae. If however phosphates levels are increased by slow addition of monosodium phosphate, or a similar phosphorus compound, to levels of 8 to 10 mg of measurable PO4, hair algae on the glass and on the gravel, started reappearing gradually. We did not carry the experiment further as we did not wish to increase the Redox potential levels above 500 mv. This experiment too was repeatable in other tanks.

Remember that to obtain such levels maintenance is very important, and that the water used in the tank, and the water used to make water changes, needs to be of excellent quality. If need be, use distilled or chemical free water.

This is discussed in another chapter. If your mains water is of particular bad quality this may be the way to go.

## 9.6 Redox Potential Meters

Several kinds of Redox potential meters are now commercially available, mostly from Scientific instrument Companies. Three companies however market units that are specifically made for the marine hobby : Sanders, Selzle and Dupla Usa.

These meters offer considerable advantages over the ones that can be bought from other companies, as they allow the aquarist to control ozone output at the same time, and pre-set a desired redox potential level.

The principle is simple. The aquarist determines the Redox potential level at which he or she wants to run the Reef Tank. This number is entered into the Redox potential meter. How this is done, depends on the unit. The probe is immersed in the Reef Tank. The ozonizer is hooked up to the Redox potential meter. Again, how this is done depends on the type of unit.

Once the desired Redox potential is reached, the meter automatically switches off the ozonizer. If the Redox potential decreases, the ozonizer is automatically switched on again. This becomes a continuous process. In the long run it obviously stabilizes the Redox potential level. Using such a unit is a major improvement in Reef Tank keeping. Although this equipment is expensive, it is worth every penny one pays for it.

We wish to make an important remark here : if you are presently running your Tank at low Redox potential levels, you should not increase that level rapidly, rather you should do so slowly, perhaps 25 to 30 mv per week. This can be done by gradually increasing the amount of ozone that is dispensed in the skimmer, making sure that no excess amounts however are added to the Reef Tank at any time. Refer to the section on ozone if necessary for more details.

With a meter that allows for the control of the Redox potential level this can be achieved very easily. Increase the setting every week or so by 30 mv, and the redox regulator-meter, will automatically ensure that no rapid increase occurs. If you do not have a redox meter regulator, we suggest that you start by setting the ozonizer at 0.75 mg per gallon of water, and decide whether or not to increase it, based on whether or not that amount you can smell any ozone above the water line. If so, decrease the amount, if not let it run for a week. Then increase it by 5 mg per hour for another week and so on, until you start seeing improvements in the tank's outlook. Refer to the ozone section in this book for more details. Using ozone has to be carefully planned. Please remember that.

## 9.7 A Redox Potential Control experiment

This experiment was conducted in a 500 liter glass Aquarium, running at pH 8.16, 25 degrees Celcius, S.g. 1.020, dKH 15 degrees, Klaes IV skimmer, ozonizer by Sanders, 45 mg per hour, Carbon dioxide is added for macro-algae growth. Lighting is by 2 individually positioned 175 watt metal halide, 4300 K degrees spectrum. A Dupla Redox potential regulating unit is used, and is set gradually higher, in increments of 25 mv, every 5th day. Feeding occurs once a day, early in the morning, approximately 2 hours after the lights, which run 10 hours a day, have gone on.

Fish population consisted of 12 medium sized clown fish, one cleaner wrasse and one cleaner shrimp, 4 domino damsel fish, approximately 60 pounds of live rock, obtained from a Florida supplier, 6 medium sized anemones, clumps of several kinds of Caulerpa species. When the experiment started, this tank had been running, without problems, for approximately 4 months.

Following Redox potential readings were obtained :

| Day | 7.00 am | 7.00 pm |
|-----|---------|---------|
| 1   | 412     | 387     |
| 2   | 411     | 391     |
| 3   | 413     | 389     |
| 4   | 411     | 378     |
| 5   | 409     | 390     |
| 6   | 405     | 378     |
| 7   | 404     | 378     |
| 8   | 404     | 377     |
| 9   | 402     | 374     |
| 10  | 399     | 370     |

The above numbers are indicative of a rather stable Aquarium, at least up to day 6, when the values start going down, ever so slightly, but down nevertheless.

This is an advance warning that something is probably wrong in the aquarium and should make us look for a cause. This is in fact the one and very important use of redox potential measurements in aquariums.

Once we have determined the level at which our tank normally runs, any deviation of more than 20 mv for more than 2 hours, should be cause for concern. Not panic. Just concern. It means that something is happening in the aquarium that is pulling the redox potential level down. Said differently, excessive pollution is being created, and at a level that the filtering that we have installed can obviously not deal with. If it could, the redox potential would not be going down. This is very important to remember. Taking immediate action when such drops in redox potential occur, will save many fish and invertebrate lives, and many dollars as a result.

In our case we knew what the cause was, as a dead fish had been introduced in the aquarium to determine the filter's capacity to deal with this form of pollution, and also to monitor its effect on the actual Redox potential of our Reef Tank.

Readings taken on subsequent days showed the following pattern :

| Day | 7.00 am | 7.00 pm |
|-----|---------|---------|
| 11  | 392     | 367     |
| 12  | 390     | 366     |
| 13  | 386     | 362     |

What we notice here, is that as decomposition increased, the Redox potential was affected more markedly. When the source of pollution was removed, at least what was left of it, Redox potential levels started to rise slowly again, and on day 18 morning readings were 403 mv in the a.m. and 387 mv in the p.m. measurement.

This is nearly back to the values at which the experiment started. Approximately 2 weeks later the values were higher than what had been measured originally.

The experiment was then slightly altered.

Instead of using approximately 10 percent of the water volume in equivalent Bioball quantity, this amount was raised to 15 percent.

The first measurements listed, were taken after 30 days of operation of the newly sized trickle filter.

All other conditions were left identical.

Here are some measurements :

| Day | 7.00 am | 7.00 pm |
|-----|---------|---------|
| 30  | 417     | 389     |
| 31  | 419     | 388     |
| 32  | 427     | 407     |
| 33  | 429     | 414     |
| 34  | 431     | 415     |
| 35  | 443     | 420     |

This would indicate that the extra amount of filter media used resulted in better water quality, since no other parameters were changed.

Eventually when we stopped recording the measurements the redox levels were at respectively 476/433 mv. When the experiment started nitrate levels were at 24 mg per liter. When we discontinued the experiment nitrate levels had fallen to below 11 mg per liter.

Do we therefore advocate the use of larger quantities of media in trickle filters? Not really, but we seemed to have laid our finger on an a subject that needs to be researched more : does increasing the available area for bacterial growth result in higher redox levels, on a repeatable basis, and if so does it change other water quality parameters. Needless to say, we have begun such testing as we find this to be a promising area of research, especially the nitrate reduction part of it.

# 9.8 What does this all mean ?

In essence, what experimenting with redox potential levels demonstrates, is that its management is an important water quality control factor on one hand, and that higher water qualities lead to better running aquariums.

Is there then such a level as an ideal redox potential value? No there is not. What we are concerned with is ranges of values, and fluctuations of the values we can measure in our tanks. First we need to make sure our tank's redox is in the right range,  350 to 380 mv or 380 to 425 mv depending on which author one follows.

Subsequently we want to make sure that we maintain the level in that range, by using some or all of the means available, and discussed, to do so.

Lastly, we should react to any changes immediately and look for the causes of the drop, without waiting till disaster strikes. Lowering of the redox levels is one of the best  advance warning signals that something is wrong in the aquarium.

# 9.9 Using Redox Potential Levels

1. Determine the redox level of your particular tank,

2. Make at least two measurements in a 24 hour period,

3. Appropriate times to take measurements are : as soon as the lights go on (this will the day's high level), and in the evening before they go off (this will be the low level)

4. Keep monitoring the redox potential at regular intervals,

5. If a variation of more than 25 mv occurs, look for the cause. Perhaps regular maintenance will solve the drop. Do not let time go by however. You need to get the level back up.

6. Test to find out how much the redox potential drops after feeding, and monitor how long it takes for it to get back to the original level. This part of the test might take about 2 hours of your time. It is time well invested however.

If your aquarium is doing well, and for as long as it does well, the following guidelines will apply :

- Redox levels will stay within the same general values as you initially measured,

- fluctuations after feeding will not deviate much from the measurements you made,

- the trend should be stable or upwards (some meters have little arrows ---> and <--- that indicate this trend). If the trend in your case in <---, make sure that you monitor more frequently to ensure that no significant drop occurs.

- watch this tendency at all times, either by looking at the arrows, or by looking at the actual daily values.

If the redox level goes down, and keeps doing so for several days in a row, or rapidly in a short time, clean the filters, look for dead fish and so on, and check whether the skimmer is running properly.

As a patch, you may wish to turn the ozone output up temporarily, and determine whether that solves the problem. Look for the real cause however.

If adding another fish or invertebrate makes the level drop significantly, your tank is obviously overloaded. This too requires corrective action on your part. It means that you have a tank that is on the verge of overload, and although you probably do not want to, you will have to remove some fish or invertebrates.

Redox potential trend is thus a good indicator of whether your filter simple can handle the bioload, or not.

If adding animal life makes the level go down, and if after a day or two it has not gone back to its original level, you are looking for potential trouble.

Redox potential meters and electrodes are not an inexpensive. They provide very meaningful data about the reef tank however, and should therefore be on your wishlist, if you do not have such a meter yet.

Some meters allow the testing of both pH and Redox potential, if bought with the necessary probes of course. If you do not presently have a pH meter either, such units can perform both tasks for you, at less than the cost of two individual instruments .

# 10. Heating

Heating is treated extensively in most of the existing aquarium books that you have already read. We will therefore not go into great depth. If you wish more detailed information, check one of the existing references that you already own

We wish to make a few general remarks, and discuss low voltage cable heating. This new form of heating uses cables, made out of a silicone material, which can be placed permanently in the aquarium, and which operate on only 42 volts, making them extremely safe to use.

## 10.1 Introduction

The temperature at which we keep our aquarium reef, determines the metabolic rate of the biomass we keep in it. Unlike humans whose body temperature is not dependent on the environment, fish react differently and adjust their own to that of the external medium, the water in the aquarium.

As the temperature goes down, the rate of metabolism slows down. Of course if the temperature goes too low, all life will cease. The same will happen if the temperature goes up to high.

An aquarium needs therefore to be kept, temperature-wise, within a pretty narrow range. Introducing invertebrates and corals complicates the picture somewhat, and requires that we keep the temperature as stable as possible, between 24 and 27 degrees celcius, or approximately between 75 and 80 degrees Fahrenheit. Do not exceed 28 degrees Celcius.

## 10.1.1  Temperature conversion

Converting temperatures from Celcius to Fahrenheit, and from Fahrenheit to Celcius is not complicated. One applies a simple formula in both cases. These formulas will be useful to most aquarists reading this book, because very frequently, temperature recommendations, and measurements, that accompany pictures in other books are given in Celcius. This is often the case because the text was translated from some European book or article, or because the author elected to use the scientifically more acceptable notation, which is Celcius degrees.

**The mathematical formulas are as follows :**

You have seen them before, but never thought you would have any use for them :

|  |  |  |
|---|---|---|
| Celcius | = | 5/9 of (Fahrenheit minus 32) |
| Fahrenheit | = | 9/5 of Celcius, plus 32 |

| Examples : | 25 degrees Celcius |  |
|---|---|---|
|  | 9 times 25 | = 225, |
|  | divided by 5 | = 45, |
|  | plus 32 | = 77 degrees Fahrenheit |

| Example : | 28 degrees Celcius |  |
|---|---|---|
|  | 9 x 28 = 252, |  |
|  | : 5 | = 50.4, |
|  | + 32 | = 82.4 Fahrenheit |

As you can see from these conversions, the maximum at which we should keep our corals and invertebrates is only slightly over 82 degrees Fahrenheit. Running the tank at higher temperatures not only endangers the life of the invertebrates and corals in the long run, but will practically make it impossible for you to have a reef tank that looks "real", where corals are wide open, anemones spread and stretched, and just gives the impression of a tank that is doing well.

Although, on the reef, certain areas will be warmer, at certain times of the day, or at low tide, the animal life growing there is specialized and can withstand these greater temperatures, and the wider swings. You are unlikely to want to duplicate such a mixture of biomass in your aquarium, and need therefore to stay with the generally recommended temperature ranges.

Different authors will suggest different "ideal" temperatures. This is not contradictory, but might have to do with the type of biomass they experimented with. Generally however the extremes recommended do not vary much.

Some more conversions :

| Celcius | Fahrenheit | Fahrenheit | Celcius |
|---------|------------|------------|---------|
| 19      | 66.2       | 66         | 18.9    |
| 20      | 68.0       | 68         | 20.0    |
| 21      | 69.8       | 70         | 21.1    |
| 22      | 71.6       | 72         | 22.2    |
| 23      | 73.4       | 74         | 23.3    |
| 24      | 75.2       | 75         | 23.9    |
| 25      | 77.0       | 76         | 24.4    |
| 26      | 78.8       | 77         | 25.0    |
| 27      | 80.6       | 78         | 25.6    |
| 28      | 82.4       | 79         | 26.1    |
| 29      | 84.2       | 80         | 26.7    |
| 30      | 86.0       | 81         | 27.2    |
|         |            | 82         | 27.8    |
|         |            | 83         | 28.3    |
|         |            | 84         | 28.9    |
|         |            | 85         | 29.4    |

Not selecting the right kind of pump can result in the temperature increasing and exceeding the 82.4 degrees indicated, as some magnetic drive pumps transfer the heat of the motor to the water, to cool the latter down, and allow it to continue to operate without overheating.

One can of course use a cooling unit to bring it back down, or one can use a pump that does not transfer heat to the water, and this might solve the problem. Cooling units can be quite expensive though, and you might therefore not wish to acquire one.

There is another rather simple method of cooling the aquarium water. It is not expensive and involves little labor. Buy a second hand small freezer. Drill 2 holes through the side, using a drill bit that is meant to go through soft metals.

Cooling units/frezers have thin walls with a thick layer of foam or some similar material in between, that acts as insulating material. It is rather easy to drill through them.

Take thin flexible hose, with an internal diameter of 1/4 inch. Coil it up inside the freezer, making sure there are no kinks, as this would impede the flow. Put as much tubing as you can possibly get inside. Push the beginning and the end of the coil through the two holes you have drilled. Attach a small low output pump, e.g. a power head, to one end, and guide the other end to the bottom of the trickle filter.

When you push water very slowly through the flexible tubing coil, it will be cooled off inside the freezer, before it returns to the tank. This system which should not cost you more than 100.00 dollars to make, will certainly reduce the temperature by several degrees.

If the temperature reduction is too great, adjust the temperature setting button inside the freezer, or push the water through a little faster. Even if you do not use this system year round, it might come in handy during the hottest part of the summer.

Lights can also transfer heat, especially high intensity discharge lights that hang too close to the water, e.g. metal halides that operate at high wattages. Be careful when selecting such lights and make sure they can be hung away from the surface, as this will ensure that no heat transfer occurs.

Some of the lights now sold have built in heat extractors. This will of course reduce the risk of heat transfer, and might be a less expensive alternative to buying some of the other lights on the market. Durability if however a factor that also needs to be taken into account, besides aesthetics of course. If you like to look into your aquarium from the top, and do not wish to move the light every time maintenance is due, hanging lights have the advantage. Remember also that light fixtures get hot, and that before moving them, you will need to let them cool down for a while.

Salt water conducts electricity extremely well; it is therefore important that anything electrical be safe, and well protected from the corrosion that saltwater occasions. This obviously applies to heaters, but also to lights, and any other electrical devices used.

Remember that most commercially available heaters are not grounded, and therefore constitute a serious hazard if anything goes wrong with them.

Rubber suction cups used to affix them inside the aquarium will have to be replaced regularly, as they will harden and eventually break the seal attaching them to the glass, making the heater fall in the water and possibly break, if it hits a rock. The better kind are made out of stainless steel, or a quartz like material, and prevent such a potential problem.

If the water levels falls too low, the heater could burst, as the glass is too far out of the water, heats up too much, and shatters. This is potentially dangerous, and can be prevented by using a float switch with the heater. If the level goes down too low,the heating will auto- matically switch off. This may seem a far out protection, but is guaranteed to work.

How much heating (wattage) is needed depends on several factors besides the size of the aquarium :

— do you use a cover over the tank?
— what is the temperature of the room in which the tank is?
— how much does this temperature vary between day and night?
— what is the difference in temperature between seasons?
— as the sun shining on the tank at anytime during the day?
— what kind of pump are you using?
— what kind of lighting have you installed?

Establishing how much wattage of heating is required, is therefore something you will have to determine empirically.

Incidentally, the sun should never be allowed to shine on the aquarium, as this will only bring about complications, especially with micro-algae. We shall discuss this more at length in the chapter on macro and micro algae.

## 10.2  Methods

There are a variety of types of heaters on the market. Most aquarists still use the traditional glass stick heater types. In Germany this is no longer so, especially in marine hobby. Several other types of heaters are available in the United States and Canada too, not a every pet store perhaps, but a little research will allow you to find them. Of course hobby magazines are an excellent source to look for them.

### 10.2.1  Stick  heaters

The most commonly used means of heating the aquarium. Some units even have temperature settings. Most are made of glass, which can lead to problems, especially if bullish fish are in the aquarium.

Of course it would be better to place the heater in the sump of the trickle filter, in which case it will more than likely have to be laid down, and you will therefore need a submersible heater.

One way to protect a glass heather, is to place it inside a piece of pvc pipe, drilled with holes all around. The pipe should be at least 3 times the size of the heather's width, and the holes should be 3/8 to 1/2 inch each.

This will prevent some breakage. Place the whole device in an area with good water flow, to allow the water inside the pipe to be thoroughly mixed with the rest, as it escapes through the holes.

One can also buy heaters made out of 316 stainless steel, which is salt water resistant and does not leach any noxious products in the water. Such heaters are obviously better than the glass variety, but are more expensive.

From an accuracy point of view, many heater units are not very precise, and great improvements could be made. In reef aquariums we would recommend the use of quartz heaters, and a separate and highly accurate thermostat. Both such instruments can be obtained from Scientific Instrument Supply places. They are not particularly expensive either.

## 10.2.2 Quartz heaters

The principle is the same as the glass heater, the only difference being that the part that heats up, is made out of quartz. The result is a more uniform heating, and not as hot as glass heaters in any given spot of the stick. A word of caution with glass and quartz heaters : snails which happen to settle on them will get burned.

Again, precision is usually better than with glass heaters, but can still be improved, e.g. by connecting them to an electronic heating controller. Dupla makes such a unit that can be obtained with or without a digital display, or as indicated by using a commercial thermostat, set for the temperature that you wish to maintain as the minimum in your reef tank.

## 10.2.3 Cable heating

From as security standpoint, the best you can obtain. A cable is strung underneath the substrate, or is placed against the back of the aquarium, or placed in the bottom of the trickle filter.

Make sure, if you plan on installing cable, that you get the low voltage version. These cables which require a transformer, operate at 42 volt, which is safe, even if the cable ruptured.

Cable heating will also result in the most uniform heating. This will prevent areas in the tank where the temperature is different from the main body of the tank. This is very desirable, as it will stress the fish much less.

Cable heating is however expensive. A control unit can be attached to the transformer to obtain very accurate temperature settings. This unit comes with or without a digital read-out, and has either one or two sensors, one to

## Two types of Heating Cables
## The long one is for bottom installation
## The short one is for supplemental heating or can be affixed to
## the side or back of the aquarium

Photo Dupla Aquaristik Gmbh

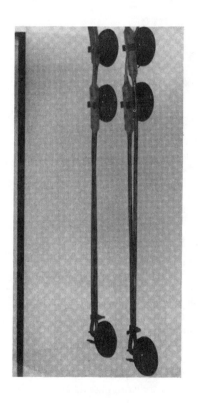
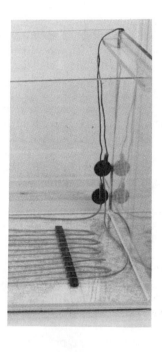

measure the actual aquarium temperature, and one to switch the heating on and off, based on the setting that you have made. This is hi-tech equipment, but gives the best results and the most accurate control. If you are prepared to go all the way, and wish the best heating alternative available, that is what you need.

Cables can be obtained in various sizes, delivering different wattage ratings, and the resulting heat.

## 10.3 Recommended temperature

As you might have surmised from the preceding sections, it is desirable to select a temperature in the right range, and then to keep the tank at that temperature all the time. Stability is one of the keys to success in the reef tank, as we have indicated many times.

Keeping your tank at a slightly lower temperature seems to benefit both fish and invertebrates, and our recommendation is that you try to stabilize the tank at 75 to 76 degrees Fahrenheit, but definitely stay within the minimum of 73.5 and a maximum of 82.4.

If necessary, review the lighting set up, the pump you use, and consider using a cooling unit if the temperature really gets out of hand.

Aquarists report that this is hard to achieve in many parts of the country. As aquariums take on the ambient temperature, in the summer they exceed, and in the winter they are lower than the range recommended.

There are no magic tricks to resolve this problem. From too cool to the right temperature is easy to solve. Use more heating cable or more heaters, and place them in different locations, to minimize temperature differences in parts of the aquarium.

In this respect we prefer to use four 50 watt heaters, rather than one 200 watt, as we can distribute the heating better over the entire aquarium, which reduces stress and unevenly heated water.

If the water is too warm, the only viable alternative, after other causes such as pumps and light have been eliminated, is using a cooling unit. Perhaps the type that you can easily build yourself is what you should experiment with first. We know many aquarists who have followed our advice and are extremely satisfied with the results. The set up is rudimentary, but it does the job and is inexpensive.

Two last remarks which are often overlooked , and apply to both temperature and salinity :

– the water used for water changes, and top-offs, whether from the mains, distilled or other, should first be brought to the aquarium water temperature. Do not use it at other temperatures, you will stress the biomass

– when acclimmating fish observe the above rule as well !

## 10.4 Making an inexpensive Cooling Unit

1. Acquire an inexpensive or second hand stand-alone small freezer. These units are not expensive, especially if you buy a second hand one.

2. Buy 1/4 inch flexible tubing. You will need at least 50 feet and preferably more.

3. Drill two holes through the side of the freezer with a regular drill. Make the holes about 1/8 inch larger than the outside diameter of the flexible hose. This is not difficult as most freezers have thin metal sheet plates, then some foam or other insulating material, and then usually plastic, which is what you see when you open the freezer door.

4. Place all the flexible tubing inside the freezer, nicely coiled up.

5. Push flexible hose through the 2 holes you have made. One will be the in, and the other the out of course. So use both ends of the tubing that is coiled up.

6. The return end is guided to the sump of the trickle filter, or to the aquarium.

7. The in end is attached to a power head or small submersible pump.

8. The flow through the coil has to be slow, to allow the water to cool down as it moves through the coil in the freezer.

9. Start by setting the cooling unit a medium range, and if the temperature adjustment is not large enough, meaning if the temperature of the water does not go down enough, increase the setting to cooler.

10. Adjust the flow rate to make the water remain in the tubing longer if necessary.

11. You now have an inexpensive cooling unit.

# Cooling Unit with Titanium Coil

Photo Dupla Aquaristik Gmbh

1  Long lasting refrigeration/cooling unit
with titanium parts. It is used specifically
for cooling aquariums in warm countries. It
can regulate the temperature automatically between 15° and 30° C.

# 11.  Maintenance

Throughout this book we have indicated, on several occasions, the importance of good and regular maintenance techniques.

Here for your easy reference are the recommended frequencies for the various components of the Reef Tank.

If you are using additional equipment, e.g. ultraviolet sterilizers, denitrification equipment different from what we suggested, or any other devices, these should be cleaned and maintained as well. You may feel that this is too much work. It is however necessary if you wish to keep your reef tank well balanced. Deaths and problems due to lack of maintenance should not exist. They are too easy to avoid.

| | |
|---|---|
| Obtain water analysis | : Call local Water supply company |
| Mechanical Filters | : at least once a week |
| Chemical Filters | : check once a week using carbon efficiency test |
| Dead material | : remove at once, as soon as you notice it |
| Pump | : at least every 3 months |
| Ball valves | : at least every 3 months |
| Check valve | : every 6 weeks |
| Skimmer if used | : once a month |
| Ozonizer if used | : once every 2 months |
| Airstone in skimmer | : renew every month |
| Tubing on ozonizer | : check for leaks once a month |
| Overflow box | : clean every week |

Syphon overflow if used : once a week
Uneaten food : remove as soon as noticed. Remember that fish have a fast metabolism and sometimes excrete uneaten food. This happens if you feed too much or do not leave enough time between feedings
Foot valve if used : clean screen once a week
Power heads if used : check every week, clean every two weeks
CO2 reactor if used : dismantle and clean once a month
Oxygen reactor if used : dismantle and clean once a month
Spray bar if used : clean once a month
Drip plate : check every week, clean monthly
Sump bottom : remove obvious dirt once a week, clean thoroughly once a month
Air pump : check diaphragm regularly
Bioballs : do not touch at all
Other filter media : check regularly, ideally you should never have to clean your trickle filter media
Pipe and flexible tubing : no cleaning should be necessary
Bottom of tank : any visible dirt should be removed at once
Micro and macro-algae : remove any dead or dying ones at once
Lights : if you use fluorescent tubes, change them every six months. Metal halide bulbs will last several years, before they change spectrum to such an extent that they need to be replaced.
pH electrode : visual check once a week, cleaning about every 8 to 10 weeks
Redox electrode : visual once a week, clean every 6 to 8 weeks
Heaters : inspect every week and clean if necessary

| | |
|---|---|
| Aquarium glass/acrylic | : as needed, more often if your redox potential is low, as you will have to deal with micro and other such algae |
| Resins | : no way to determine. Check manufacturers recommendations |
| Substrate | : if thin, as suggested, irregularly |
| Air dryer | : follow recommendations given by the manufacturer U.V. |
| | : if you use a UV, change bulb about every six months. We do not recommend their use however. We prefer ozone. We suggest not to combine them. |
| Decorative material | : as needed, by visual inspection |
| Glass heaters | : as required, check every 3 weeks |
| Carbonate Hardness | : once a week if CO2 is used every 3 weeks if no CO2 used |
| pH | : check pH meter daily If reagents are used: once a week |
| Phosphates | : once a week |
| Iron | : once a week |
| Dissolved oxygen | : once a week |
| Nitrite | : initially once a day. Then once a week, after tank has matured, once every 2 to 3 weeks |
| Nitrate | : after tank has matured once a week |
| Redox | : Check daily, twice a day is better. Take a morning and an evening reading. As with all tests, keep notes |
| CO2 supply | : if you are using carbon dioxide make sure to check the bottle regularly. It is a good idea to have a spare small bottle which can be used while the larger one is being filled |

# 12.Chemistry in the Marine Hobby

Since so many words are used when writing or talking about our hobby, and since many do not always mean much to the reader, or the listener, we have included a section that explains some of them in what we have tried to keep laymen's terms.

This is not a scientific dissertation. If you need the exact chemical definition, refer to a chemistry book, preferably organic chemistry. Your local library will probably have several of them that will interest you.

Chemistry is a rather complex science, but in our hobby we do not need to understand a great deal, and certainly not to the degree that scientists look for.

What is of interest to us is, in most cases, to be found in books on water chemistry, and in books on organic chemistry, mostly in the chapters that deal with oxidation of protein, the nitrogen cycle, and sections on biological decomposition.

Some of you might wonder why we included this section. It is the direct result of many conversations with hobbyists asking more comments on these subjects over and over again.

We hope that it will be useful, and that you will be able to put it to work for you. Better understanding of the terminology will certainly lead to more meaningful conversations between aquarists, if nothing else that is a major step forward we feel.

We have tried to be as complete as possible, we are sure however that some terms you would have liked to find in here are missing. We apologize. Finding the definition of a term is however as close as the nearest good dictionary.

## 12.1 Elements :

a pure substance which cannot be broken down into anything simpler by chemical reaction. There are 104 such elements known to man. They are classified in the " Table of Elements", previously known as the Table of Mendeljeff, which can be found in many books.

Most of them occur naturally, but some can only be made in laboratories, sometimes even only by nuclear reaction. There are 3 classes. Metals, non-metals and metalloids. Some examples that relate to our hobby : iron, a metal; oxygen, a non-metal; and arsenic, a metalloid, which is found in traces in both the water we add to the tank, and in the salt mix we use.

As already indicated, most elements known to man are found in sea-water. The salts we use to prepare our tanks contain many of them, usually 70, and some manufacturers even list them on their packaging. Those present in very small, should we say minute, quantities, are known as trace elements.

## 12.2 Acid :

a substance that releases hydrogen ions when added to water, and thus lowers the pH. Acids in pure form are dangerous and should be treated with care.

In our aquarium however they only appear in very diluted form, but are still strong enough to reduce the pH of the water. Acid will turn blue litmus paper red. Acids give off carbon dioxide when added to carbonates, this is the reason why adding a dilution of sulfuric acid to a carbonate, will produce CO2. This method is no longer in wide use in aquarium keeping however. Acids also neutralize alkalis (see). Our aquariums also contain organic acids -amino type-, as explained in the filtration section of this book.

## 12.3 Air :

the mixture of gasses that surrounds us, and that we use for several purposes when running tanks. Air contains 20.9 % oxygen, 78.1 % nitrogen, 0.03 % carbon dioxide, and some minor amounts of rare or noble gasses such argon, neon, krypton, xenon, as well as some water and pollutants.

Some of the latter include :

| | |
|---|---|
| sulphur dioxide.... | source, burning coal and gas |
| carbon monoxide.... | source, cigarettes, engines |
| dust............... | source, outdoor, clothes, pets |
| pollen........... | source, trees and flowers |

Note the large amount of oxygen and the very small amount of Carbon dioxide air contains.

## 12.4 Alkalies :

opposite of acids. An alkali is a base (see) which is soluble in water. They usually are metal hydroxides, such as sodium hydroxide. The latter is used to raise the pH of the water, and can be bought in pet stores in diluted form. Ammonia solution or ammonium hydroxide is also an alkali of course, and is present in our tanks as a result of the breakdown of nitrogen products from various sources, e.g. food protein, feces, plant material, fish and other biomass metabolism, etc. Alkalis have a pH which is higher than 7.00, as opposed to acids which have a pH which is lower than 7.00

Strong alkali compounds will burn your hands, the same way strong acids will do. Most of the time however, hobbyists only get to handle diluted forms of these.

## 12.5 Allotrope :

Elements that can exist in different forms. The chemical properties are the same, but the physical ones are different. A good example is carbon of which two allotropes are diamond and graphite. Phosphorus and sulphur can also take on allotropic states, and are elements found in tanks in the form of phosphates and sulphates. Both are undesirable and need to be removed, or the tank needs to be set up differently, to ensure that they cannot build up. Sulphates are not a compound that we usually deal with, as no test are available for aquarists to use. We would anyway not be interested in the Sulphate, but in the Hydrogen sulfide that could be present. Phosphates can pose serious micro-algae problems as we have seen

## 12.6 Amino-acids :

these are organic compounds, the building blocks of protein. When protein breakes down, these amino-acids appear as by-products, and some can be noxious. Our own bodies need about 20 different ones, some of which we cannot produce ourselves, but have to eat (idem for our fish). When combining, amino-acids form what is known as peptides or poly-peptides, which when they form chains result in various proteins. The acid part of the compound has the formula COOH, and the amino part the formula NH2 (where the nitrogen is that eventually turns up in the water. We cannot and do not wish to avoid these acids, as we have to feed the fish, metabolism has to take place, and chemical reactions will take place in the tank whether we want it or not. What is of interest to us, is ensuring that the break down chain of events does not get interupted, as such could cause problems in the aquarium.

## 12.7 Ammonia :

NH3, is a colorless gas that we all know and that needs to be removed from the water by biological filtration. Ammonia is used in fertilizers, pharmaceuticals, cleaning industry, in the manufacturing of Nylon and even in the

fabrication of explosives (Ammonium nitrate). We have also seen in the filtration section that nitrogen can be present in many forms. This is only one
of them. At low pH levels the amount of ammonia is extremely low, ammonium ions however are present, but do not concern us as much as they are not
considered toxic, except if they bind into Ammonium Hydroxide. This is the
reason why ammonium is a greater problem in marine tanks, indeed a greater
amount is converted to the gas form at a higher pH level, and the gas is very
noxious, even in very small quantities.

## 12.8 Base :

a substance that reacts with an acid to form a salt and water. The ones best
known to us are probably sodium hydroxide and ammonium hydroxide (NaOH
and NH4OH). Anytime such a compound is added or produced in the tank, the
pH will rise. This can occur for instance in a tank in which a lot of macro-algae are kept, and not enough CO2 is available.

The macro-algae will look for their carbon supply in the carbonate and hydrogen carbonates, and possibly produce hydroxides in the process, not directly of course, but as a chemical side reaction occurring in the water. When
this happens, calcium precipitates can also been seen in the tank, a good example is the white rim around the glass at the water level.

This process is also refered to as biogenic decalcification.

## 12.9 Boron :

a non metallic element which is added to glass, as an oxide, (B2O3) to make
glass stronger, such as for instance Pyrex glass, or other similar types  that
can be put on stoves etc. Such glass is often used to make retort and flasks
used in testing liquids etc.

## 12.10 Brass :

brass is a mixture of copper and zinc, and can therefore not be used in salt
water aquariums, as the copper will slowly be released in the water, with all
the damaging effects we know. Most aquarists know this, but sometimes brass
parts are found inside other devices that we use. Watch out therefore.

## 12.11 Bronze :

is a mixture of copper and tin, and can therefore also not be used in the reef
aquarium. It is unlikely you would anyway, as it is not the type of material
used in the hobby.

Beware when you buy products that were not developped for the marine
hobby, but that you are using anyway. Make sure that you know what they
contain, and that no compounds included are noxious.

## 12.12 Calcium :

Calcium is a soft metallic element. It is fairly reactive, and gives a steady stream of hydrogen when added to water. Calcium is present in many forms, and some of these compounds are of importance to us : calcium carbonate, calcium hydrogen carbonate, calcium hydroxide, calcium sulphate, aragonite, calcite and various other such, the names of which you will frequently find in hobby literature. Calcium magnesium compounds are also often referred to, e.g. coral itself. Dolomite is another such compound that contains calcium. Marine aquariums require such compounds to assist in stabilizing the pH, by raising the buffer. The buffer is the sum total of all elements that do so.

## 12.13 Carbohydrates :

organic compounds which contain the following elements : carbon, hydrogen and oxygen. Some better known ones are the sugars such as glucose, sucrose etc... starch and cellulose, all elements that are to be found in the aquarium as a result of the various breakdown processes that occur there. Sugars are not found as such, but are used in certain systems that advocate denitrification, the removal of nitrates, by the use of lactose, another sugar, or other chemicals. We personally prefer to let denitrification run its own, natural course, by setting up the trickle filter in a specific way. See filtration.

## 12.14 Carbonates :

$CO_3$, such as in limestone $CaCO_3$, dolomite ($CaMg(CO_3)_2$), malachite $CuCO_3.Cu(OH)_2$ As we have indicated, carbonates and bi-carbonates, also called hydrogen carbonates, are part of the buffering system of seawater, as well as of the water in our aquariums.

A loss of carbonates will lead to Calcium precipitating, forming white residue on the water rim line on the glass . This is also referred to as biogenic decalcification.

## 12.15 Caustic :

strong alkalis, that burn organic material. Examples that apply to us are NaOH sodium hydroxide, used to raise the pH, also called caustic soda when in pure form, and caustic potash or potassium hydroxide KOH. The variety that you buy in stores is strongly diluted and will not cause the burn associated with caustic soda, used to unclog pipes for instance.

## 12.16 Celcius :

unit of temperature, where 100 degrees equals boiling point, and zero degrees equals freezing point. One degree celcius = one degree Kelvin. See section on heating for conversion to Fahrenheit formula. Scientific notations are always given in Celcius degrees. So are most articles, translated from another language. Conversion is simple, and you should take the time to write the formulas down somewhere. They will come in handy.

## 12.17  Cellulose :

a carbohydrate which is a polymer, and of which the cell walls of plants are made up of. As indicated, carbohydrates are organic in nature, meaning they contain carbon. This is a product that breaks down in the aquarium and pollutes the water.

## 12.18  Chalk :

rock formed from shells of marine animals. It is softer than other calcium compounds, its formula is also CaCO3. Added to water it makes a milky cloud, until it settles on the bottom. It does not dissolve by itself, and is therefore not suitable as such, without intervention, to raise the carbonate hardness of the water. Some similar compounds can be used in reactors, in which water and carbon dioxide are mixed, much like a CO2 reactor. The difference is that in this case, a carbonate is used, which in contact with the carbon dioxide containing water, lower in pH, will slowly dissolve and raise the carbonate hardness somewhat, on a constant basis.

## 12.19  Chlorophyll :

the green pigment in plants and algae, which is responsible for the absorption of carbon during the photosynthesis process. Photosynthesis require light, and some of the macro-algae we wish to keep require a great deal of it, and light of a certain spectrum at that. There are several types of chlorophyll, all of which synthesize at different peaks of the light spectrum. They are referred to as chlorophyll a,b, and c. Chlorophyll reacts to light up to 700 nanometers, not just the 420 nanometers as indicated by some sources who advocate the use of actinic light. All Chlorophylls are magnesium centered.

## 12.20  Compound :

a compound is a pure substance which is made up of 2 or more elements that are chemically bonded. The properties of the compound are different from the properties of the elements that it is made up of.

The one we know best is probably water H2O and another one we are very familiar with is NaCl, Sodium chloride, the main component of the salt we use to prepare our reef tanks.

Many other compounds, some intermediate ones, are formed in the aquarium as part of the complex closed eco-system chemistry taking place all the time.

## 12.21 Dry ice :

solid carbon dioxide, we recognize it or know of it by the white fumes it makes when immersed in water for instance. It is often used to produce special effects in the theatre, but is also used in the hobby, for instance to keep frozen foods, frozen for longer periods of time, when transporting them. It will stick to your fingers, so handle it with care if you come accross it.

## 12.22 Formalin :

a aqueous solution of formaldehyde, also called methanal. It is used in certain medications sold in pet stores, for the treatment of fish diseases. It should not be used at all in reef tanks. In fact medical treatment of fish should always occur outside of the tank. We know that it is very hard to catch any fish out of a reef set up, however adding any kind of medication is extremely dangerous to the chemistry of the water and of the filters. Methods to catch fish include using 2 nets rather than one, and chasing the fish with one net towards the other one, or using a clear plastic container, place some food inside, and wait -or shoud we say hope- until the fish goes inside. Of course the problem with that system is two-fold : sick fish usually do not eat, and invariably fish you do not want to remove enter the container.

## 12.23 Hydrogen Carbonates :

part of the buffering system of the aquarium water. Probably the best known one is calcium hydrogen carbonate, also known as baking soda, with a chemical formula of $Ca(HCO3)2$. Hydrogen carbonates are also called bi-carbonates, the former terminology is however preferred nowadays. You cannot add them directly to the aquarium, as they will cloud the water, since most of the time you will only find them in powder form. Several such products, specifically made for reef tank use, are found in pet stores.

## 12.24 Hydrogen Peroxide H2O2 :

Both a powerful oxidizing agent, and a compound that can be used to quickly raise the oxygen levels in salt water tanks. The result is however only temporary, and will not solve low dissolved oxygen level problems. Can be obtained in drugstores in a 3 percent solution. Hueckstedt(1969) is in favor of its use whenever fish seem to suffer from lack of oxygen. Kipper(1987) recommends against it. Three percent solutions are not strong enough for the purpose described, and stronger ones cannot easily be obtained by aquarists. We recommend against its use.

## 12.25 Hydrogen Sulfide H2S :

a particularly strong smelling gas, that is very noxious and easily diffuses in the aquarium water. Recognized by the so-called rotten egg smell. It occurs when organic material that contains sulphur decomposes in an oxygenless environment. To be avoided at all cost, as it will strongly affect invertebrates and corals. Best remedy, ensure that there are no areas in the tank where anaerobic activity can take place. Good maintenance practises are part of this process.

## 12.26 Hygroscopic :

a substance that absorbs water very easily, and can take up to 70 percent of its own weight up, without showing signs of moisture or getting wet. Well known examples are sodium chloride, silica gel, copper oxide etc. Deliquescence on the other hand is the ability to take up so much water that melting occurs as a result, calcium chloride and iron chloride are examples. The water, by the way, can be taken up from the air. This is one of the reasons that containers with unused aquarium salt should be closed tightly. It is also frequently the reason why containers of reagents that are left open, will go bad. Test reagents can then no longer be used.

## 12.27 Indicators of pH :

a substance which changes its color under different conditions. Used in testing for pH with dry reagents, or with strips of paper that have been treated with such compounds.

The following are three that are commonly used : phenolphtalein to test for wide range pH e.g. a pH 4 to 10 test; methyl red or litmus used for pH ranges of 4 to 12; and thymol blue which is used for pH ranges of 7 to 12, the one we are interested in.

## 12.28 Kelvin degrees :

unit of temperature that is equal to celcius degrees. The scale however is different. For instance, absolute zero is -273 Celcius, but zero degrees Kelvin. Freezing point is equal to zero degrees Celcius, but 273 Kelvin degrees. Boiling on the other hand is 100 degrees Celcius and 373 Kelvin. It should be clear from this that Kelvin degrees are usually used by scientists to express negative celcius degrees, e.g. boiling and freezing temperatures of many gasses and other chemical elements.

## 12.29 Nanometre :

a unit of length, used for instance in the expression of the length of light waves. One needs 100 million nanometres to obtain one meter.

Sometimes found in hobby literature that deals with the analysis of the spectrum of various light sources, e.g. halide and actinic lighting, or when talking about photosynthesis. 1000 nanometers = 1 micron.

## 12.30  Nitrates :

all nitrates contain the NO3 group. Nitrates are one of the end decomposition products of the nitrogen cycle. They are not easy to remove from our aquarium water. Denitrification is one method, changing water another, adding more macro-algae yet another. Nitrates can be broken up by heat, but this is not practical in the aquarium. We  have dealt extensively with nitrate removal methods, as well as with phosphate, in another section.

## 12.31  Oxidation :

a substance undergoes oxidation if it gains oxygen, or loses hydrogen, or loses electrons. Oxides are the compounds that result from a union between an element and oxygen. Oxidizing agents are substances that cause the oxidation of other elements. Common oxidizing agents are oxygen, chlorine, ozone, hydrogen peroxide, potassium permanganate. Strong oxidation potential in the aquarium, will ensure that the water is of high quality, resulting in a much more balanced aquarium.

## 12.32  Peptides :

when 2 or more amino-acids react together, they form peptides, more than two amino-acids reacting together form poly-peptides, and chains of poly-peptides form protein. The way the chains are linked determines which protein is formed. Protein is of importance to us because of the many ways it breaks down, and the potential problems this can bring about for the aquarium ilife forms. Protein chemistry is a fascinatingsubject. Those wishing more details should look the subject up in the library.

## 12.33  Phenols :

phenols are white and crystallic soluble solids. They can result from protein breakdown, or from the use of resins to treat the aquarium water. Phenols are corrosive and poisonous. Phenols contain carbon, hydrogen, oxygen and another element, e.g. sodium. Using activated carbon of superior quality greatly reduces the danger from phenolic compounds. Avoiding using medication in the aquarium is another one. Carbolic acid is the legal name of phenol. Cresols, Xylenols, Resorcinols, and Naphtols are all types of Phenols. They are called Aromatic organic compounds.

## 12.34  Some Decimal length measurement units

| One meter | = 100  centimeters |
| One centimeter | =  10 millimeters |
| One millimeter | = 1000 microns |
| One micron | = 1000 nanometers |
| pico | = one million millionth of |

micro                                    = one millionth of
nano                                     = one thousand millionth of

## 12.35 Classification of the Animal Kingdom (Phyla)

Phylym Protozoa                          microscopic unicellular animals
                                         e.g. Amoebe or Paramecium
Phylym Porifera                          Porous animals e.g. sponges
Phylym Coelenterata                      Tentacle bearing animals with
                                         stingers e.g.Hydra,Sea
                                         Anemomes, Jelly Fish
Phylum Platyhelminthes                   Flatworms such as Planaria and
                                         tapeworms
Phylum Annelida                          Segmented worms : earthworm,
                                         leech
Phylum Mollusca                          Soft bodied animals with shells
                                         e.g. snails and clams
Phylum Arthropoda                        Insects and crustaceans, spiders
Phylum Echinodermata                     Spiny skinned animals e.g. stars,
                                         urchins

Complete lists, -there are several interpretations-, can be found in any good
Zoology or Biology book

## 12.36 Aerobe  –  Anaerobe :

aerobes are organisms that require oxygen to survive, e.g. nitrobacter. Anaer-
obes on the other hand do not, and survive without it, e.g. sulphur bacteria.
There are  also bacteria which are called facultatively aerobic anaerobic,
meaning they can behave in both ways. These bacteria can also survive in areas where oxygen is very low, and are of interest to us because they are able
to assist in the breakdown of nitrate NO3, by removing one of oxygen
molecules, leaving us with NO, which is a gas which escapes (it is also
known as laughing gas). This process can be duplicated in the aquarium by
setting up the trickle filter in a particular way. Refer to that section for more
details.

## 12.37 De-amination :

the process by which excess amino-acids are disposed of by the liver, since
amino-acids cannot be stored.This happens to amino-acids which have not
been converted to protein.

We have mentioned the word "amine" in the section on biological filtration.
This de-amination process can produce some noxious by products as we have
seen. This involves the removal of the NH2 group and its conversion into
NH3, and then into urea which is excreted into the water (at least in our case).

## 12.38 Autotrophic bacteria :

bacteria that require simple inorganic substances for growth, they convert the latter to complex organic ones. Macro-algae and plants are good examples of the process. They use carbon dioxide and through photosynthesis convert it into the materials required for growth. See also heterotrophic bacteria.

## 12.39 Eco-system :

a community of organisms interacting with each other, as well as with their environment, for instance an eco system is a complex system where fish interact with each other, with the invertebrates, the plants and algae, and also with the environment, the tank, light, food etc..

## 12.40 Heterotrophic bacteria :

organisms which obtain organic compounds (food) by feeding on other living organisms. All animals, humans, fish, and most bacteria are heterotrophic, meaning such bacteria can only survive if natural foods are present (foods that contain protein). Nitrosomonas and Nitrobacter are autotrophic not heterotrophic.

## 12.41 Metabolism :

the sum of all chemical and physical processes taking place in a living organism. Catabolism is the process of breaking down compounds, anabolism is the process of synthesizing compounds. This is an important concept in aquarium keeping. Most of the activity we are dealing however is of the catabolic type, certainly when we look at what happens with protein, which breaks down to amino-acids and amines and so on, as we have seen in the chapter on biological filtration.

## 12.42 Plankton :

Microscopic animal and plants, respectively called zooplankton and phytoplankton, both of which can float freely in the aquarium water. Outbreaks of phytoplankton are more frequent than zooplankton ones. They can be observed by the discoloration of the aquarium water. They result from insufficient maintenance, overload of phosphates and nitrates. Fine filtering, e.g. diatom filters easily remove both types. Aquarists should however look for the cause, and adjust conditions as required, to avoid their recurrence.

## 12.43 Saprophyte :

organism that feeds on dead material, usually fish, plants, micro and macro-algae, bringing about decomposition. These fungi and bacteria are important in the recycling of nutrients in open systems. In our aquariums however we should do all possible, through good maintenance techniques to avoid such decomposition from happening. It requires regular filter cleaning and the removal of all dead material from the water.

## 12.44 Runner :

a term used to describe the growth of macro-algae. Runners are branch-like extensions that are visible to the naked eye, usually end in a point which is frequently whitish. Most species of Caulerpa reproduce in this way. First the runners, then new branches with the typical leaf. Runners and stolons are very similar and both result in the creation of a new plant or a new macro-algae.

## 12.45 Bar :

a measure of atmospheric pressure.Especially applicable if you use carbon dioxide on the aquarium, as the pressure inside the bottle, and the pressure at which the carbon dioxide is pushed into the aquarium is usually expressed in Bar. Pressure is also expressed in pounds per square inch : psi. 1 Bar is equal to 14.5 pounds per square inch, or also 29.53 inches of mercury pressure.

## 12.46 Ampere :

a measurement of the flow of electrical current. Pumps for instance carry such a reading. Exceeding the total amperage allowed on a given circuit, will blow the fuse. Many other instruments have amperage ratings, for instance float switches. Using a float switch of a lower rating than the pump that it is controlling, will result in  float switch failure. Beware when buying such control switches therefore.

## 12.47 Gallons vs liters

One US gallon equals 3.7125 liters.

Standard type aquariums in Europe include 100, 200, 300, 500, 750 liters. This corresponds to  respectively  26.5, 53, 79.25, 132, 198 US gallons.

Often the question is asked : how many Bioballs per gallon. The correct answer is 55, giving a 23 square feet surface area.

## 12.48 Spectrum, Kelvin degrees, as applied to Light

Units that are used in the analysis of the type of light waves emitted by a particular bulb or light source. Light waves or series of light waves correspond to a certain color, e.g. red, green, blue, violet, ultraviolet. The predominance of one or more of these determines the color of the light : very white, blueish, reddish, yellow, etc. This color, called warmth is referred to in Kelvin degrees. The higher the number the cooler the light, the lower the warmer.

## 12.49 Cavitation

Water contains gasses. When a water pump, inside the volute, the area where the impeller rotates, moves too little water, the water is broken up and the dissolved gasses come out of solution. The resulting stream of water coming out of the pipe, characteristically will be whitish, as thousands of tiny bubbles were coming out at the same time.

This happens when the water is restricted at the intake. Not enough water reaches the volute, the impeller breaks it up, and bubbles come out on the other end. This is both unsightly and dangerous. Too long of this regimen will ruin the pump. Moreover, nitrogen bubbles may create problems for the fish.

This may also happen if a fine filter is attached to the pump intake, and that filter is so dirty that it restricts the water from reaching the pump in sufficient quantities.

Alternatively, reducing pipe size to below the pump manufacturers re- commendations can  also result in cavitation.

## 12.50 Slurping noise from standpipes

If this happens, enlarge the size of the pipe. As a rule of thumb, do not use anything less than 1.5 inch.

Standpipes can replace overflow boxes of course. They do however not allow you to pre-filter the water. A pre-filter will then need to be built elsewhere in the system.

## 12.51 Uneaten food and food excesses

Overfeeding is the source of many problems. How can you know what the right amount to feed is ?

Most authors recommend that it should be no more than what fish eat in a few minutes. That is of course correct, except that certain fish do not come to the food right away, and you can therefore not judge when to stop.

You must use judgement. What you think is enough, is probably too much. It is not much of a guideline, but basically means that you are more than likely overfeeding, although you think not.

Do not feed too frequently, and not too close to each other either. Fish have a fast metabolism, and can excrete uneaten food if you feed them too rapidly in succession. This uneaten food increases the pollution in the tank.

Liquid foods are very hard to deal with. Most of the quantities put in the aquarium are usually lost, and end up polluting the tank, and stressing the filters. If you use such food, do so in another tank. We have explained the procedure elsewhere in the book.

Making your own food is not complicated :

Buy some fresh seafood at the supermarket. The more varieties the better. Cut this in small chuncks. Put them in a blender. Add vitamins if you wish. Chop the mixture up. Drain the excess liquid. Put all this on a flat surface. Spread it out and flatten the lot. With a large knife, make small squares of food. Place the plate in the freezer. Wait the necessary time. When frozen you may wish to package the food in small packets, using plastic foil.

## 12.52 Cleaning Live Rock

Live rock is often full of undesirable material. Some of the lifeforms are dead. Some is detritus. Some of it you do not want : e.g. fire worms (they eat coral).

Take water from the aquarium and fill a bucket. Take the rock gently, and move it back and forth through the water, until you are satisfied that it is clean enough. Do this with every piece before placing them in an acclimating vat or bucket.

After the rinsing - cleaning session is finished, go through the bottom of the bucket, there might be some lifeforms crawling in there that you may wish to put in the tank.

## 12.53 Increasing Biological filtration when other methods are not feasible

If all else fails, and you cannot increase the size of the trickle filter, or replace the packing material with one that has a larger surface area, you may have to add a second filter to your system.

Alternatively, take a cannister filter, fill it with e.g. Bioballs and use that as additional filtration.

There are, of course, many more terms and units of measurement used in the hobby. We have tried to cover those that we felt would benefit from some explanation and how they apply to keeping fish and invertebrates.

# 13.  Light

## 13.1 Introduction

No subject is perhaps as controversial as the type of lighting to be used over a reef tank. We can not determine the reasons for this, and do not really want to concern us with it too much,  but the debate regularly heats up.

Advocates of various lighting systems portray the equipment that they work with, or sell, as the one and only safe way to go, using beautifully looking aquariums to make the point.

Different types of lighting are mixed, and new terminology suddenly appears out of nowhere. Qualities even the manufacturers of certain bulbs are unaware of, are given prominent display and labeled as required for good and continued invertebrate life in the reef tank.

Frankly, we suggest to take all this with a grain of salt. Perhaps many of the statements made are correct, and will in the long run turn out to be better methods than the ones used now to keep reef tanks.

In fact we hope so. Once the dust settles everyone will be better off, and the hobby will have progressed another large step.

Do we wish to get involved in this controversy ?

No, we would rather like to take a different approach,  and let you decide what kind of light is best for your tank, using the criteria we have developed to evaluate a particular light source.

No doubt, some of the newer types of bulbs introduced in the hobby have their benefits, but we believe that these qualities can be derived from more common and less controversial types of lighting as well.

Untested methods may seem appealing, but we would like to see more research, and more evidence that in the long run such lighting is not detrimental. especially to invertebrates, since most react very negatively to Ultraviolet light, especially of the A type.

## 13.2 Requirements

To properly maintain reef aquariums full of invertebrates, live rock etc, and to promote photosynthesis we need light of a particular kind.

The light source used has to meet two main criteria :

**Criterion 1** : the intensity obtained needs to allow us to keep invertebrates, macro-algae, and other life forms that we place in the aquarium, without harm,  and for continued lengths of time,

**Criterion 2** : the spectrum obtained must be of a kind that is ba- lanced enough to benefit all of these lifeforms, and not just a few.

Which light form one uses to obtain these results is therefore, in our opinion, not relevant, as long as the above two criteria are met on a continuous basis.

This can conceivably be achieved with fluorescent tubes, with metal halide lamps, vapor-arc lights, mixtures of fluorescent tubes etc..., but excludes certain types of light, as they will not fit the above definition. The latter include incandescent and the so-called spot lights, as well as certain vapor lights whose spectrum is not at all in the right range, e.g. sodium vapor and tungsten halogen lights, which are too dominant in the yellow spectrum.

Does this mean that all the money you have spent on Halides and Mercury vapors, Arc lights, Actinics etc is lost, or wrongly invested ? Of course not, since any light that meets the above criteria is all right to use.

We could add a third criterion, and that would be cost efficiency. This would be calculated as lumen per watt, per dollar spent.

This is an interesting calculation to do for comparing several types of light, and in certain cases yields extremely interesting results.

It would turn out indeed that the most economical lights that can be used, that still allow us to achieve the right spectrum and intensity are indeed the newer type of fluorescent tubes manufactured for instance by Osram under the name of DuLux tubes. We are presently using such lights over an aquarium and will report the results in Marine Reef, the newsletter that is published by Dupla USA Press.

## 13.3 Intensity

All reef tanks that we have seen contain a mixture of animal life that has a thoroughly different photo-period –the length of time the light is actually on– and intensity requirements.

Corals that only open at night, are placed in the full target of strong metal halide lighting, others that require very strong light are placed low in the aquarium, perhaps even under a shelf -like structure made of base rock, or some other form of "filler" rock placed in the aquarium.

Can the aquarist be so discriminating in his or her selection of invertebrates to avoid this problem ? The answer is obviously no. For one, the choice of inverts offered for sale is wide, and the specific requirements of many are unknown. Compared to nature, the aquarium is so small that attempting to duplicate what happens on a reef seems impossible.

What we are attempting to say of course is that we cannot, in a reef tank, provide the ideal amount of light for every single specimen. Nei-ther will it be possible to provide enough of the right spectrum for every form either. Trade-offs will have to exist, and approximations, and testing where a particular piece of coral does better, will be necessary.

Reading articles and publications, and finding out more about the bio- mass that is kept, will of course help a great deal. Unfortunately not many articles are available, and the information found is often not
complete enough to allow us to draw any definitive conclusions.

Some intensity levels are known however, for instance the amount of Lux ( a unit of how much light reaches a particular spot) reaching the water, at the water level, on the reef, with full sun, is far in excess of 100.000 units.

When we go down somewhat, this intensity diminishes rapidly, and at a level of 5 feet under the water, this has dropped to 40 to 50 000 Lux, going even deeper reduces the Lux to around 8 000 at 25 feet, and so on.

It should be clear from this that depending on where an invert is positioned, more, or less, light will reach. Lifeforms, inverts, etc. will do best in similar conditions in our reef tank.

For this reason we advocate having at least TWO different types of areas in the reef tank :

— One with high light intensity, and

— one with low light intensity.

This will allow us to position certain inverts, in the light zone where they
belong, and move others around, and experiment to see where they do better.

This may seem like "work", it is in reality not, as one figures out rather
quickly what the correct placement is. And it is after all exciting to experiment and find solutions.

Animals that do not fit in either of the two zones may be placed in areas
where some shadow exists from overhanging rocks, to deter -mine if that
location will make them react more positively and look better.

If you are not sure which corals come out at night, the solution is simple,
go down and check your aquarium about two hours after the lights have been
turned off, and you will know.

The greater majority of macro-algae require strong light intensities, often in
excess of 15 000 Lux. They should therefore always be placed in highly lit
areas. Caulerpa type prefer  locations close to the top, with not too strong
water movement

You may find out where they do best, by simply looking at several bunches
that you have spread around the reef tank, and observe in which locations
runners are growing. Spreading runners would be an indication that such a
spot is desirable, and that future additions of such algae, or other bunches of
them should be placed in similar spots.

Most corals that harbor symbiotic algae (See section on algae), require relatively strong light, and should be placed in that light zone in your aquarium.

Most anemones of course do best in high intensity light, and sponges and
tubeworms do better in the lower light zone. They do extremely well in arc-
vapor light (a type of metal halide).

We are not too concerned about fish, as they are mobile enough to seek out
places that are convenient and meet their light requirements.

To achieve the intensities needed strong lights will be required, or alternatively, several of them which, when combined, will give us the desired Lux readings.

This can be achieved by mixing a number of high wattage fluorescent tubes (we will discuss spectrum later), or using some of the high intensity discharge arc-vapor lights on the market.

Which option you select is a matter of economy. Both the initial price and the cost of running both kinds differ. Fluorescent tubes are less expensive to run, and their purchase price (the bulb) is lower too. They do however lose their spectrum rather rapidly. Such tubes should be replaced about every 6 months. Calculate that too in the price equation, if you will be doing one. The initial outlay may be lower, but...

A word of caution regarding halide vapor-arc lights : Arc-vapor metal halide lights are known to generate ultraviolet A light, unless they have been either fitted with a protective special glass, or the bulb manufactured in a particular way, to screen such UV light out. If ultraviolet A is emitted the corals and invertebrates will react quite negatively. This is not a major problem, and is quite  acceptable, providing you do not remove the ultraviolet screen, or make sure the bulb is treated to eliminate such radiation.

This is perhaps what hobbyists refer to when they indicate that their corals burned while using Halide lighting! Another reason why corals change color of course, and an important one, is that when corals receive the right kind of light, symbiotic algae grow, and color the invert. The type of color depends on the dominant pigments of the algae. Coral burn would however occur as a result of A-type UV radiation.

This is not due to the type of light used, but to the fact that either the protective glass was removed, or to the fact that the wrong kind of bulb was used. Check  and make sure. And remember the terms metal halide, halide, and so on, are generic terms, and refer to the type of light, but do not identify the type of bulb.The same of course applies to fluorescent tubes, as that is a generic term as well, since so many different ones can be bought.

When buying new lights you should ensure that the output is high in Lumen (a unit of total output), which will reflect in a high Lux reading, in the tank, in a given spot. High lumen output is necessary to achieve the desired Lux readings that corals and macro-algae require to do well in our reef tank. Typically strong halides will have outputs in the range of 10 to 15 000 Lumen.

**Modern and Esthetic Lights**
**Top : Dulux Osram Tubes**
**Bottom : HQI Osram Power Stars**

Photo Dupla Aquaristik Gmbh

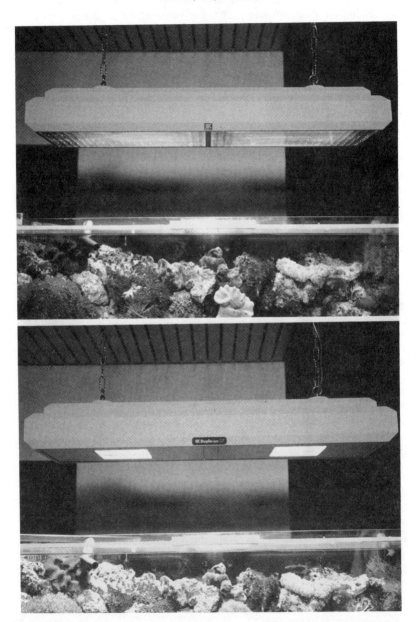

**The intensities we recommend are as follows :**

At the water level : irrelevant, since this can change considerably once the light penetrates the water.

| | |
|---|---|
| 3 to   5 inches in the water | : 15 000 to 20 000 Lux |
| 8 to 12 inches below the water line | : 10 000  to 15 000 Lux |
| At the substrate level | : 3 000 to 4 000 Lux |

Usually, if you can achieve one of these levels, the other ones will be quite close to those numbers. If the amount of light in certain areas of the substrate level is too high, then such areas can be also used for co -rals and inverts that require high lighting.

If not enough darker areas are available, position base rock used in the filling of the tank, in  a way that  create such areas. This is not complicated but might require that you re-arrange some of the deco- ration, or add some extra pieces.

You may obtain these levels by mixing fluorescent tubes, or by using metal halide, or other such high intensity discharge lights.

Often we are asked, how many watts per gallon of water, are required. Such a measurement does not really make sense. You can of course calculate one, but it will apply to your tank, and not necessarily to some one else's. It is therefore not a good yardstick of required lighting since it cannot be generalized. Different aquarists, keep different life forms and decorate their reefs in quite different ways, and this excludes generalizations. It would be nice to be able to suggest one, but it is not realistic to do so.

## 13.4 Spectrum

Our second criterion was spectrum. This is as important a criterion as the intensity, as it determines the type of light waves that reach the invertebrates and macro-algae.

The spectrum depends on what type of color predominates. White light, e.g. day light, is made up of a mixture of colors. An analysis of these, giving exact amounts of each color, expressed in wavelengths, give us a spectral analysis.

Sunlight is obviously a very complete form of light. As this light penetrates the water, certain wavelengths, meaning colors, are filtered out, and do not reach the reef life. As one goes deeper, more and more colors are filtered out, leaving only blue, at greater depths.

Of course most of the life forms we keep, are not found at such great depths and benefit therefore, on the real reef, of a rather good mix of all colors emitted by sunlight.

Photosynthesis, which takes place in the aquarium whenever the lights are on, and is the catalyst for all the chemical and biological processes occurring, peaks at different wave lengths, depending on the type of chlorophyll that is generated in the process.

One of these is in the 420-430 nanometer wavelength, and is the reason for some sources to advocate the use of Actinic lighting.

Photosynthesis however peaks at more than one wavelength, since different types of chlorophyll need to be produced to sustain life in the tank. Isolating one type of light and administering it in massive doses is therefore not correct. To use an analogy, your car runs on gas, but needs oil too. Providing a light spectrum that incorporates not only the three wavelength peaks of chlorophyll synthesis, but does so at the desired intensity, would therefore solve all our problems.

**Such a perfect light does not exist,** except in nature. Anything we use over the tank is an approximation, a light source that comes close, but not just totally what we want. This is obviously the reason why mixing several kinds of fluorescent tubes will give such good results, providing enough space over the tank exists to attain the required intensity as well. And that is where often the problem with fluorescent tubes exists. There just usually is not enough space.

Some stores and some aquarists we know, have solved this problem by building their own light box, which has 6 or more fluorescent tubes inside, and sits over the aquarium. All ballasts are remotely mounted. This is an excellent solution, but unfortunately no commercial units allowing you to do that are available, to our knowledge. Moreover if you build such a unit, many safety factors -electric shock-wize- have to be dealt with. It is however a viable solution.

Full spectrum lights, mixed with warm daylight will give excellent results. The ratio suggested is 1 daylight for four full spectrum bulbs. The number of bulbs needed depends on the size of the tank, and should really be measured with a light meter that allows spot mea-surements. This can easily be obtained from a friend who is into photography, or sometimes they can be rented from stores that sell camera equipment. All you need it for, is a day or two, maximum.

Place your fluorescent tubes over the tank. Measure the intensity at various depths, and decide whether you can reach the required in- tensity by adding more tubes. Depending on the conditions you might be able to do so. If not you may have to go the metal halide arc-vapor way.

It is also recommended to stagger both the on and off timing of the lights, to provide a semblance of rising and setting sun. This can be done with timers. Several articles on this subject have appeared in FAMA both in 1987 and in 1988 issues.

To supplement the requirement for blue wavelength light, hobbyists are now using Actinic bulbs, and running them for many hours a day.

Although the last word on this type of lighting has not been heard, we do not recommend strong actinic lighting, and suggest that if used, the bulb should not be run form more than one to tow hours per day.

The type of bulb used, the Actinic O3, as there are many, was designed for totally different purposes, e.g. the breakdown of Bilirubin in certain new born infants, and also for Diazo blueprint machines. Other types of actinic bulbs are used in insect zappers, and in tanning lights. At the time of this writing we were not able to determine exact levels of ultraviolet A emission of the 03 bulbs. Dr.S.Sascha (1987) recommends not exceeding 14 percent of total wattage. For every 100 watt of total light, no more than 14 watt actinic.

Alternatively, you may wish to use Metal Halide arc-vapor type lights, that emit a spectrum that is between 4300 and 5000 Kelvin ( a unit expressing the mix of colors and as a result the relative warmth of light) degrees. We personally prefer bulbs emitting in the range of 4300 to 4500 K degrees, but excellent reports with bulbs in the 5000 and even 5500 K have been reported as well (Kipper,1986). The latter bulbs are the Osram HQI Power Star bulbs.

Some lights that are sold as metal halides, but that are not vapor-arc type bulbs, are of the incandescent type, and will usually give a very yellow light, e.g.tungsten quartz bulbs. They should not be used.

The bulbs that we use, incorporate a larger fraction of the blue spectrum, we could say that they are skewed towards the blue, than other types of metal halide arc-vapor lights. With such lights no Actinic lighting is necessary. All the blue wavelength needed is provided.

How many such bulbs will be required, we cannot tell from our vantage point, as we do not know your particular conditions.You should use the intensity levels given as a guideline. This will require a spot light meter as we have explained earlier.

You may feel that we have not given you the magic number, and you are correct, because there is no such number. Only evidence, that can be observed for any length of time, determines whether or not you have the right kind of light and the right intensity.

Hopefully following these guidelines will get you there, or confirm that what you have presently set up is not only adequate, but beneficial as well. If you are in doubt, measure and then decide what to do. It is much more professional.

As you experiment, you will be able to determine for yourself that some of the lights that you are now using to do fit the criteria we set forth. Fortunately, switching to the right kind is not a major undertaking.

Availability is not a problem either, judging from the advertisements for lights presently found in magazines.

**Bulb Types Used in modern Lights : a. Dulux Tube Osram
b. Vapor arc Light, c. Power Star by Osram**

Photo Dupla Aquaristik Gmbh

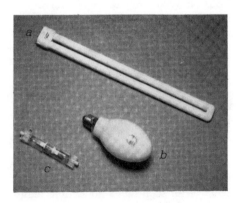

# 14. Micro and Macro-Algae

## 14.1 Introduction

The term algae means different things to different people. Botanists and Bi-ologists find the term elusive of definition too (Bold,1985). Sometimes re-ferred to as slime, scum, seaweed, and many other names, even the pronun-ciation of the name is not always clear : some say algae with a hard "g", others prefer a soft one.

Algae share a lot in common with plants, but they are unique, and therefore define easy definitions that are all encompassing, often because of a number of very unique features.

Some algae are in fact very similar to bacteria, and some scientists classify certain algae as such : Cyanophyta and Prochlorophyta, referred to as Cyanobacteria. They are known to us as Blue-green algae.

Algae can be aquatic, sub-areal (exposed to air), or live in soil. Aquatic varieties appear in both fresh, brackish and saline waters, even in extremely high salinities of 100 per mille, which is three times as saline as our tank water is.

Algae are very resilient and can adapt to many milieus, e.g. Enteromorpha can easily live on the hull of ships and navigate with them from saline to fresh water milieus, without any serious damage. Enteromorpha is one of the hair like algae that is found in aquariums and that we refer to as micro-algae.

Aquatic algae may be suspended (planktonic), or attached (bentic), and some live on the surface of the water (neustonic).

If classified according to how they attach to a host, algae go by adjectives such as :

– Epilithic         meaning living on stones
– Epipelic        meaning living on mud and sand
– Epiphytic      meaning attached to plants
– Epizoic         meaning attached to animals : yes, even that.

Algae, especially the blue-greens have been around for some 3 billion years. Cell structure goes from single cell to the complexity of the kelps and rockweeds. From the very small, e.g. M.pusilla at 1 to 1.5 micron, to the very large kelps which can grow 180 feet tall, and can do so extremely fast. Several classifications exist, one of the most common and well accepted is Kingdom Plantae, Monera, and Protista, further divided into the :

Cyanophyta            Blue-green algae
Prochlorophyta
Chlorophyta            Green algae
Charophyta            Stoneworts
Euglenophyta         Euglenoids
Phaeophyta           Brown algae
Chrysophyta           Golden yellow-green algae
Pyrrhophyta           Dinoflagellates
Cryptophyta           Cryptonomads
Rodophyta             Red algae

Obviously, we are not particularly interested in the majority of them, since they do not appear in reef tanks as a matter of course.

The one we are concerned with are the Brown, Red, Green and Blue green algae.

The study of algae is a science referred to as Phycology, and recognized authorities such as V. J. Chapman, D. J. Chapman, F. R. Trainor, H.C. Bold and M.J. Wynne have written long treatises and in depth studies. Unfortunately these are much too complicated and contain material that is of no use to us. They also do not deal with the types of species that we are most interested in, e.g. Caulerpales, Chlamydomonas –another of the undesirable ones–, Ulva –also called sea lettuce–, Chladophora and for instance Valonia, in depth.

What we would like this chapter to achieve is to give you a better insight in the types of algae that can be kept in our reef tanks, some of the factors that influence their growth and survival, and some of the nutrients that need to be provided, and what actions to take to rid your tanks of undesirable ones.

Scientific names are given where appropriate.

We hope to publish a book in late 1988 dealing solely with macro-algae, based on the experiments conducted in the author's tanks, and information collected and exchanged with hobbyists in Germany. This should prove very interesting and rewarding a project.

## 14.2   Micro-algae

Micro-algae are what hobbyists call most of the undesirable algae that grow in reef tanks. This is however a misnomer, since some of these provide many fish and grazers with the necessary food sources. Such algae also perform the valuable task of removing noxious materials from the water, and act as a cleaning plant in many ways. Not every type of micro-algae is therefore to be scraped off and discarded.

Micro-algae, as their name implies would be small, so small in fact that many cannot be identified unless a microscope and superior reference textbook is available.

Rather than attempting to describe types that found in aquariums, let us rather deal with what should be done when they turn up, and make your reef tank look unsightly.

### 14.2.1  Why do micro-algae appear ?

Micro-algae, like any other life form not placed in the aquarium on purpose, as the result of a purchase decision you made,  come in attached to rocks and other algae that you acquire.

This is unavoidable, most micro-algae spores and the algae themselves, are extremely small as individual entities, and cannot be removed from the host, without destroying the latter at the same time.

As conditions in the reef tank become propitious for their proliferation, they will start growing rapidly and multiply at sometimes alarming rates.

Propitious conditions in their case, means bad quality water to us. Water that contains excess amounts of the Nitrate and Phosphate compounds are excellent for micro-algae reproduction. Light that includes certain types of spectra will also benefit such algae greatly.

It would therefore seem obvious that if we want to limit the growth of such undesirable algae, we need to maintain extremely high water quality levels.

This has been demonstrated over and over again, and most aquarists are aware of this as well.

The problem seems to be that no one manages to maintain the water at levels of quality that such micro-algae dislike, and waters in which the competition for scarce food sources works to their detriment. By the latter we mean that other algae forms deplete nutrient levels fast, and keep micro-algae blooms in check in the process. This happens to be a very efficient way of controlling micro-algae growth, and is frequently both practised and recommended in German circles.

## 14.2.2 What should you therefore do ?

1.      Adhere to a strict and regular maintenance program
2.      Test for nitrate and phosphate levels regularly
3.      Take immediate corrective action if the nitrate levels
        exceed 15 mg per liter, and if phosphate levels exceed 1 mg per
        liter. How this is done was explained elsewhere.
4.      Do not use water additives that contain either phosphate or
        nitrate, or both
5.      Ensure that your tap water does not contain nitrates and
        phosphates either
6.      Plant the tank heavily with macro-algae, to ensure competition for
        scarce food sources
7.      Do everything that is necessary to raise the redox potential level of
        your tank to over 325 mv, and preferably over 350 mv, during the
        day time
8.      If this requires a skimmer and an ozonizer, you need to
        install such devices. If you already have them, refer to the
        redox potential section on how to raise the redox potential in your
        tank.
9.      Scrape off any algae on the glass, and other decoration that you
        can scrape, while the redox potential building process is going on.
        This will make the disappearance of excess micro-algae proceed at a
        faster rate.
10.     Do not expect immediate results. G. Bepko(1987) reports that it
        can take more than 6 weeks, after the redox   potential has reached
        the desired level for most of the undesirable algae to
        disappear.Thiel(1986) reported that only 3 weeks after redox

potentials had reached 370 mv did he notice that micro-algae of the red and slimy type had disappeared from his 180 gal. tank, and that only manageable amounts of small hairlike algae remained.

11.    Place several more algae eating fish in the tank.
12.    Reduce food quantities for a while until the situation is
       under control.

It is quite possible that in your reef these conditions will take longer. The reasons can be :

–     high nitrate levels to begin with
–     high phosphate levels to begin with
–     overfeeding
–     no grazers and algae eating fish are present

Do not get discouraged, keep the 12 points in mind and continue to do all that is necessary to raise your redox potential level. The micro-algae will disappear.

Kipper(1987) reports that silicic acid, and perhaps sodium silicates can play a role in the appearance of red slimy algae. Many German aquarists agree, many disagree. This is a wide-open area and will have to be investigated further. It is also not quite clear how silicic acids would form in the aquarium. Most are gels, which are formed from Sodium silicates and sulfuric acid.

Red undesirable algae, the patches sometimes seen in aquariums are often the result of simple organic overload of the tank water, and can easily be eliminated by ensuring that the water quality is higher. This is done by means, again, of a protein skimmer and an ozonizer. Checking for organic load can be done easily using an oxygen test.

The procedure is as follows :

–     Take two water samples
–     one is used immediately for the dissolved oxygen test
–     the other one is stored in a sealed container that cannot trap any air.
      This is very important, as oxygen from that air will   falsify the
      test
–     store this container for 48 hours, in a dark place, for instance   in a
      cabinet
–     perform the oxygen test on this sample again after the   48
      hours have elapsed
–     deduct the oxygen level found from the test result of the
      sample you did 2 days earlier

if the result is more than 2.5 mg, you have too many organics in the water.

Of course the addition of activated carbon, in the quantities suggested earlier, will also reduce organic loads.

If the micro-algae you wish to rid the tank of, are growing on dead coral, on other macro-algae and such, your problem is real difficult to solve in a short matter of time.

Several water changes will be required, stick to a rigid maintenance and testing program, and follow the steps above. Add several weeks to the time frame given, as it will take longer for such a tank to get to the right redox potential levels. The situation is however not desperate.

No need to dismantle the tank and start all over again. You will need to soak the rock that is overgrown in some bleach and then let it sit in the sun or outdoors, to kill of the algae, and you will need to discard macro type algae that are overgrown with micro ones.

If hair-like and very long strings of algae appear in the tank, do not remove them, just keep them in check. They are desirable.

If bubble type algae appear, and the bubbles are green with a shiny look, usually Valonia species, they are excellent too, and attractive as well. If the bubbles have a dotted appearance the algae is called Bornatella and is desirable too.

Chaetomorpha appears as a bunch of hairlike threads that are undulated, and grow in all directions, with no apparent pattern.

It is not possible to give a list of the micro algae that you might find in your tank because on one hand there are so many different types, and on the other we cannot tell what come in with the rocks and such you bought at some point.

Often however we have found Lyngbya, Microcoleus and Oscilatoria to be present in many tanks.

## 14.2.3 Blue–green Algae

These algae which are really a link between bacteria and plants, are photosynthetic micro-organisms. They might look unsightly but are great producers of oxygen in the tank.

Whether you see them or not, you can be sure that they are always pre sent. Individually they cannot be seen, but since they live in groups, or clusters and colonies that you can observe them with the naked eye.

Their color varies from blackish, through brown to deep green. They form gelatinous masses, cushions, and sheets that look like skin. Messy is probably a good description.

We are sure that you know what we mean. At some point or another you have had them in your tank, in quantities that could hardly make you miss seeing them.

What most aquarists wish to get rid off are indeed these type of algae. They grow on glass, on the substrate, on other algae, in short on any -thing they can get to.

Nostoc is a form of blue green algae. Some examples of colonial filamentous ones include :, Oscillatoria, Spirulina, Phormidium and Schizothrix.

Branched, filamentous forms also occur :
Westiella, Fischerella, Nostochopsis and many others.

Both light and the availability of NH3 plays an important role in the propagation of blue-green algae. Light sources with excess amounts of the red spectrum (650 nm) promote the growth of most (Fay,1983).

Many blue-greens are also chemoheterotrophs, meaning that they can propagate using organic sources of nutrients. This explains why they will reproduce so quickly and easily in aquarium water loaded with organics.

Riddance steps to be taken are described earlier in this section, follow especially the organic load pattern of the water, by taking regular organic load tests.

## 14.3 Green Algae

These are type of algae that we all wish would be the only ones in the tank. And rightfully so, most of them look really appealing and decorative. It is also a great pleasure to watch them propagate.

The availability of such algae in good pet stores is usually assured and many varieties can be bought.

Often this includes Caulerpa species. Caulerpa is a family of algae. To give you an idea of how large it is, here are some forms of Caulerpales that we have seen :

C. clavifari
C. trifaria
C. verticillata
C. serrulata
C. pellata
C. crassifolia
C. crassifolia mexicana
C. sertularioides
C. prolifera
C. racemosa
C. racemosa macrophysa
C. cupressoides
C. cupreiformis
C. floridana
C. okamurai
C. brownii
C. geminata
C. taxifolia
C. paspaloides
C. asmeadii

Quite an assortment indeed. And we have only mentioned some. There are a great deal more. And of course this is only one macro-algae of the Caulerpales group.

Incidentally the name Caulerpa comes from Caul (kaulos) = stem, and erpa (herpo) = creeping.

Caulerpales like shallow areas, high light intensities, and mud or sand to root in. They will attach to rocks too. Do not float them, but make sure when you put them in the aquarium that they are stationary.

Caulerpa species are among the easiest to keep. They also grow quickly, by sending out runners, whitish looking tips at the end of the branch like main part of the algae.

Caulerpa like many other green algae require high intensity light, in excess of 15 000 Lux. What this means is that to be sure you are providing enough light, you will need to take a spot measurement of how much light is reaching the actual spot where these algae are located. Make sure to place them in the high light zones of the tank.

The spectrum they prefer is a wide and full spectrum, this also hap- pens to be a rather white white spectrum close to daylight. Vita-lite is such a light source. If you have no access to this type of bulb, you will need to mix several bulbs to arrive at a final spectrum that is around 4300 Kelvin degrees. This is an area where enough blue is coming through to eliminate the need to add strong actinic bulbs. You may wish to do so for the corals however, but for no more than one to two hours a day (see section on light).

Many fluorescent tubes are required to achieve this, and you may find that unless you have a light box that can hold 6 or more tubes, you will need to switch to metal halide vapor-arc lighting.

The recommended spectrum is from 4300 to 5500 Kelvin degrees. If you kept only algae the higher number would be better, but if you also keep invertebrates, which we assume is the case, the 4300 K light should be your choice.

Besides light for photosynthesis Caulerpa species and other macro algae require carbon dioxide and fertilizers, especially iron. $CO_2$ can be provided by the manual or automatic addition. Check elsewhere in this book for pointers on how to set such carbon dioxide addition equipment up. You will need to maintain carbon dioxide levels of between 3 and 4 mg per liter.

Fertilizers containing iron can be bought at pet stores. Make sure that iron is included, and that it is chelated. If not, it will precipitate and fall out.

When using iron containing fertilizers, expect the formation of iron oxide. This will be seen as a brown reddish substance inside pipes and flexible hoses. It is not harmful and no a matter to be concerned about.

To maintain healthy and deep green looking macro-algae, high redox potential levels are advocated (see chapter on redox).

Green algae can be free floating, attached and parasitic. We are mainly concerned with the attached ones of course.

Green algae can reproduce by propagation : sending out runners, or by sexual means : a small green cloud that suddenly forms around the algae. This is not a frequent occurrence though in reef aquariums. Conditions are usually better for the algae to grow by means of their runners.

Some other forms of algae that can be found in aquariums are :

Codium species, Halimeda species, Bryopsis species, Ulva species - especially U. fasciata-, Cladophora, Penicillus species, Valonia species, and Udotea species

All require intense lighting and need areas where they can attach their holdfasts to. Do not indiscriminately float macro-algae in the water therefore. Make sure they are placed in an area with good lighting, and that will allow for the holdfasts to attach themselves, e.g. substrate, or rock.

One requirement that needs to be strictly adhered to is not to continuously change the pH, this affects algae negatively.

Keep the carbonate hardness at 12 dKH or better. Maintain iron levels of 0.05 to 0.1 mg/l, and add carbon dioxide if necessary.
It should also be clear that if you wish to grow macro-algae, you will need to pay attention to the type and number of algae eating fish kept in the tank at any one time. Initially, when the algae are taking hold, and growing, few of them are required. Once they take off however, you will need to introduce such fish to keep the amount of algae in check.

Algae that turn whitish, translucid, have died because of lack of nutrients. If this happens to you, remove all the dead algae, and perform a 30 percent water change. The exact amount is really dependent on the quantity fo algae that died. If only a few died off, a small water changes will obviously do.This will reduce the amount of toxins that have re-entered the water as a result of the algae die-off. Replace newly acquired algae in the tank, and re-adjust all nutrient levels. If this happens to you and you are not using carbon dioxide addition equipment, it is probably a good time to look into it.

If you acquire calcareous algae, e.g. Halimeda and Penicillus species, make sure that they are placed in a sand type substrate. They will not attach to rocks. In a 30 gallon tank that we ran for about 9 months, we made both grow new circular shaped leaves and blades respectively, using CO2, iron supplements, and a 150 watt Osram metal halide arc-vapor bulb of 5500 Kelvin degrees.

If you follow the recommendations and you find that suddenly your macro-algae take off, and start growing all over the tank, you should not get concerned. This is good and very appealing too. You should however introduce algae eating fish, e.g. Tangs that do a particularly good job at it, and above all, very regularly monitor your nutrient levels : both iron and carbon dioxide. The more algae the more quickly the reserve gets depleted of course. This will require adjusting the levels dispensed for instance by a dosing pump if you are using one.

If you remove algae from the tank, you will always rip the stem, and stored fluids and other elements that the algae have absorbed and taken out of the water, will re-enter the aquarium. This requires that you change water to reduce the levels of these toxins. This is not just a recommendation, it is a must. We have seen several large tanks go sour as a result of taking out large quantities of algae, and not doing so.

To be successful at growing algae, you need to start with a good seed bunch of such algae. If what you see in the pet store does not look deep green and healthy, do not buy it. It will only die in your tank a few days or weeks later. Good quality stock, to begin growing algae is as important as adding nutrients.

We have not covered the brown algae, as most of the ones that appear in tanks are really classified in the blue green variety and occur as a result of poor water quality  management. Although brown macro-algae do exist of course, they are not the kind usually kept by aquarists.

Some types of brown macro-algae  may also be of the red macro vari- ety, which we are not covering in this book.

Gracillaria, an algae which is sold in some pet stores, in its red and green variety is not recommended. The clumps that are collected do not usually regenerate, die-off, or more frequently break up in small pieces which end up being spread all over the tank, and in the filters. We do not recommend that you place them in the reef tank.

# 14.4   Symbiosis-Mutualism : Symbiotic Algae

It has been known for many years by a great number of aquarists that certain corals and a great number of other invertebrates have created a very useful relationship with a much lower form of life: certain forms of algae.

This relationship, which benefits both, is referred to as Symbiosis, or Mutualism. The host and the Symbiont have formed an intricate biological and chemical relationship between themselves, which has evolved over time, to allow both to cope more effectively with the environment.

Symbiosis is found in invertebrates, corals; sponges; fungi, lichens; and even in some plants. It is thought to be the result of the necessity of both to cope with the relatively low nutrient levels that are common around Reefs. This may seem contrary to what you had expected, as the rich life on the Reefs could have given the impression that food sources must be abundant. This however not so.

Reef waters are low in many nutrients, as can be evidenced easily by looking at a water analysis of such Reef water. Typically nutrient levels around Reefs are powers of ten lower than similar levels in aquariums.

Notwithstanding that fact, life thrives, because these low levels are constantly replaced, and a lack therefore really never occurs. The only way for us to duplicate that situation in a Reef tank would be to add very small amounts of nutrients, and doing so constantly. This is of course practically impossible to achieve.

The closest we can come to matching Reef conditions is to carefully monitor water chemistry, and make regular water changes as indicated elsewhere in this book, to replenish some of the nutrients and trace elements that have been removed by the use of carbon and by the life that is present in the Reef Tank. Of course some additives may be used to achieve this result too. It is unfortunately not possible to determine accurately whether these products satisfy the requirements of the life that is kept in the tank.

Symbiotic relationships can take on many forms. They can be intra-cellular, inter-cellular, or even just on the surface of the host. In some cases the relationship can be parasitic, rather than symbiotic.

Much research is still necessary in this area to determine the exact nature of many relationships between lower life forms. as many of the mutualistic relations are far from understood. Ch. Delbeek of the Ma-rine Aquarium Society of Toronto has written several highly informa- tive articles on the subject. This is of course a trend that should be encouraged as it spreads knowledge and results in more hobbyists becoming proficient in keeping macro-algae and reef tanks.

The area that concerns us however, has been studied extensively, especially the relationship of Zooxanthella microadriatica, which is one of the most commonly found algae in sea anemones and corals.

Although we are not concerned with it in this analysis, symbiosis occurs as frequently in freshwater organisms, as it does in marine environments. A good example of the latter being the relationship that exists between Chlorella and Platymonas, and some lower animal lifeforms, e.g. freshwater Hydra viridis and Paramecium bursaria.

Relationships between host and symbiont are not necessary for survival, as in most cases both can live quite independent lives. Studies have shown that algae can alter their carbon exchange and absorption processes, showing a return to independent life. Some Invertebrates can live on plankton and thus thrive independently as well. It has however been demonstrated that many reef building corals cannot survive on plankton alone, mainly due to the poorness of such plankton around the reef (Darley,1982).

Speculation as to how the symbiotic relationships came about a- bounds. One theory holds that as algae were ingested they continued their photosynthetic activity until digestion would kill them off. Over evolutionary periods of time the algae adapted and managed to survive for longer and longer. As photosynthesis continued, the algae produced metabolic products such as "organic" carbon, usually in the form of glycerol, and other nutrients, e.g. organic acids such alanine, which benefitted the host.

As relationships become more mutually meaningful, they obviously evolved to a balanced state, where both the alga and the host were able to derive considerable advantage from the relationship. This then led to the development of permanent symbiotic relationships, as we know them now.

It has been demonstrated that symbiotic algae can adapt to some degree to changing light conditions, mainly by producing more Chlorophyll a. This has the result that the symbionts that grow in hosts exposed to higher light sources, will be clearer in color than those that have adapted to shade conditions. Clearer in this respect means brighter colors. This can observed in the Tridacna clam, where symbionts range in color from dark brown to the very bright colors we have seen in many photographs, or perhaps even in aquariums that were using metal halide vapor-arc, or some other form of high intensity lighting.

This is also the reason that many invertebrates that contain symbionts, change color as the light conditions are altered. This is sometimes erroneously interpreted as "burning" of the invert. Of course this is not the case. It is in fact the direct result of providing more beneficial quantities of light, to which the algae react, producing brighter pigments, and coloring their hosts correspondingly.

Most of the benefit derived by the host seems to be in the area of organic carbonic transfer from the alga to the host. Oxygen transfer does not play a significant role, more than likely because the host lives in an oxygen rich environment to begin with.

Muscatine and Porter(1977) were able to determine that in one type of coral, 87 percent of the daily carbon intake of the coral had passed through the algae first. This is of course of major significance to us, as it illustrates the need to ensure that photosynthesis is promoted by providing adequate lighting levels. Of course, although the host can "feed" on its symbiont for its carbon requirements, vitamins and other nutrients still need to be extracted from the surrounding water, zoo-plankton, or from other food sources that we provide. This should be a confirmation of the fact that providing a varied diet is most important.

One of the reasons that these symbiotic relationships are so frequent in marine reef environments is that they are based on a very efficient recycling of nitrogen and phosphorus compounds between the host and the symbiont. This is then supplemented by additional quantities that can be taken up from the environment, which as we have indicated is relatively poor in such nutrients.

The more efficient the symbiotic relationship is therefore, the less the "partners" have to rely on this environment. This is important for long term survival of course. It is assumed that the algae are the uptake medium of these nutrients, from where they pass to the host. Some of the nitrogen and phosphorus are recycled between the symbiont and the host, excess minerals are released back into the water. The net result is that both the symbiont and the host are less dependent on outside conditions than other forms of life, in which this kind of relationship does not exist.

Zooxantellae are also thought to be important in the building mechanisms of the reef itself. The process is not really clearly understood, but it is a fact that all reef building corals contain zooxantellae, that light is part of photosynthesis and promotes the formation of calcium carbonate by corals.

Algal cells are found in varying ratios to coral cells: from 1 to 300 according to Darley(1982), accounting for the fact that some corals or anemones can be either drab in color, or bright and multicolored in some cases, especially when lighting is correctly set up over the Reef tank. Higher concentrations, in bright light, will give brighter colors to the host. This is of course providing the host has a high incidence of symbionts per cell. It is also dependent on the type of zooxantellae found in the host. The latter fact accounts for the great diversity of colors found in the invertebrates that we keep in our Reef Tanks, and is related to the type of chlorophyll and pigments that are found in the symbiont.

Since the symbiotic relationship between the invertebrate animal life and the algae is of such importance, and in essence not so complex as it might appear, maintaining correct light levels in the aquarium should be a major concern of every aquarist. You may wish to refer again to the section on lighting to decide if your Reef is receiving the right kind and enough lighting.

Recently the addition of actinic 03 fluorescent tubes has been widely publicized and advocated. We are not in total agreement with these statements and recommendations for various reasons. You may personally have found that they work well on your reef. We have heard several positive and also several negative comments on their long term effect however.

The final word on actinic lighting has obviously not been written and we wish to reserve full judgement. Many hobbyists report excellent results. We have found however that these results can be duplicated using non-specialized bulbs that are skewed towards the blue spectrum but still provide a rather complete overall spectrum as well. We are of course experimenting with them, and will draw some conclusions once both the experimental and control tanks have ran for about 9 to 12 months.

Many symbiotic relationships involve blue-green algae, for instance Richelia, but these are in most cases not with invertebrates, but with lichens and diatoms, and are therefore of less interest to us and are not within the scope of this book.

We are most interested in promoting such symbiotic relationships in our Reef tanks, for obvious reasons. We should therefore carefully select the lighting used. Based on our experience, metal halide of the arc-vapor type lighting, in the 4300 Kelvin degree range, still seems to work best.

Let us hope that, as time goes by, more and positive evidence will be collected on the exact long term effect of such specialized sources as Actinic O3 and Super actinic lighting. It could even motivate manu- facturers to put lights on the market that serve our purpose even more.

## 14.5  Zooplankton

Although obviously not algae, as the name implies, hobbyists frequen- tly mistake the appearance of zooplankton for undesirable free floating algae blooms.

Zooplankton in a reef tank is the result of the sudden growth explo- sion of small animalcules that have been brought in with the live rock that is now used so often.

It includes many copepods and siphonophores. Most of them feed on phytoplankton, diatoms and dinoflagellates.

Such outbreaks should not be a cause for concern, indeed many fish , invertebrates and filter feeders will feed on the zooplankton present. Outbreaks do not usually last for very long, as nutrient levels which caused the outbreak become quickly depleted, and the colony dies off or is reduced to levels commensurate with nutrient supplies available.

Of course it would be a different matter if the type of copepods that appeared were parasitic and infested the fish. Such however are the risks we run when we use live rock. It is indeed not possible to determine whether it harbors any undesirable life forms, until it is too late usually. If however we ensure that high water quality standards are adhered to, such risks will be considerably alleviated.

## 14.6  Summary

Following a regular maintenance program and ensuring adequate light and nutrient levels, will take a lot of the guess work out of keeping macro-algae.

Since they so nicely decorate the tank, we feel that the incentive to do so is certainly there, and that the results certainly justify the effort.

Ulva species and many of the Caulerpales can easily be obtained from local pet stores, and even through the mail from some sources in Flo-rida and Hawaii.

Excellent results are obtained with high intensity lighting. Such lighting sources are now also readily for sale.

Progress in keeping macro-algae should therefore be achievable by anyone taking the time, and investing the money to do so. We hope that you who are reading this, are one of them.

# 15. Protein Skimmers And Ozone

## 15.1 Ozone

Ozone is probably the most misunderstood additive used in marine aquariums. When ozone is used, hobbyists are quick to blame ozone for any of the many problems that can occur in an aquarium, even though the problems might have nothing to do with ozone at all. It just seems that ozone is a convenient scapegoat.

Ozone is an allotropic form of oxygen. A very unstable one. Under normal circumstances it is a bluish gas. It is very soluble in water. When ozone is mixed with water, especially in a tank which is full of organic pollution, it starts breaking down, and in essence disappears from the water, pollutants that are present, because it is such a strong oxidizer. In nature ozone is formed by discharges of atmospheric electricity during storms; by the oxidation of resins in coniferous forests, as is often found in coastal areas, where it is liberated from oxidizing seaweeds.

Pure ozone has an ORP of 2076 mv, this compares for instance with chlorine which has only an ORP of 1360 mv. We all know what chlorine can do, so one can visualize how powerful the oxidation of ozone can be.

Excesses of ozone are harmful, both in the aquarium and in the air. The EPA sets maxima for noxious compounds, including ozone, whose maximum concentration in the work place has been set at : 0.1 mg per cubic meter, which is 1000 liters.

### 15.1.1 When should you use ozone ?

If you determine that your redox potential is low, that dissolved oxygen levels are low (the two usually go hand in hand anyway) and your tank just does not look right, it may be a good idea to consider the use of ozone to try to improve conditions.

If your tank is overcrowded, whether the above conditions exist or not, but you are suffering from continuous outbreaks of disease, or the tank is infested with micro-algae and red algae, you may also wish to use ozone.

Ozone can also be used in small quantities to increase the water quality in general.

If your tank is running at redox potential levels that you deem too low, and you would like to increase the ORP somewhat, or even a great deal, in all likelihood, the only alternative available to you, save for changing conditions in the tank considerably, is the use of ozone.

If you wish to control the outbreaks of disease, and keep them in check, ozone will eliminate most of the free floating parasites, before they can re-infect other fish.

This does not mean that when using ozone no diseases will break out however. We said "it will keep it in check", and if your fish are healthy enough, they will be able to rid themselves of the parasites.

If excess nitrite is present, for any reason, and you wish to reduce the level, ozone will do so too. Of course, you should look for the real problem, and not use a palliative. Excess nitrite can be attributed to many causes, and they should be eliminated. Using ozone however will temporarily lessen the stress on the fish.

Ozone reduces the organic load of the water, and makes protein skimmers work more efficiently.

## 15.1.2 How do we dispense Ozone ?

Various devices, mostly made by a German company : Sanders, are available in pet stores in the United States and Canada.

These units deliver 25, 50, 100, and 250 mg per hour. The size you will require depends on the tank, and on the tank conditions, as we will see later.

Ozone is produced by a high intensity electrical discharge inside a chamber through which air is blown.

Output of ozone is dependent on both the amount of air, and the humidity of that air. Setting an ozonizer at a particular value, does not therefore guarantee that such is the amount of ozone that you will get.

Air can be dried, using a device made for that purpose. Good quality ones are expensive, and unfortunately because the humidity in a room with an aquarium is so high, they do not last for very long.

We have tried using silica gel capsules, in a small container through which the air first needs to go. This helps, but you have to remember to change the capsules about every week. This becomes costly. Small air dryers are available from Scientific Instrument Suppliers. If you do acquire such a unit make sure that access to supplies of the drying agent is easy, as you will need to change such agents frequently.

We would rather recommend that you make sure that you are pushing the right amount of air through the unit. To know whether this amount is correct, you will need to check the manufacturers recommended air flow rates. If in doubt, or if you cannot find the instructions, check with someone else or call the manufacturer.

Ideally you will blow the air-ozone mix into a protein skimmer. Alternatively you may use a device sold by Dupla, which gives off extremely fine bubbles, a diffuser basically, which is completely ozone and carbon dioxide resistant. It can also be easily be dismantled for cleaning. Such a unit would be placed in the sump of the trickle filter, in the front, not in the back, and you would maintain activated carbon in that same area, to ensure that residual ozone is removed before the water returns to the aquarium. Invertebrates react negatively to residual ozone.

### 15.1.3 How much ozone should you use ?

This is a very gray area, indeed, conditions in every tank are different. Some hobbyists have excellent maintenance practises, others have not. Some tanks are overcrowded, some not. Some filters are sized correctly, others are too small. Some tanks contain lots of invertebrates and few fish, others just the opposite. Some mains water is good, some is not so good, others use distilled or chemical free water, or use reverse osmosis to purify it first. We hope that you can see our point.

Of course every aquarist would like to have something to go by. We understand this concern, and would therefore like to make some recommendations.

Be sure however to verify that such recommendations give the results we point out in your tank too. If they are different, too high or too low, you will need to make adjustments in your ozonizers output. Remember ozone is toxic and needs t o be handled with care.

### 15.1.3.1 The tank is in bad condition

Redox potential levels are below 200 mv, the tank is full of micro and other undesirable algae. Fish die or get diseased regularly. Inverts do not live for long. Macro-algae die off.

In such a case, it is unlikely that ozone will do much for you.

The first and most important matter to take care of, is to get conditions back in shape. A thorough maintenance cycle is recommended, and to be maintained for at least one month.

Conditions need to be re-evaluated after that.

Ozone in this case would only make things marginally better, but would more than likely not resolve your problems.

You need to look at :

– feeding techniques
– overcrowding of the tank
– dirty filters, mechanical and chemical
– too small filters, biological
– dead material decomposing
– and anything else that resulted in the condition the tank is in.

### 15.1.3.2 The tank looks all right, but....

If you can measure the redox potential, and if the values are over 200 mv, preferably around 230 to 240 mv, ozone is for you.

Technically speaking your tank is not out of balance, but on the edge. You should improve on your maintenance schedule, do some testing, and take some remedial actions in that area.

Adding ozone will, in all likelihood, result in a gradual increase in the redox potential level, meaning in the quality of the water.

To determine how much ozone to use, first set the ozonizer at approximately 0.5 mg per gallon of water. E.g. on 110 gallon tank, this means 55 mg per hour.

Observe what happens to the redox potential. Is it rising ? Is it stationary ? Or is the level still showing a downwards tendency.

Depending on what you find, either increase or decrease.

Let us assume that the redox is starting to rise. You will now need to wait until you know exactly how far up the scale the redox potential value will go, and whether that level of ozone will maintain the ORP at that level.

If this is the case, you have determined the ideal level to use.

If this is not the case, increase the amount further, making sure however that no ozone can be smelled. Higher levels will of course do a better job, but since the oxidation process is not always as efficient as it should be, some ozone will not break down. That is the residual ozone. That ozone is noxious and needs to be removed, by either turning down the unit, or flowing the water over activated carbon.

Of course one of the decisions you will have had to make is at what level to run your tank. We refer you to the redox potential section for that decision.

Finding the right level can take some time. A few weeks ! Not a few hours or a few days. You will need to be patient and experiment.

The efficiency at which the ozone will work in your tank, depends on the method by which you are diffusing it into the tank. The best method is inside a protein skimmer. Next best is the use of a diffuser that allows only extremely small bubbles to escape in the water, indeed, the smaller the bubble for any given volume of air-ozone the greater the contact surface with the water, and as a result the greater the larger the oxidation that will take place.

If you do not have a redox potential meter, you will need to buy one, rent one, or borrow one.

Making recommendations, based on gallons per liter, and visual inspection is possible, but haphazard. If you wish to follow that technique, go very slowly, start at extremely low levels of ozone, and based on the results seen

# Protein Skimmer

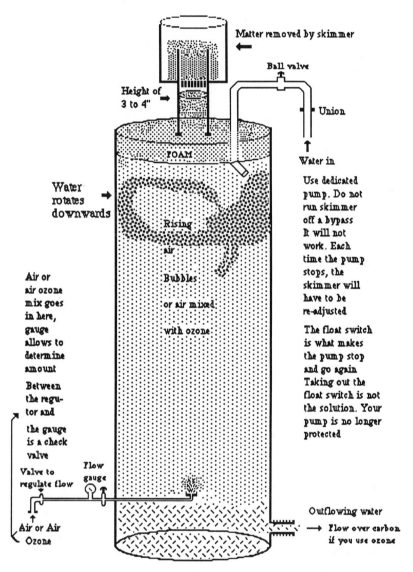

Matter removed by skimmer

Ball valve

Union

Height of 3 to 4"

FOAM

Water in

Water rotates downwards

Rising air

Bubbles

or air mixed

with ozone

Use dedicated pump. Do not run skimmer off a bypass It will not work. Each time the pump stops, the skimmer will have to be re-adjusted

The float switch is what makes the pump stop and go again Taking out the float switch is not the solution. Your pump is no longer protected

Air or air ozone mix goes in here, gauge allows to determine amount

Between the regutor and the gauge is a check valve

Valve to regulate flow

Flow gauge

Air or Air Ozone

Outflowing water

→ Flow over carbon if you use ozone

Make the skimmer as large as you can. Diameter should be 4 to 6", and height should be 3 feet or more. The longer the contact time, the better the efficiency. Small bubbles increase the efficiency as well. Use large wooden air diffusers. Change them frequently as they smudge up and start producing larger bubbles. The latter is an indication that they need changing. All pieces can be bought from an acrylic tube or pipe re-seller.

in the aquarium, gradually increase the output. Wait at least 2 weeks between output changes to determine the change. Make a picture of the tank, to be able to compare. Two weeks down the line, you will not remember what the tank looked like today.

Remember : if you smell ozone, or if fish and inverts react negatively, reduce the output immediately. When you use a redox potential meter such a situation is not likely to happen, and you have much greater control over tank conditions.

### 15.1.3.3 The tank is doing great, but....

Perhaps your tank looks just fine, or perhaps you have been using ozone already, and water conditions are good to excellent.

Is ozone still for you ?

It depends on the redox potential level, and whether you are able to maintain the conditions for any length of time. Are they fluctuating ? Sometimes the tank looks great and sometimes not.

More than likely your tank too will benefit from using ozone. Water conditions can be stabilized, or slightly improved. Redox potential can be raised somewhat higher, and perhaps your fish will do better, eat more often, without difficulty, and those hair-like micro-algae, usually Enteromorpha species, will start to diminish and not grow everywhere, especially in places where you do not really want them.

The principle is the same as the one already described. Take a redox potential reading. Decide which value you want your tank to be at, and start adjusting the ozone output until that value is reached and you are able to maintain it.

Increases should be made infrequently, space them at least one to two weeks apart. As tank conditions improve, small amounts of ozone will have a greater effect. So watch what is happening carefully.

### 15.1.3.4 Remarks

As the water quality improves, an equal amount of ozone, will have a greater effect. With less pollution to deal with, the quality improvement occurs faster.

It is important therefore, if your tank runs at redox potential levels that are already high, e.g. over 325 mv, that you be extremely careful and monitor more frequently what is happening.

In the end this results in the unit that you have acquired being over-sized for the job, but that is unavoidable, as in the beginning of the treatment you need to be able to run it at higher levels of output.

Carbon will need more frequent changes as a result of using ozone. Since more organics are broken down, more quickly, the carbon will become exhausted more rapidly. Remember to test more often.

When initially introducing ozone in a tank that has up to now not been treated with it, you must start with minimal doses and increase in small increments. This requires patience. Nothing happens quickly, and rather than risking adverse effects, you should take all necessary precautions not to upset an existing system, by the rapid introduction of a totally new element.

## 15.2 Protein Skimmers

The use of protein skimmers, also called foam fractionnators, is not as common in the United States and Canada, as it is in Europe.

Protein skimmers, of all sizes, have been used by marine aquarists in Germany for many years.

Companies such as Sanders, Eheim, Klaes, Optima, and others offer a wide variety of models.

Strangely, and even though respected authors such as Stephen Spotte and others have written about protein skimming extensively, the hobbyist has only reacted with moderate enthusiasm.

We cannot find a particular reason for this phenomenon either. Perhaps it has to do with pricing, since the models available on the market are all imported from Germany, or perhaps with the fear that a protein skimmer will remove too many "good" substances, besides the noxious ones it takes out very efficiently.

We do not know. We regret this, as protein skimmers definitely perform a very valuable function in the reef aquarium. We recommend their use highly.

## 15.2.1 What does a skimmer really do ?

As water and air mixtures are circulated inside the skimmer column, the air bubbles that rise, or their skin to be more precise, picks up detritus and organic matter.

This creates foam at the top, and as that foam becomes more concentrated with dirt, it is able to keep rising higher and higher above the water level of the skimmer.

The design is such, that the neck of the skimmer is much narrower than the actual body; this forces the foam inside a narrower area, concentrating the bubbles more, and pushing them gradually upwards, as foam from beneath keeps exerting an upward pressure.

Eventually this foam reaches the top of the neck, and flows into a beaker built for that purpose.

The principle is simple, and works.

To convince yourself that skimmers remove all kinds of material from the water, one need only look into the beaker once in a while.

**Does this action remove elements that we do not want removed ?**

The answer is : yes it does. Should we therefore discontinue the use of a skimmer, or not even install one to begin with.

We think that the benefits that can be derived from the use of a properly sized skimmer, far outweigh the disadvantages, and that one can always replace trace elements if needed.

Skimmers remove proteineous matter before it can break down and pollute the water.

Skimmers remove other substances that are noxious and that can adhere to the bubble skins, these include some of the intermediate breakdown products referred to in the filtration section.

Skimmers allow us to purify and clean the water and raise the redox potential level of the water. They should therefore be a welcome addition to a reef tank.

## 15.2.2 Features to look for in a skimmer

The column should be tall and not less than 4 inches wide. Preferably more. Of course the size you will use depends on the tank size, and small skimmer therefore have narrower bodies.

The water should enter the skimmer at the top and whirl downwards in a strong circulating motion. This increases contact time between the air-water or air-ozone water, and increases efficiency.

The beaker or cup at the top should be large. This will necessitate less frequent cleaning.

The neck should be narrow and a few inches long. The larger the skimmer the longer the neck should be, within limits of up to about 6 inches. This prevents wet foam, that is actually not carrying too much pollution from not reaching the top. It will concentrate further and then reach the beaker, taking out more pollution in the process.

The air inlet should be able to handle a through put of several hundred liters of air per hour. It should therefore be of the same size as the outlet of the air pump that you will use to run it.

If airstones are used in the bottom, they should be made of wood, easily accessible so they can be changed without too much difficulty, and they should be able to handle the amount of air pushed into the skimmer. This will, in certain cases, require that two such wooden air diffusers be used. Wooden diffusers will produce a smaller bubble.

Ensure that all parts are ozone resistant, if you plan on using the latter. We recommend that you do, as ozone improves the efficiency of the skimmer in more than one way. It should be able to handle the flow of water that you will require, based on the size of your tank.

## 15.2.3 Skimmer Efficiency

Protein skimmer efficiency is dependent on several factors :

- bubble size
- contact time
- adhesion-attraction capability of the bubbles
- water flow

Bubble size should be small, around 1 mm preferably. Wooden air diffusers will produce such bubbles.

Contact time is determined by the size of the bubble, the smaller it is the slower it will rise, and by the height of the column.

Adhesion capability and adhesion are determined and influenced by factors outside of the hobbyists control. The use of ozone will however increase this important factor

## 15.2.4 Size of skimmer and flow rates

Water flow is dependent on the size of the tank, and all manufacturers that we know of, recommend for what size tank their units should be used. Our experience is that they err. The models recommended are usually too small. Experiments conducted with skimmers built ourselves, indicate without doubt that larger skimmers perform better, and enabled us to reduce the dissolved organic levels, measured as total organic carbon, more efficiently.

Air input can be increased to just the point below the appearance of strong turbulence on the top of the water in the skimmer. This will be different for every model, and you will have to test your skimmer with various air pumps to find the right amount in your particular case.

Water flow, although it cannot be expressed as a gallon per hour figure, because of the variety of skimmers, is important inasmuch as turnover of aquarium water through the skimmer is involved. Our recommendation in this respect is to turn all aquarium water through the skimmer 1.75 times per hour. This needs to be done using a dedicated pump of course. If the skimmer you use allows higher throughputs you may wish to do so, making sure that, as you increase the flow, no residual ozone is returned to the tank.

The skimmer should be tall, as this is the critical factor influencing contact time. We do not use skimmers smaller than 3 feet. They will not fit underneath the aquarium of course, but have to be placed in a dedicated cabinet, or in some remote location, as the place where you put the skimmer, really has no bearing on its efficiency. Doing so might require the use of a stronger pump, especially if height is involved and many fittings are included in the piping set up.

Building your own skimmer is not very complicated, but it is highly likely that commercial models will run more efficiently, as their shape, and the relation between input and output, the height of these, and such things as pipe diameter, neck size and length have been worked out through much trial and error, before they reach the market.

## 15.2.5 Cleaning and Maintenance

A few observations that might be of value to you :

- Skimmers need to be serviced frequently. Cleaning of the beaker is no fun, but needs to be done at regular intervals. How often depends on tank conditions, skimmer efficiency. When the cup is dirty and full of brownish or greenish liquid, empty it.

- Attaching a flexible hose that is connected to a drain, makes life easier. Detritus and concentrated organics flow away automatically. Such a set up also prevents the skimmer beaker from overflowing. This should not happen, but does. Using water additives can change the surface tension of the water, and suddenly very liquid foam starts erupting from the skimmer, fills the cup in no time, and then flows onto the ground (carpet?).

- New skimmers will produce wet foam of the type just described for a while. This stops when the inside of the neck and the top are coated with a greasy type substance which makes too wet bubbles burst. You may of course add a little grease to prevent this from happening, to break your skimmer in.

- Ozone greatly reduces this problem because it enhances the oxidation of organics and produces a different kind of bubble-pollution reaction.

- Adjusting a skimmer, to get just the right kind of flow to enter the beaker, not too wet, but still enough to overflow, can be tricky, and you will need to spend a fair amount of time doing so.

- Skimmer adjustments, meaning regulating the amount of water going in, and the amount of water leaving the skimmer, which determines the height of the water inside the column, takes time. Minute changes take a long time to show their true effect. If you only slightly alter the amount of water entering or leaving the skimmer, it may take 20 or minutes before you can actually see where the new water level inside the skimmer will be. Keep that in mind, as it will prevent both overflows, and the level inside being too low.

- the skimmer should run 24 hours a day. Use a good and reliable pump.
- remember that if the pump stops, the water inside the skimmer will want to flow away. If the skimmer is at the same level as the bottom of the trickle filter, make sure that the sump can hold that quantity of water.

- Both the beaker and the inside of the skimmer should be cleaned from time to time. Slime and oxidized organics will settle on the walls, and need to be removed.

- If you return the water from the skimmer directly to the aquarium, you must make sure that it does not contain any residual ozone, if you are using an ozonizer that is.

- Change the airstones regularly. They accumulate slime too, when that happens the bubble size will change, and the output of air will be restricted more and more.

- Whenever you add anything to the aquarium, e.g. trace elements, water conditioners, KH generator, and the like, make sure that their effect, when dissolving, does not make the skimmer produce wetter foam and overflow.

## Carbon Dioxide Reactor

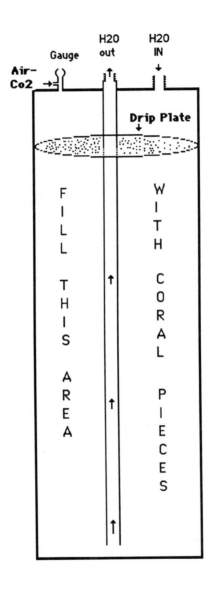

# 16. Newer Reactors

## 16.1  CO2 Reactors

### 16.1.1  Large  models

The principle that governs the functioning of a carbon dioxide reactor is based on the fact that the latter forms carbonic acid when it mixes with water. The water mass where this happens, inside the carbon dioxide reactor, has a pH that is more acidic. This mixture, when in contact with the carbonates and bicarbonates that are placed inside the reactor, slowly dissolves some of these, and as a result increases the buffer of the water, ensuring a better and longer pH stability. In addition of course, carbon dioxide is available to macro and symbiotic algae as well.

The drawing, elsewhere in the book, shows the cylinder filled with pieces of broken up coral. You may use any other material that is high in carbonates and bicarbonates. Water enters from the top, and is dispersed by the drip plate, much like what happens at the top of the trickle filter. This is a circular plate, siliconed in, to made it water tight around the edges. Water can only go further down in the cylinder through the 3/16 inch holes drilled in the plate.

A mix of air and CO2 is pushed in the column, or just CO2. As a slight over pressure is created inside the cylinder, the mix of air and CO2 is forced in the water to some extent. This ensures that the process will work. Whether you want to use air mixed with carbon dioxide, or just carbon dioxide, is a matter of debate. Our recommendation is to use a mixture of both. Indeed, otherwise too much carbon dioxide would be necessary to achieve the desired over-pressure. Such an amount of CO2 would make more checking of the KH necessary to prevent pH drop. Mixing the two, does not do away with having to test the KH regularly, but  certainly less frequent are necessary.

The problem is not in setting up the reactor itself, rather in adjusting the output of air - CO2 or just CO2, in such a way that the water never rises more than about 2 to 3 inches inside the cylinder. We have found that in most cases only about 0.1 bar differential is required. To make it easier to adjust, we therefore suggested to mount a gauge on top of the reactor. This should be a low pressure gauge of course. Models reading from 0 to 1 bar are available, and cost only a few dollars. They will need to be threaded in a piece of pvc, that is itself glued into the top of the cylinder. What you will need, usually, is a 3/8 inch threaded female reducing fitting. This fitting has a lip. Drill a hole in the top plate that is the exact diameter of the outside of the fitting. Slide the whole gauge and fitting assembly trough the hole and glue the lip of the fitting onto the plate, with pvc bonding agents.

If no water stays in the cylinder, meaning that all the incoming water is pushed back out through the middle piece of pipe, you have created too high a pressure inside the cylinder. Reducing it somewhat will solve the problem. Finding the exact level however might require two or three different attempts.

If too much water remains in the cylinder, you have not created enough internal pressure. Again a few attempts might be necessary to get it right.

Once you done so, write down what exact is required. Of course this will only apply to the water output that you are now providing to the cylinder. If you change that output, you will again need to adjust the pressure. This is one of the reasons that such devices need to be run with a dedicated water pump.

Before using a carbon dioxide reactor you will need to test the carbonate hardness of the water, to ensure that no pH drop will occur. Keep the dKH at 15, and no lower than 12 at any time.

How much $CO_2$ needs to be pushed into the cylinder ?

The principles to be followed were described in the section dealing with instrumentation, and need to be adhered to here as well. There is no magic number. Use the guidelines already given and you will be all right.

If an air pump is used, and we recommend you do, place a check valve between the pump and the cylinder.

To make the mixture of air and carbon dioxide, you will need an air pump, and a bottle of $CO_2$. With a T-connector inject a little $CO_2$ in the line. If you wish to be absolutely sure of how much carbon dioxide goes in the cylinder, use a bubble counting device, e.g. Dupla's.

The water going to the cylinder should be pre-filtered water. You may for instance use water from the sump of the trickle filter. A submersible pump will be able to run this set up satisfactorily. Place it in the sump, use pvc or silicone hose.

## 16.1.2 Using two small reactors S

This is a much easier system to set up. No need for a gauge. No need to make difficult adjustments. Install the two reactors as shown in the diagram elsewhere in the book. The outflow of the first reactor is connected to the inflow of the second one.

Only the CO2 inlet of the first one is used. In this set up you may use straight CO2. There is no need to mix it with air.

The adjustment to be done is based on the information already given in the chapter on the use of carbon dioxide. The only difference is that in this type of set up, we are using two reactors instead of one, and we are changing the material inside the reactors to pieces of broken up coral, or another such compound.

Do not forget to check the dKH and adjust it before using carbon dioxide if necessary.

The reactors can be placed inside the aquarium (not very appealing), inside the sump of the trickle filter (might get a little crowded in there), or on the outside. Use flexible tubing to do all connections, and secure them with clamps. Make sure to use CO2 resistant tubing. Preferably silicone or pvc hose. Clear plastic tubing will not last for a long time. It will start to harden.

The water going to the reactors needs to be prefiltered. Use water from the sump of the trickle filter.

## 16.2  Activated Carbon Reactor

The reactor used is the same as the one described in 16.1.1, but is of a smaller size. No drip plate is necessary. Just the inlet, and the pipe in the middle through which the water returns to the aquarium. No pressure gauge and no air inlet holes are necessary either.

The holes in the central pipe are smaller, and a piece of cheese cloth, or a similar material is wrapped around the pipe. The cylinder is filled with carbon of superior quality.

As water is pushed in the cylinder, the latter fills, and the only way out for the water is through the carbon, then the cloth, then the pipe and back to the aquarium.

The cylinder needs to be of the size that can hold the amount of carbon that is necessary for your tank (see recommendations elsewhere).

This is a device that will give you superior chemical filtration, and we highly recommend it. It is also easy to build yourself. You may even have cannister filters, or similar, built using the principle described standing around.

Remember to regularly change the activated carbon ! Use the carbon efficiency test frequently.

If you do not use a cannister filter to achieve this result, an acrylic tube about 2 feet tall and 4-6 inches in diameter will do an excellent job for you. Remember that the contents will be under pressure from the water that is pushed into the cylinder, so make sure that all parts are bonded for strength in addition to for water tightness.

## 16.3 Oxygen Reactors

The principles and cylinder are the same as the ones described for the large model carbon dioxide reactor. Only air is injected however.

The material inside the cylinder can be Bioballs, or a similar packing medium. Most units available in Germany however use Bioballs, because they break the water up much more than some other media, and as a result, the finer droplets can better absorb oxygen better.

Again, it will take you a little time to find the exact amount of air that needs to be injected to maintain water at the 2 to 3 inch level.

Those of you using trickle filters that already contain Bioballs will only marginally benefit from the addition of an oxygen reactor though, as the nature of a trickle filter with Bioballs is that it increases oxygen as one of its side-benefits.

## 16.4 More on Ion Exchangers

The device used to run water over Ion exchangers is identical to the one described for activated carbon.

There are many resins on the market. You will need to select the one that you decide will do the job for you.

Ion exchangers are "specific", they will remove a certain type of compound from the water. You therefore buy the resin that you need to remove whatever it is that you wish to remove.

Remember what we have said earlier in the book, make sure that no phenols are liberated in the water in the process. Resins or Ion exchangers that use the sodium ion as an exchange ion obviously will not work in salt water tanks, because the concentration of sodium in the tank water is already so high. Ensure that you are not buying an ion exchanger of that type.

It is rumored that Dupla Usa will shortly introduce a totally new ion exchanger which can be used in these cylinders. Introduction date had not been set at the time of this writing, as testing was still going on.

The product will, amongst others, remove *nitrate*. This would of course be a good step forward, again, in water chemistry for reef aquariums. This product is tentatively simply called : X-Nitrate.

Other resins are available. Chemical supply companies should be able to clue you in, and send you specification sheets. You should get these for any such ion exchangers that are advertised, or that you plan to buy. Indeed many do not work in salt water. And that is of course the most important factor to watch for.

Sometimes ads will claim : works for salt water tanks too. What they really mean, is that you can use them on the water from the mains, before the salt has been added. After the water is treated, the water is then adjusted for salinity and added to the tank. This is a play on words, and not really what we need. We need a product that can be permanently used on the tank.

Last but not least : products that do the same job may come in different qualities. Get the best you can. Resins usually last a long time, so the extra few dollars do not really make a big difference. Additionally some resins can be regenerated, extending their use for even longer.

# Summary

*We hope that you have enjoyed this second printing of the Marine Fish and Invert Reef Aquarium.*

*The first printing sold out in 3 weeks time, between March 4 and March 25 of 1988.*

*Many many Hobbyists have called to express their satisfaction with contents of the book, and we hope that you have enjoyed it too.*

*Hopefully we will have contributed to a better understanding of such concepts as Redox Potential, the use of Carbon dioxide, Protein Skimmers, Ozone, Trickle Filters, and other such concepts.*

*This book does not imply that you have to use all this equipment to be successful. It gives you the option, and discusses what they can do for your Reef tank. As you become more of a "serious" hobbyist, you will probably find that you will want to add a least some of them to your Reef.*

*Good luck in your endeavors.*

*We appreciate your comments.*

*Albert J. Thiel*
*31 Eversley Avenue*
*Norwalk, CT 06851*

---

*Should you wish to be placed on Dupla Press' mailing list, please send us your name and address.*

*Dupla Press has started a technical newsletter for serious Hobbyists called :*

*MARINE REEF*

*You may subscribe for $ 48.00 for 17 issues per year (one every 3 weeks)*

---

# Appendix 1

## Actual Testing using Dupla Tests

### Introduction

Some aquarists who have acquired Dupla's complete Test Kit cases, or just individual tests, have observed that the English translation of the instruction sheets is not always as clear as they would like them to be. They have indicated that these sheets sometimes need to be re-read several times to clearly understand what is actually required to perform such tests correctly.

We thank Hobbyists for bringing this to Dupla's attention. At the same time Dupla apologizes for any inconvenience that this might have caused.

For those who have brought the matter up, and for all others who might benefit from a review , a section that re-explains all the basic tests, such as NH4, NO2, NO3, Cu, as well as some of the more Dupla specific tests, such as KH (carbonate hardness), GH (general hardness), PO4 (phosphate), O2 (Oxygen), CO2 (carbon dioxide), Fe (iron), and the organic load and carbon efficiency tests, has been included as an Appendix.

This will hopefully clarify any misunderstandings, and give everyone wishing to check on how they were performing such tests, a chance to review the instructions.

Many of you will ask whether such elaborate testing is really required. And rightfully so. Our answer is two-fold. If you are serious about the aquarium(s) that you are keeping, and want to be able to stay on top of things, then you should definitely perform these tests on a regular basis. Some are required more often than others in fact (see individual tests for recommendations). If you want to maintain your tank in good condition, but are not particularly concerned about knowing every detail of the water chemistry, the answer is no. In such a case however, there are still a number of tests that you should perform at regular intervals. Examples of the latter include : testing the pH, the KH and the NO3 and PO4 levels.

Doing so will allow you to pinpoint potential problems before they actually occur. An important one that can be avoided by regular testing, for phosphates e.g. is the appearance of slimy algae blooms.

Of course, since you will be investing some time in actually doing all this testing, and since you will want to be able to compare what parameters have changed from one testing session to the next, you should keep records.

Dupla, for one, produces a "Diary of the Aquarist", that enables you to record all all values tested. In doing so you are creating a historical record of tank conditions. This is a valuable piece of information, not only in the immediate sense, but also when trying to determine what happened to your Reef over a period of time, should things suddenly go wrong. And as you well know, they sometimes will for no apparent reason. As someone once observed : aquarium problems never really stop, they just cease to continue, only to suddenly start all over again, at the least expected time. Although this sounds a little pessimistic, it does not have to be so. Keeping a tab on what happens over time, will enable you to refer to test value data to try to determine the causes of problems, and perhaps avoid making mistakes in the future.

In the immediate, the test results will tell you whether corrective action is required in certain specific areas, e.g. carbonate hardness, or dissolved oxygen levels for instance.

The Dupla line of tests, besides being complete, offers the innovative approach of "expiration" dates. on all tests. This ensures that the test reagents used are chemically stable, and are thus able to give the accurate results that they were designed for.

This is a process which is costly, as only small quantities of any given test can be manufactured at any time. The advantage derived however is well worth the effort.

## 1. pH Test 4, 6, and 7.3

Dupla offers three aquarium specific tests for pH measurement, and an additional general purpose test pH 4-10. Since it is unlikely that we would use the latter ,and the pH 4 and pH 6, in Reef tanks, we will limit ourselves to the discussion of pH 7.3 test, which is the one used for salt water. pH 4 and pH 6 are used in fresh water tanks only, and pH 4-10 is used mainly in community tanks, giving a broad range testing capability.

The pH 7.3 test is simple to use. Required are : the test reagent, a test cylinder or a small container that can hold 6 and 12 milliliters of water and the test comparison colors. You need not necessarily buy Dupla's test cylinder by the way. Any vial that has milliliter graduations will do the trick. The reagent and the colors however will have to be obtained from a Dupla dealer. The colors can of course be used over and over again. Dupla sells such color charts individually, or in a packet that contains all color charts for all the tests that the company makes. Buying the latter would obviously be a better buy.

The test is very simple : take 12 ml of aquarium water, add 5 drops of the reagent, wait a few moments, gently shake the mixture somewhat, and then compare the color this mixture has taken on, with the color comparison chart. The best comparison is obtained by looking at the sample from the top. In the packet of comparison colors, Dupla has included a special "window card" that allows for easier comparison as well. Based on the result obtained, decide whether corrective action is required. You may also look at the sample sideways. Light conditions in the room where the test is made determine which is the best viewing angle.

## 2. KH test : Carbonate Hardness

Testing for carbonate hardness is important, as we have seen elsewhere in this book. This is especially the case if one keeps corals and wishes to maintain a stable pH at all times, especially when Carbon dioxide is being used.

The KH test can be performed without the use of any comparison colors. The color change that is indicative of the carbonate hardness level will occur very visibly.

Required are the KH reagent, a test cylinder, or a vial that can hold 6 ml and 12 ml of aquarium water.

Take 6 ml of water. Start adding drops of the KH reagent, and count the drops you add. As this is done, the water color will first turn to blue. After adding each drop, gently stir the solution to evenly distribute the reagent. After adding a certain number of drops, the blue will change to a reddish or purplish color, that cannot be mistaken. As soon as the sample is of a uniform new color, stop adding drops of the KH reagent.

The number of drops  that you have added corresponds to the KH or carbonate hardness. This number can be anywhere from 7 to 18 depending on the quality of your aquarium water. Refer to the chapter on carbonate hardness to determine whether the KH in your tank needs to be adjusted. You may also perform this test by using 12 ml of water. In that case, each drops only represents one half degree of Carbonate hardness.

Note : an error factor of 0.5 dKH occurs if the water used for the test contains more than 10 mg/l of phosphates. The error is on the + side.

## 3. GH Test   (General Hardness)

As a matter of practice we do not test for general hardness in marine tanks. There are in fact multiple reasons : in the majority of cases the general hardness will be very high anyway, and general hardness is not a factor that we wish to control and adjust in a Reef tank. Should you decide to attempt testing anyway, you may find that the contents of one bottle of GH test is not sufficient to obtain a result. GH testing is really only used in fresh water tanks, especially in areas with very soft or very hard water. Both might need to be adjusted in freshwater tanks, depending on the kind of fish population that is kept. E.g. in tanks with Discus sp. fish we would want to eliminate it as much as possible, and in community tanks we may wish to raise it somewhat.

## 4. CO2 Test : Carbon dioxide

Carbon dioxide testing in marine tanks is done by measuring the amount of milligrams per liter of CO2 present. Required are the reagent itself, and a test retort or vial that can hold 100 and 200 milliliters of water.

The retort is filled with 100 ml of aquarium water. Drops of the reagent are added slowly. Count the number of drops added. Every time a drop is added the water will take on a slightly pinkish color, which will disappear within seconds. To determine whether the sample is still pinkish, look at it sideways, holding it up so that you can get a good view.

The test is completed when the adding of drops keeps the water pinkish for more than one minute or so. This means that the pinkish color stays and does not disappear after a few seconds. The number of drops it took to achieve that, multiplied by two is equal to the CO2 content in mg per liter. If you use 200 ml of water to perform this test, each drop added corresponds to one mg/l. This method will give a more accurate result, but will also use more drops.

Check elsewhere in this book to determine whether you are in the right range.

Be careful as the reagent stains and is hard to remove. After the test is completed, clean the test retort carefully by rinsing it in fresh water. Left over reagent will falsify the next test.

Although Dupla sells a "visual-qualitative" CO2 test, which is designed for fresh water tanks, such a test does unfortunately not exist for marine aquariums. The existing one cannot be used in Reef tanks. The color you obtain would always be blue, indicating a lack of CO2. The reagents used in the test are not of the proper type for salt water.

## 5.Cu Test : Copper

The Dupla copper test is a highly sensitive one, and can be used in both fresh and salt water. The reagent is the same, the comparison colors are different.

This remark applies to all Dupla tests. Make therefore sure that you are using the right set of comparison colors when you test your Reef tank. In fact when buying tests make sure that you also buy the salt water comparison colors to go with it. The test kit case that contains all tests, can be obtained with either fresh or saltwater color charts. Specify which one you want to your dealer.

Required : the Cu reagent, the color chart and a test cylinder or vial that can hold 6 or 12 ml of water.

Take 12 ml of aquarium water and add 5 drops of the Cu reagent. Wait at least 3 minutes. Stir gently. Compare the color your sample now has with the color chart. Decide whether you are in the right range, and take corrective action if necessary. The Dupla copper test detects only non-chelated Copper, which is the toxic kind. Copper that is not in solution cannot be detected.

A side remark is apropos :

heavy metals, such as copper, precipitate at high pH levels, which is the reason why copper solutions found in pet stores are usually chelated. Chelators, or chelating agents, such as EDTA, are used to stabilize these solutions and make the heavy metals stay in solution for much longer periods of time. Not forever, just for longer periods of time.

When, over time, this copper falls out,and is therefore no longer in solution, tests will not detect it. Just think for a minute to convince yourself of this fact. If you threw a copper penny in a tank, and measured for copper content immediately, you would not be able to detect its presence, because that copper is not in solution.

Both slow and rapid changes in pH can however bring about a dangerous situation, insasmuch as heavy metals will go back in solution, if the pH changes downwards. It is therefore important to ensure that, when lowering the pH of your water, no copper levels that might be toxic suddenly develop. This could be the case if you used copper at one time or another, in an aquarium that had coral pieces in it, and you are now using these same pieces in a reef tank where the pH is lower than in the original tank. This would cause precipitated copper  attached to these coral pieces, to go back into solution, and harm the reef inhabitants. The recommendation often made is never to use coral that came from other tanks in a reef aquarium, as you can never be sure that no copper was ever used in that other tank.

## 6. NO3 test (Nitrate)

Required : Test cylinder and NO3 test reagent. Possibly a chart that gives dilution factor calculations. The latter is necessary if the NO3 content is higher than 5 mg per liter.

Fill the test cylinder with 12 ml of aquarium water, add a rounded spoonful of the reagent to the water. Shake gently to mix properly. You will need to wait a few minutes before actually taking a reading. If what we suspect is the case, your reading will be higher than 5 mg/l which is the highest that you can compare with the color charts.

The reason no color charts for higher readings are available, has nothing to do with an omission on our part, or the fact that we consider 5 mg to be the highest level that the aquarium should have. As the nitrate content increases, the color of the test solution becomes darker and darker after reagent is added.

Distinguishing between shades of a dark color is very difficult. It serves no purpose therefore to even make them available. The better and much easier way to determine NO3 content exactly, is to make dilutions of the aquarium water, and use the existing color charts, which can easily be compared with the tested fluid. The dilution factor required depends on conditions in your tank. The heavier the water is loaded with nitrates, the more you will have to dilute it.

Let us explain the principle and the testing method by using an example. You can use this example for your own tank conditions, by substituting values as required. This will become clear to you in a short while.

a) Instead of taking 12 ml of aquarium water, let's take only 6 ml and add 6 ml of Dupladest marine, or distilled water adjusted for specific gravity. The test cylinder now contains half aquarium water and half of the other liquid. If you test this new sample for Nitrates, you would have to multiply the result obtained by two, since you diluted your aquarium water by 50 percent. The total sample of 12 ml had only 6 ml of aquarium water in it.

b) If diluting the water by 50 percent does still not give you an acceptable reading, meaning the color of the test water is still too dark after you added the reagent, you will need to dilute the water even further. This can be done by taking 3 ml of aquarium water, and 9 ml of Dupladest marine, or distilled water. After the test is done, you now need to multiply the result by four. This is because the total sample tested contained only 25 percent aquarium water.

c) further dilutions might be necessary, depending on your tank's conditions.

d) if you are using less water from the aquarium, and more Dupladest marine or distilled water that has been salinity adjusted, the method is as follows : determine what percentage the aquarium water represents of the total 12 ml. For example, if we use 1 ml and 11 ml, the aquarium water represents 1/12 of the total. Take the test, then multiply the result by 12.

If you used only .5 ml of aquarium water, and 11.5 of Dupladest marine, you find that the aquarium water is only 1/24 th of the total water, and the result needs to be multiplied by 24.

You can make further dilutions if required, and calculate the factor yourself, using the above examples.

Of course if such high nitrate levels are measured, corrective action needs to be taken urgently. In all likelihood the tank will not look in too good condition, micro-algae might be overgrowing the glass, the substrate, the macro-algae and everything else in the tank as well.

Water changes with nitrate free water are a must, more macro algae need to be introduced, and the trickle filter needs to be outfitted with a denitrating (denitrification) foam block, as explained elsewhere.

Although nobody seems to be able to provide sufficient evidence of what exact level should be allowed as a maximum, it is a fact that progressive increases of nitrate levels make tanks look unhealthy. Fish do not seem to react as quickly as invertebrates do. We do not have a definitive number to advance either, but can state that 40 mg/l is too much high, that at 30 mg/l excessive growth of micro-algae is often reported, that at 20 mg/l often micro-algae have appeared, that less than 20 mg per liter seems to make invertebrate look better and micro-algae growth less of a problem. We recommend less than 15 mg at all times

We have no firm basis for the reasons for this, but are basing these statements purely on observed conditions, in several aquariums, over a period of several months of monitoring and talking to other experienced aquarists.

What seems to make sense to everyone knowledgeable about tank conditions, is that the fewer nitrates are present, the better the tank runs, meaning that tank maintenance management is again taking on a more important role. Do not therefore let conditions run out of hand. Take both preventative and corrective measures by changing water regularly, maintaining substantial amounts of macro-algae, and ensure that the water that is used for water changes does not contain any or very little nitrates.

## 7.Carbon Efficiency test

The carbon efficiency test is a quick and simple way to determine whether the activated carbon you are using needs replacing. The test is performed by using a two-colored piece of plastic, holding it under water, and looking at it from a distance of about 2 feet. If you cannot distinguish the difference between the white and the yellow, you know that, either your water needs to be treated with carbon, or if it is, that the carbon you are using is exhausted and needs to be replaced.

It is a pretty straight forward test that requires only the two- colored chart. If you wish to make such a card yourself, make sure that the yellow is a faint one.

## 8. Cleaning a pH electrode

Required : cleaning solution and a small vial. The cleaning solution can be obtained from your Dupla dealer, or you may  wish to use an acid solution that you have readily available.

Immerse the probe in the cleaning solution for 30 to 45 minutes and then rinse the probe under tepid tap water. Re-immerse the probe in the cleaning solution for another 15 minutes and rinse again.

After the probe has been cleaned, it will need to be re-calibrated. Electrodes should be cleaned regularly. At least every 4 to 6 weeks. This will ensure that the reading you obtain is accurate. This is especially important if you use the probe in conjunction with the Dupla pH digital regulator.

## 9. pH Electrode Calibration

In Reef tanks the pH electrode needs to be calibrated for a high pH reading. This is achieved by using two distinct solutions, pH 7 and pH 9. These solutions are guaranteed to be of the pH listed on the label. Extreme care needs to be taken not to pollute the calibrating solutions, as doing so will falsify your next calibration. This is also the reason that the liquid used to do the calibration has to be discarded after the calibration is finished. Do not, we repeat, do not re-add it to the calibrating solution bottle. Doing so will definitely pollute the solution and will give erroneous subsequent calibrations.

pH meters have either one or two calibrating knobs. The ones Dupla features have two. The left one is used in conjunction with the pH 7 solution and the right one in conjunction with the pH 9 solution. It is important not to invert these.

The calibration ensures that the probe and the meter are adjusted to each other and give accurate readings.

The procedure is as follows : attach the electrode to a pH meter and place it in a small amount of pH 7 solution. Let stand for at least 10 minutes. Now look at the display on the meter. If it does not say 7.00 exactly, adjust the display by turning the calibrating know until it does.

Rinse probe and throw the pH 7 solution in the vial away. Rinse vial and dry it out thoroughly. The latter is important. If the vial still contained tap water, it would pollute the pH 9 calibrating solution that we will use next.

Fill the vial with a little pH 9 solution and place the probe in it. Wait at least ten minutes. Check the read out, if it does not say 9.00 exactly, adjust it with the knob until it does. The left knob is used with the pH 7 solution and the right knob with the pH 9 solution. Other instruments might only have one knob however. Refer to the manual that came with the meter if need be.

After the calibration is finished, throw the solution in the vial away, rinse it and dry it thoroughly, then store it.

You may now place the electrode back in service. Your pH reading will now be accurate.

pH electrodes should be calibrated regularly. This will ensure accurate readings. Once every 2 to 3 months is recommended, and every time the probe is cleaned.

Be very careful in how you handle the pH electrode, it is a scientific piece of equipment and does not take abuse. Do not let the tip of the electrode dry out. It will ruin the probe and you will no longer be able to adjust it correctly. Most pH probes cannot be totally immersed. The top portion of it needs to remain out of the water. Refer to the manufacturers instructions if need be. When the electrode is not used, e.g. stored for some reason or another, it should be placed in KCl, potassium chloride. This is usually achieved by placing a special cap that can be filled with KCl over its tip. Such a tip usually comes with the probe when you originally buy it. Do not throw it away, as at some point you will need it again. KCl can be obtained from Dupla dealers and from chemical supply houses.

When installing your pH meter and probe, try to keep the lead that is attached to the probe away from other electric cords. This will eliminate "jumping" of the read-out, due to electrical interference from the other wires. Away means several inches, not feet. Static electricity can do the same thing, before adjusting the meter touch a piece of grounded metal or so.

## 10. Setting up a manual CO2 system

This has been described in detail in the chapter on Carbon dioxide use, in the main body of the book, and we refer you back to that section.

## 11. Using CO2 Reactors

Dupla has two types of carbon dioxide reactors. Basically a small one, and and a large one.The small one is mainly used in fresh water tanks, and in small marine ones, e.g. up to 55 gallons. The large reactor, referred to as Reactor S, is used on all other marine tanks, including Reefs.

The function of the reactor is to ensure a more efficient mixing of the water and the carbon dioxide. This saves CO2 and give a more uniform distribution of the carbon dioxide in the water.

To make a CO2 reactor work, two things are required. A supply of Carbon dioxide and a supply of water. Inside the reactor, both are mixed efficiently. The small reactor can only be placed inside the filter sump  or inside the tank. The Reactor S can be placed inside the filter sump, inside the tank, or just plainly outside the aquarium. When placed outside, additional hose is required to guide the water that comes out of the reactor, at the bottom, back to the aquarium or to the sump. This process is clearly illustrated in documentation that comes with it.

The water required for the functioning of the reactor can be guided to it in several ways. The simplest way would be to use a T-fitting in the water return

( the water line from the pump to the aquarium). The  T-fitting is stepped
down to the size of the reactor intake which is 1/4 inch. A valve to regulate
the flow is inserted, and with hose, the valve is connected to the top of the
reactor. To regulate the flow, a needle valve, or a flat C-clamp type device can
be used. The flat C-clamp valve will be the less expensive way to go. The
needle valve however allows for more accurate water flow control. Make sure
that all hose connections are reinforced by using hose clamps, and make sure
that they are saltwater resistant.

$CO_2$ is supplied to the reactor from a $CO_2$ bottle. If your system is an automated one, you will control this flow by means of a magnetic valve and a pH
regulator. This is described elsewhere in this book, in the section that deals
with the automated addition of carbon dioxide to the aquarium.
$CO_2$ reactors can  be used in series, to make the addition of $CO_2$ even more
efficient. This entails placing two of them one after each other. Refer to the
diagram dealing with $O_2$ reactors.

Of course the Reactor S can be used to add other gasses to the water, for instance small amounts of Ozone. To do so you substitute the $CO_2$ supply
source with an air pump and small ozonizer. Make sure that the hose you use
when doing this is ozone resistant. The air pump needs to be able to put out
more pressure than the one created by the water that is entering the reactor.
The size of the air pump will therefore vary depending on the amount of water
that you plan to push through the reactor.

Make sure that both the air pump and the ozonizer are above the water level
of the tank, or of the sump of the filter, depending on where you plan to
place the Reactor S, or the series of Reactor S's used for this purpose.

## 12. NO2, Nitrite test

Required : a test cylinder, or a vial, and the nitrite reagent. Add the reagent to
the 6 ml of water in the vial which will be tested and let stand. Compare the
new color of the sample with the test colors and read off the content. If excess nitrite -we maintain that anything over 0.1 mg/l is too much- is present,
look for the possible causes immediately. A heaping spoonful of reagent is
required. Use the spatula side.

Reasons for excess nitrites include :

- overcrowding and the resulting inability of the filter to cope with the
excessive amounts of nitrite produced.
- excesses in feeding.
- dying biological filter, possibly due to the use of medication, such as antibiotics.
- too small a filter, or the wrong filter medium. Suggestion : substitute a
medium that offers more surface area.
- dead fish or invert decomposing somewhere behind rocks.
- faulty reagent. Check whether expiration date is passed, or perhaps the
reagent has been polluted by some foreign material, or has been left standing

open and has absorbed water. The reagent, usually sodium sulfite, is hygroscopic.
- pollution in fine filter and mechanical filter. Clean these filters regularly to prevent this from occurring.
- lack of sufficient bacteria to convert the nitrites to nitrates. This can happen when filters are not correctly run in, or when excess ammonia is present, since the presence of excess ammonia inhibits the growth of the Nitrobacter.

## 13. PO4, Phosphates

Required : test cylinder, or vial, and test reagents A and B.
Take 12 ml of water, add 4 drops of reagents A, shake gently to mix the drops with the water. Add 4 drops of reagent B. Wait a few minutes and compare the color of the test solution against the color charts.

Recommended level : less than 2 mg per liter. PO4 is a very desirable nutrient for micro-algae, and excess phosphate will result in the tank overgrowing with such undesirable algae very rapidly.

Dilution of the sample may be necessary here too. If this is the case for your tank, refer to the Nitrate section and apply the same multiplication factors.

Phosphate levels are hard to reduce. Test the water you are using to make water changes, to ensure that you are not adding PO4 without realizing it. Alternatively, increase water change amounts until conditions are back to normal. Use distilled or chemical free water, if necessary, for a while. Kipper(1987) in fact recommends that this is the only water that should be used for water changes. Adding more macro-algae is another method of reducing the phosphate levels, as macro-algae use PO4 as nutrients.

Check PO4 levels regularly to ensure that you can keep the increase in check, or at least that you are aware at what rate they are increasing, and determine how you need to adjust tank conditions to cope with this situation.

If you wish to avoid micro-algae blooms, the type we all wish we never had, you will need to include this test in your regular testing habits, and be prepared to take the corrective actions that we suggested. Whether this should include the use of distilled or chemical free water will depend on the quality of the water that you have access to.

## 14. O2, Oxygen

Dupla's battery of tests includes an Oxygen test, which is really a two-fold test. The first test is the actual amount of dissolved oxygen in the aquarium water, and the second test is referred to as the BSB2, which translated to English stands for the Biochemical oxygen demand in 48 hours.

Dissolved Oxygen : This is not as complicated a test, as it would appear from the instruction sheet. It is however a test which takes a little more patience than other Dupla tests. It is extremely accurate, and gives us a measurement that is most important to monitor in reef aquariums.

Required : a test cylinder and reagents A,B,C, and D.

Fill the test cylinder to the top. This means 20 ml of water. Add 5 drops of reagent A. Shake gently. Add 5 drops of reagent B. Now close the test cylinder, but first remove the little pin in the cover. When you then close the cylinder a little water will come out. That is required to ensure that no air is trapped in the cylinder. Such air would falsify the test, as air contains oxygen.

Let stand for 10 minutes. A brownish sediment will form, and start settling towards the bottom. Now comes the part that many aquarists are confused by. The actual amount of sediment is dependent on the amount of oxygen your water contains. If this is low the sediment will settle below the 6 ml hole. But maybe yours is high and the sediment will settle at a higher level. If the sediment is below the 6 ml hole, open that hole and let the excess water flow out. If it is higher, open the 12 ml hole and let the excess water flow out. Add 5 drops of reagent C. Shake gently and let stand for 5 minutes. The brown sediment dissolves and turns yellowish.

To this solution add drops of reagent D. Count the number of drops it takes to turn that yellowish liquid to a clear liquid. Each drop equals 0.5 mg oxygen.

## 15. Iron test Fe

Add 12 ml of aquarium water to the test cylinder, and using the spoon, add a heapful to that water.

Wait about 3 minutes and the tested water will take on a shade of blue. The bluer the more iron is contained in the tank.

Recommended level for reef tanks with macro-algae is 0.05 to 0.1 mg per liter. If your level is too low, use Duplaplant 24.

## 16. Determining how much Duplaplant 24 is required

Test the aquarium for iron content. Write the number down. If the level you determine is zero or very close to it follow this procedure :

Remove any carbon from the tank or the filter.

Add 1 drop of Duplaplant 24 per gallon of water. Wait 1 hour and re-test your aquarium. If the level is still close to zero, repeat the procedure.

Continue doing this until you can at least measure some degree of iron content, e.g. 0.05 mg/l